Decoloniality, Lan[guage]
and Literacy

STUDIES IN KNOWLEDGE PRODUCTION AND PARTICIPATION

Series Editors: **Mary Jane Curry**, *University of Rochester, USA* and **Theresa Lillis**, *The Open University, UK*

Questions about the relationships among language and other semiotic resources (such as image, film/video, sound) and knowledge production, participation and distribution are increasingly coming to the fore in the context of debates about globalisation, multilingualism and new technologies. Much of the existing work published on knowledge production has focused on formal academic/scientific knowledge; this knowledge is beginning to be produced and communicated via a much wider range of genres, modes and media including, for example, blogs, wikis and Twitter feeds, which have created new ways of producing and communicating knowledge, as well as opening up new ways of participating. Fast-moving shifts in these domains prompt the need for this series which aims to explore facets of knowledge production including: what is counted as knowledge, how it is recognised and rewarded, and who has access to producing, distributing and using knowledge(s). One of the key aims of the series is to include work by scholars located outside the 'centre', and to include work written in innovative styles and formats.

All books in this series are externally peer-reviewed.

Full details of all the books in this series and of all our other publications can be found on http://www.multilingual-matters.com, or by writing to Multilingual Matters, St Nicholas House, 31–34 High Street, Bristol BS1 2AW, UK.

Editorial Board

Jannis Androutsopoulos, *University of Hamburg, Germany*
Karen Bennett, *Universidade Nova, Portugal*
Jan Blommaert, *Tilburg University, the Netherlands*
Rebecca Black, *University of California, USA*
Sally Burgess, *Universidad de La Laguna, Spain*
Paula Carlino, *University of Buenos Aires, Argentina*
Christine Casanave, *Temple University, USA*
Christiane Donohue, *Dartmouth College, USA*
Guillaume Gentil, *Carleton University, Canada*
Bruce Horner, *University of Louisville, USA*
Dawang Huang, *University of Ningbo, China*
Luisa Martín Rojo, *Universidad Autonoma, Spain*
Carolyn McKinney, *University of Cape Town, South Africa*
Françoise Salager-Meyer, *Universidad de Los Andes, Venezuela*
Elana Shohamy, *Tel Aviv University, Israel*
Sue Starfield, *University of New South Wales, Australia*
Christine Tardy, *Arizona State University, USA*
Lucia Thesen, *University of Cape Town, South Africa*

STUDIES IN KNOWLEDGE PRODUCTION AND PARTICIPATION: 3

Decoloniality, Language and Literacy

Conversations with Teacher Educators

Edited by
Carolyn McKinney and Pam Christie

MULTILINGUAL MATTERS
Bristol • Jackson

DOI https://doi.org/10.21832/MCKINN9240
Library of Congress Cataloging in Publication Data
A catalog record for this book is available from the Library of Congress.
Names: McKinney, Carolyn, editor. | Christie, Pam, editor.
Title: Decoloniality, Language and Literacy: Conversations with Teacher
   Educators/Edited by Carolyn McKinney and Pam Christie.
Description: Bristol, UK; Blue Ridge Summit, PA: Multilingual Matters, 2022. |
   Series: Studies in Knowledge Production and Participation: 3 |
   Includes bibliographical references and index. | Summary: "Through a
   range of unconventional genres, representations of data, and dialogic, reflective
   narratives alongside more traditional academic genres, this book engages with
   contexts of decoloniality and border thinking in the Global South. It captures the
   learning that takes place beyond the borders of disciplines and formal classroom
   spaces"— Provided by publisher. Identifiers: LCCN 2021037268 (print) | LCCN
   2021037269 (ebook) | ISBN 9781788929233 (paperback) | ISBN 9781788929240
   (hardback) | ISBN 9781788929257 (pdf) | ISBN 9781788929264 (epub)
   Subjects: LCSH: Education—Developing countries. | Non-formal education—
   Developing countries. | Language and education—Developing countries. |
   Literacy—Developing countries. | Teachers—Training of—Developing countries.
   Classification: LCC LC2605 .D36 2022 (print) |
LCC LC2605 (ebook) | DDC 370.9724—dc23
LC record available at https://lccn.loc.gov/2021037268
LC ebook record available at https://lccn.loc.gov/2021037269

British Library Cataloguing in Publication Data
A catalogue entry for this book is available from the British Library.

ISBN-13: 978-1-78892-924-0 (hbk)
ISBN-13: 978-1-78892-923-3 (pbk)

Multilingual Matters
UK: St Nicholas House, 31–34 High Street, Bristol BS1 2AW, UK.
USA: Ingram, Jackson, TN, USA.

Copyright © 2022 Carolyn McKinney, Pam Christie and the authors of individual chapters.

All rights reserved. No part of this work may be reproduced in any form or by any means without permission in writing from the publisher.

The policy of Multilingual Matters/Channel View Publications is to use papers that are natural, renewable and recyclable products, made from wood grown in sustainable forests. In the manufacturing process of our books, and to further support our policy, preference is given to printers that have FSC and PEFC Chain of Custody certification. The FSC and/or PEFC logos will appear on those books where full certification has been granted to the printer concerned.

Typeset by Nova Techset Private Limited, Bengaluru and Chennai, India.
Printed and bound in the UK by the CPI Books Group Ltd.

Contents

	Acknowledgements	vii
	Contributors	ix
	Prologue	xiii
1	Introduction: Conversations with Teacher Educators in Coloniality *Carolyn McKinney and Pam Christie*	1

Part 1: De/coloniality in Schooling

	Leaving Home at 10 *Harry Garuba*	21
2	De/coloniality in South African Language in Education Policy: Resisting the Marginalisation of African Language Speaking Children *Xolisa Guzula*	23
3	Navigating Hegemonic Knowledge and Ideologies at School: Children's Oral Storytelling as Acts of Agency and Positioning *Pinky Makoe*	46
4	Identity Meshing in Learning Science Bilingually: Tales of a 'Coconuty Nerd' *Robyn Tyler*	63

Part 2: Delinking from Coloniality in Teacher Education

5	Visual Essay: Teaching and Learning beyond the Classroom: What Can We Learn from Participating in Struggle with our Students? *Kate Angier, Carolyn McKinney and Catherine Kell*	81
6	Learning Science from umaGogo: The Value of Teaching Practice in Semi-rural School Contexts *Annemarie Hattingh*	98

7   Engaging Deficit: Pre-service Teachers' Reflections on
    Negotiation of Working-class Schools   117
    Rochelle Kapp

8   Thirdspace Thinking: Expanding the Paradigm of
    Academic Literacies to Reposition Multilingual Pre-service
    Science Teachers   136
    Soraya Abdulatief

9   Delinking from Coloniality and Increasing Participation in
    Early Literacy Teacher Education   155
    Carolyn McKinney

10 Reinventing Literacy: Literacy Teacher Education in Contexts
    of Coloniality   173
    *Catherine Kell in conversation with Xolisa Guzula and
       Carolyn McKinney*

    **Part 3: Conversations with Teacher Educators in Brazil,
    Canada and Chile**

11 Teacher Education amid Centralising/Colonial and
    Decentralising/Decolonial Forces   197
    Cloris Porto Torquato

12 Education for Depth: An Invitation to Engage with the
    Complexities and Challenges of Decolonizing Work   207
    Vanessa Andreotti and Sharon Stein

13 Transnational Connections in the Global South: A Reflection
    on this Book's Reception   215
    Natalia Ávila Reyes

    Index   222

Acknowledgements

We gratefully acknowledge funding received from the National Research Foundation (NRF), South Africa, to support this project.

This book went through a series of peer-review processes at proposal and full manuscript stages. We are extremely grateful to all the reviewers for the depth of their engagement with our work, and their insightful reviews. We also sincerely thank the series editors Theresa Lillis and M.J. Curry for their invaluable critical feedback and support of this project.

Contributors

Soraya Abdulatief is a PhD candidate in Education at the University of Cape Town. She holds a Master's degree in English Literature from the University of the Western Cape. She has lectured in English Communication at a university of technology and worked as an online editor and technical writer. Soraya's PhD research is on teaching academic literacies practices to Postgraduate Certificate in Education students learning to be science teachers. Her other research interests include decolonial and multimodal theories, using technology in education, and debates around race, gender, language and literacy.

Vanessa Andreotti is a Canada Research Chair in Race, Inequalities and Global Change and Professor in the Department of Educational Studies at the University of British Columbia. Drawing on different critiques of colonialism and human exceptionalism, her research examines the interface between historical, systemic and ongoing forms of violence, and the material and psychoanalytic dimensions of unsustainability within modernity. Vanessa's pedagogical practice seeks to open up new possibilities for cognitive, affective, relational, economic and ecological global transformative justice, healing and well-being. She is one of the founding members of the Gesturing Decolonial Futures Collective (decolonialfutures.net).

Kate Angier is a Senior Lecturer in History Education at the University of Cape Town. She is a teacher educator, graduate student supervisor and a convenor on the Postgraduate Certificate of Education (PGCE). Kate's research interests include initial and in-service teacher education, historical consciousness and the history of history education. She currently serves as an external moderator within the national examination system, and is a member of the Ministerial Team tasked with rewriting the national history curriculum

Natalia Ávila Reyes is an Assistant Professor of Education at Pontificia Universidad Católica de Chile. She holds a Master's degree in Linguistics (PUC, Chile), a Master's degree in Teaching and Learning and a PhD in Education with a specialisation in Language, Literacy, and Composition

(University of California, Santa Barbara). Natalia's primary scholarly interest is in writing across educational levels, using both educational and linguistic approaches. Her most recent research project explores the experiences of university students with writing and the dynamics of agency, voice, engagement and identity negotiation in expanding higher education systems.

Pam Christie is an Emeritus Professor at the University of Cape Town and is currently Honorary Professor at the University of Queensland, Visiting Professor at the University of Johannesburg and foundation member of the Wits UNESCO Chair Forum on Teacher Education for Diversity and Development. Working in both South Africa and Australia, Pam has taught and published in the sociology of education, education policy, school organisation and change, and classroom practice. Her driving interest is in social justice and schooling. In 2020 she published *Decolonising Schools in South Africa: The Impossible Dream?* (Routledge).

Xolisa Guzula is a Lecturer in Language and Literacy Studies with a focus on multilingual and multiliteracies education at the University of Cape Town. She is an early biliteracy specialist with research interests in emergent literacy, bi/multilingual education, language and literacy as social practice, multiliteracies, multimodality, third spaces and bilingual children's literature. Xolisa has experience in early literacy and biliteracy teacher training and community literacy training. She is one of the founders of a network of community literacy clubs emerging across the country and is a doctoral student researching third spaces as a way towards transforming language and literacy pedagogies. Xolisa is a member of bua-lit Language and Literacy Collective, www.bua-lit.org.za.

Annemarie Hattingh is Associate Professor of Science Education in the School of Education at the University of Cape Town. She is a teacher educator, supervisor of Master's and doctoral students and convenor of work-integrated learning of pre-service teachers. Annemarie researches effective and exceptional physical science teaching in diverse schooling contexts, with a special interest in innovative teaching in under-resourced learning environments. With her interest in inquiry-based learning, she was involved in a study entitled 'International collaborative investigation of beginning seventh grade students' understandings of scientific inquiry', published in the *Journal of Research in Science Teaching* 56 (4) and, locally, 'Pre-service teachers' views about the nature of science and scientific inquiry: The South African case' in the *South African Journal of Education* 40 (1).

Rochelle Kapp is an Associate Professor in the School of Education at the University of Cape Town, South Africa. She has teaching, development and supervision experience in the fields of language and literacy education, teacher education and academic development. Most of Rochelle's research has been collaborative and longitudinal, and she has published in the areas of classroom discourse, academic literacy practices, access and retention of black working-class students, teacher education, English as an additional language and the politics of English.

Catherine Kell is former Director of the School of Education at the University of Cape Town and an Associate Professor specialising in language and literacy in education. She has worked in the field of literacy and language education since the early 1980s, across the University of Cape Town, the University of the Western Cape and various universities in New Zealand. Catherine's work in literacy education draws on the tradition of linguistic ethnography and spans the contexts of adult education, worker education, schooling, higher education and academic development. Much of her recent work has focused on digital technologies and literacy education in early schooling.

Pinky Makoe is Associate Professor in the Department of Education and Curriculum Studies, University of Johannesburg. She holds a PhD in English Education from the Institute of Education, University of London. Pinky does research in multilingual school settings with a focus on English language and literacy education. Her current research interests include monolingual and monoglossic language ideologies, language and identity/subjectivity, and heteroglossic practices in contexts of diversity.

Carolyn McKinney is Associate Professor of Language Education in the School of Education at the University of Cape Town, South Africa. She is a teacher educator, graduate student supervisor and convenor of the Master's programme in Language and Literacy Studies. Carolyn's research focuses on language ideologies, multilingualism as a resource for learning, critical literacy, and relationships between language, identity/subjectivity and learning. She recently published *Language and Power in Post-Colonial Schooling: Ideologies in Practice* (2017, Routledge), and is a member of the bua-lit Language and Literacy Collective: www.bua-lit.org.za.

Sharon Stein is an Assistant Professor in the Department of Educational Studies at the University of British Columbia. Her research and pedagogical practice emphasise the complexities, paradoxes, contradictions, complicities and uncertainties related to decolonisation, sustainability and internationalisation in higher education. Through her work she seeks to support practices that can enable the emergence of more socially and ecologically accountable possibilities for knowing, being and relating otherwise. Sharon is a founding member of the Gesturing Decolonial Futures

Collective (decolonialfutures.net) and founder of the Critical Internationalization Studies Network (criticalinternationalization.net).

Cloris Porto Torquato is a Professor in the Department of Language Studies, State University of Ponta Grossa (UEPG). She is a Collaborating Professor in the Postgraduate Program in Language and Literature Studies at the Federal University of Paraná. She holds a PhD in Linguistics from the State University of Campinas (UNICAMP). Cloris's professional experience encompasses elementary, high school and higher education. She works in the areas of teaching Portuguese and Portuguese Additional Language. Her research interests include literacies, language policies and ideologies, and decolonial options in research and in teaching-learning processes. Currently, Cloris coordinates two projects at the UEPG: both are research and community engagement projects; one is related to initial and in-service teacher education and language education; the other is related to teaching Portuguese Additional Language to migrants and refugees.

Robyn Tyler is a Postdoctoral Fellow in the Centre for Multilingualism and Diversities Research at the University of the Western Cape. She is a researcher on the project 'Leveraging Languages for Science Learning in Multilingual Classrooms (2020–2022)', which seeks to develop best practice in multilingual science classrooms. Robyn supervises graduate students and student teachers and is a member of the bua-lit Language and Literacy Collective (www.bua-lit.org.za). Her research interests include semiotic repertoires for learning, translingual practice, youth and identity, inquiry-based science education and language across the curriculum.

Prologue

Coloniality and Language

'Coloniality is different from colonialism. Colonialism denotes a political and economic relation in which the sovereignty of a nation or a people rests on the power of another nation, which makes such nation an empire. Coloniality, instead, refers to long-standing patterns of power that emerged as a result of colonialism, but that define culture, labor, intersubjective relations, and knowledge production well beyond the strict limits of colonial administrations. Thus, coloniality survives colonialism. It is maintained alive in books, in the criteria for academic performance, in cultural patterns, in common sense, in the self-image of peoples, in aspirations of self, and so many other aspects of our modern experience. In a way, as modern subjects we breathe coloniality all the time and every day.' (Maldonado-Torres, 2007: 243)

'The biggest weapon wielded and actually daily unleashed by imperialism against that collective defiance is the cultural bomb. The effect of a cultural bomb is to annihilate a people's belief in their names, in their languages, in their environment, in their heritage of struggle, in their unity, in their capacities and ultimately in themselves. (…) It makes them see their past as one wasteland of non-achievement and it makes them want to distance themselves from that wasteland. It makes them want to identify with that which is furthest removed from themselves; for instance, with other people's languages rather than their own.' (Ngũgĩ wa Thiongo, 1986: 3)

'The internal enemy – colonisation – is within us all, from elites to the oppressed.' (Cusicanqui, in Dulfano, 2014)

Borderlands and Contact Zones

'The US-Mexican border *es una herida abierta* where the Third World grates against the first and bleeds.' (Anzaldúa, 1987: 25)

'… the borderlands are present wherever two or more cultures edge each other, where people of different races occupy the same territory, where under, lower, upper and middle classes touch, where the space between two individuals shrinks with intimacy.' (Anzaldúa, Preface to 1st edition of *Borderlands/La Frontera*, 1987)

'I use this term [contact zone] to refer to social spaces where cultures meet, clash, and grapple with each other, often in contexts of highly asymmetrical relations of power, such as colonialism, slavery, or their aftermaths as they are lived out in many parts of the world today.' (Pratt, 1991: 34)

Third Space

'But for me the importance of hybridity is not to be able to trace two original moments from which the third emerges, rather hybridity to me is the "third space" which enables other positions to emerge. This third space displaces the histories that constitute it, and sets up new structures of authority, new political initiatives which are inadequately understood through received wisdom.' (Bhabha, 1990: 211)

Third space is 'a transformative space where the potential for an expanded form of learning and the development of new knowledge are heightened'. (Gutierrez, 2008: 152)

References

Anzaldúa, G. (1987) *Borderlands/La Frontera: The New Mestiza*. San Francisco, CA: Aunt Lute Books.
Bhabha, H. (1990) The third space. Interview with Homi Bhabha. In J. Rutherford (ed.) *Identity: Community, Culture, Difference* (pp. 207–221). London: Lawrence & Wishart.
Dulfano, I. (2014) Decolonising the person, the image, and the collective global psyche through the lens of Silvia Rivera Cusicanqui. *Cultural Survival Quarterly Magazine*, March. See https://www.culturalsurvival.org/publications/cultural-survival-quarterly/decolonizing-person-image-and-collective-global-psyche (accessed 20 October 2020).
Gutierrez, K. (2008) Developing a sociocritical literacy in the third space. *Reading Research Quarterly* 43 (2), 148–164.
Maldonado Torres, N. (2007) On the coloniality of being: Contributions to the development of a concept. *Cultural Studies* 21 (2–3), 240–270.
Ngũgĩ wa Thiongo (1986) *Decolonising the Mind: The Language of African Literature*. London: James Currey.
Pratt, M. (1991) Arts of the contact zone. *Profession* 91, 33–40.

1 Introduction: Conversations with Teacher Educators in Coloniality

Carolyn McKinney and Pam Christie

This book began as conversations between colleagues involved in teacher education at the University of Cape Town (UCT) in a period when student protest movements calling for *Free Decolonised Education* forced a thoroughgoing engagement with the continuing coloniality of university spaces. In reflexive conversations on knowledge production and participation over the following years, we came to understand how contestations that highlighted coloniality, racism, poverty and gender violence brought moments of heightened learning for ourselves as teacher educators as well as the students.

Written against the backdrop of intense experiences of campus protests and shutdowns, the book grapples with what is required to prepare student teachers to enter a highly divided and unequal schooling system shaped by coloniality in the Global South. The book reflects on: how we as teacher educators and educational researchers grapple with the colonial matrix of power in our daily practice; how we make decisions about what counts as 'knowledge'; how we teach 'canonical' disciplinary knowledge while at the same time challenging this and acknowledging the epistemic violence wrought by the partiality of this knowledge; how we challenge the monolingual myth and enable multilingualism; and how we explore the possibilities and constraints of conducting research and scholarship in times of instability.

Our aim in this book is to build and broaden professional conversations that explore possibilities for alternative engagement in teacher education in conditions of coloniality. Alongside academic genres, the book uses a range of unconventional genres, representations of data and reflective narratives of teaching and teacher education. It sets out examples of multimodal, multilingual and embodied interactions between and among teacher educators and student teachers in science, literacy and language across the curriculum, showing our/their learning experiences and positioning. We encourage curious readers to use an automatic translation site like Google Translate for some of the reflective text that is written in isiXhosa, Afrikaans and SeSotho. In using a range of genres, the book aims to shine light on the power of participation in knowledge-making that takes place beyond the borders of disciplines and formal classroom spaces, without simply disregarding these. Significantly, the book shows that it is through the disruption of transmission modes of teaching in formal classrooms that the knowledge-making shared in this book took place.

While the research informing the chapters of the book is grounded in South Africa with its highly unequal education systems, the issues explored have relevance well beyond this context. The book contributes to broader debates about achieving social justice and equity in historically unequal contexts, particularly those of the Global South. And it opens possibilities for third space learning in engaging with the decolonial challenge of thinking *within* rather than *about* the complex power relations of border conditions.

In this introductory chapter, we address the coloniality of education in South Africa in the context of the student protests of 2015–2017, providing a brief account of issues and events. Next, we outline some of the major tensions and dilemmas in educating teachers in conditions of coloniality, considering the coloniality of knowledge and language as well as the conceptual tools of third space and pluriversality. Finally, we provide an overview of the chapters and contributions in this book, written to show a range of responses of teacher educators in schools and universities in South Africa and other places – which we describe in different ways as the border conditions of coloniality.

Our Starting Point: Education and Coloniality in South Africa

The first formal conversations that began this book project on education and coloniality took place at the end of 2017 when, for the third year running, student protests had shut down formal classes on campus towards the end of the academic year. In response to shutdown, the university had adopted a range of dispersing practices to complete the academic year, such as off-campus sessions and blended learning, and students were given the option of completing their end-of-year assessment or deferring it until the start of the next year. In what was increasingly becoming a binary choice for students and academics across the campus, we experienced competing pulls between supporting students who chose to complete their studies as well as those who favoured deferral and those who struggled with their uncertainty. A confronting symbol of the university's ambivalent response to the conflict was a large tent prominently erected on the rugby field on campus at the end of the year – fenced in and patrolled by armed security guards – to enable students who chose to write exams to do so.

As teacher education academics responsible for delivering an accredited programme under circumstances of protest and boycott, we were directly affected by student protests. Our responsibility was to complete the course accreditation requirements within the academic year for students who selected to graduate, while supporting students who chose to boycott formal classes and/or defer assessment. As a group of colleagues whose work engaged with schools as well as the university, we felt the need to create a space for dialogue across our theoretical and professional differences in order to work creatively and ethically with the complex conditions that student protests brought into focus. These protests highlighted 'decoloniality' as a rallying point, challenging academics such as ourselves to question the ways in which the culture of the university and its curriculum and language practices contributed to persistent inequalities that lingered despite the formal demise of apartheid and the launch of a new democracy in 1994.

Student protests and campus shutdowns at higher education institutions across the country during 2015–2017 shone the spotlight on experiences of coloniality. As defined by Maldonado-Torres (2007), coloniality is that which survives colonialism – the multiple unequal relationships that persist after the formal administrative structures of colonisation are dismantled. In his words:

> Coloniality … refers to long-standing patterns of power that emerged as a result of colonialism, but that define culture, labor, intersubjective relations, and knowledge production well beyond the strict limits of colonial administrations. Thus, coloniality survives colonialism. It is maintained alive in books, in the criteria for academic performance, in cultural patterns, in common sense, in the self-image of peoples, in aspirations of self, and so many other aspects of our modern experience. In a way, as modern subjects we breathe coloniality all the time and every day. (Maldonado-Torres, 2007: 243)

The demand for Free Decolonised Education made visible the limitations and stress points of the negotiated settlement that formally ended apartheid in 1994. Very briefly, the 1994 settlement brought political democratisation and formal equality before the law but did not fundamentally restructure the economy or shift the distribution of resources. South Africa is judged to be one of the most unequal countries in the world, and violence – particularly violence against women – is at shocking levels. The burdens of poverty and unemployment continue to be skewed towards black people, 'race'[1] has not diminished as a major predictor of social and educational outcomes, and the spatial geography of apartheid persists. Overall, political democracy has not fundamentally shifted the social and economic inequalities associated with apartheid and colonisation before that.

In education, systemic changes after the 1994 settlement ended the formal divisions of apartheid, but with limited reduction to the inequalities it had wrought. The field of higher education was restructured through a process of mergers, incorporations and closures, teacher colleges were shut down, and teacher education was brought under universities in a single national system for the first time. As Gillespie and Naidoo (2019) point out, the massification of higher education took place without proportional public funding, leading universities to seek revenue elsewhere, including through 'outsourcing' service workers (such as cleaners, maintenance workers and gardeners) and increasing student fees. While financial austerity has been a common experience for universities globally, what brings particular complexity in South Africa is its timing with the formal dismantling of apartheid. In effect, the removal of racial barriers to student access happened at the same time as financial barriers (fees and other costs) were raised. As Bangeni and Kapp (2017) note:

> South Africa is a particularly interesting case because in post-apartheid South Africa, considerable resources have been directed towards changing the racially-skewed pattern of university participation. Nevertheless, the participation rates for African and coloured students (in the 20- to 24-year-old cohort) have remained 'persistently very low' (14 per cent in 2011), and generally under a quarter of that of white students with 'under 5 per cent of African and coloured youth succeeding in any form of higher education' (Council on Higher Education, 2013:15). This pattern has in turn had a considerable impact on access to postgraduate studies for this demographic. (Bangeni & Kapp, 2017: 1)

In schooling, the post-apartheid policy framework replaced the multiple racially divided education departments with a single national and nine provincial departments. Fees were introduced into the public system, and extensive powers were given to school governing bodies. However, the system as a whole performs dismally, with South Africa ranked at the bottom, or close to the bottom, on all international comparative scales (see Christie, 2020). Performance patterns in the system are bimodal: there are distinctively different results for students attending different schools, and these results differ according to the poverty classification and former apartheid departments of schools. In these bimodal results, nearly 80% of students attend the poorly functioning part of the system, with a small minority (8%) attending the fee-paying schools (mostly desegregated) that achieve good results (Mlachila & Moeletsi, 2019). Almost all of the poorly performing schools are black schools in rural areas and townships. Given that these unequal patterns of resource allocation and achievement are deeply entrenched, it could be argued that they are co-constitutive, illustrating the promise of modernity together with what Mignolo (2011) calls its 'dark side' (Christie & McKinney, 2017). The curriculum exemplifies the Western episteme and its 'powerful knowledge', showing scant regard for other knowledges. Although there are 11 constitutionally recognised languages (including nine Indigenous African languages), schools provide African language as medium of instruction for the first three years only, after which all students must learn through the medium of monolingual English or Afrikaans – an issue we return to later in this chapter. As Gramling (2016) points out, the imposition of language is an innate aspect of modernity/coloniality:

> Whether we opt to call it a myth, a pathology, a paradigm, a relic, or a sham, monolingualism is woven into modernity's most minute and sophisticated political structures, and it is clearly not yet inclined to be waved off the stage by a university professor, nor even by a 'multilingual turn' in one or another discipline. (Gramling, 2016: 3–4)

These contextual conditions provide the logic for student protests and campus shutdowns across the country, 20 years after the end of apartheid. Protests point to the difficulties of shifting deep-seated inequalities – entangled intersectional inequalities of class, race, ethnicity, gender, language, geographical location and more – within a neoliberal economic policy framework. In addition, protests highlight the continuing inequalities between historically black and historically white institutions, as well as their apartheid spatial heritage, colonial knowledge hierarchies and exclusionary language practices (Editorial Collective, 2017; Mzilene & Mkhize, 2019; Xaba, 2017).[2]

Student Protests: RhodesMustFall (#RMF) and FeesMustFall (#FMF)

The protests and shutdowns of 2015 were sparked off at the historically white universities of Cape Town (UCT) and Witwatersrand (Wits), and spread rapidly to universities across the country. On 9 March 2015, a student protester at UCT emptied excrement from a portable toilet onto the bronze sculpture of arch-imperialist Cecil John Rhodes which dominated the entrance to the campus. This signalled the beginning of the #RhodesMustFall (RMF) movement, calling for the 'decolonisation' of the university. RMF's first goal was achieved with the statue's removal on 9 April 2015, but protracted struggle and protest continued around their more substantive concerns which remained simmering points of contest. In October 2015, students at Wits in Johannesburg began a protest against the proposed 10.5% fee increase at their university. This sparked the #FeesMustFall (FMF) movement, which rapidly gained national momentum across all public universities, and included a national student march on the Union Buildings (the administrative seat of government) in Tshwane/Pretoria in October. In response, State President Zuma gave an assurance that there would be zero increase in fees for 2016 – in effect, placing an additional financial burden on universities. On each campus, protests took different shape with varying demands, but what united all was the call for free, decolonised education and an end to the outsourcing of service workers. Insourcing became synonymous with FMF, and was one of the achievements of the protest movements at UCT and Wits.

At UCT, October 2015 was the first of a series of protests leading to the total shutdown of teaching and learning activities on the campus, repeated towards the end of the academic years in 2016 and 2017. It was also the beginning of what can be described as the militarisation/securitisation of the campus during protests, with the senior management employing private security and even allowing the South African Police Service onto the campus at one point. Protest marches to parliament in Cape Town were met with tear gas and stun grenades from the public order police (POPS) and, on campus, violent confrontations between police and student protestors as well as private security and student protestors were frequent.

It is significant to note that there is a much longer history of student protests against economic exclusion from universities following the changes of 1994, including annual fee protests throughout the 1990s and 2000s at historically black universities (HBUs) such as Tshwane University of Technology, Walter Sisulu University, University of Fort Hare, the Cape Peninsula University of Technology and the University of the Western Cape. However, as has been pointed out (Gillespie & Naidoo, 2019; Ndelu et al., 2017), earlier protests at HBUs had been largely ignored by the media. It took protest action at the historically white and elite institutions (HWUs) such as UCT and Wits to draw the attention of the media, general public and politicians. Xaba (2017) describes the spread of student concerns as follows:

> At historically White universities racism, exclusionary language policies and colonial symbolism form part of the national call for free education. At historically Black universities, however, other issues that form part of protest include the basic functioning of universities, better resources such as accommodation and access to technology, and the return of student activists who were excluded for ongoing protests years before FMF. (Xaba, 2017: 98)

Gillespie and Naidoo (2019) argue that the RMF and FMF protests at the HWUs of UCT and Wits may be understood as resistance to the epistemological and ontological violence of assimilating into higher education institutions that were designed to create elite, white, colonial subjectivities. As they put it, 'Black students' protest was ... against their own alienation as the new elites into a society that remains stuck in white institutional time' (Gillespie & Naidoo, 2019: 233). This is expanded as follows in the words of one of the Fallist student organisers at UCT:

> So I think the huge issue when you come to a university like UCT as a black person [is that] you see and feel very clearly the dehumanisation,

marginalisation and exploitation as a black person – whether it be as a worker, as a student, or as an academic. So we're challenging institutional racism, patriarchy, capitalism, neoliberalism and the commodification of education. We're calling for free decolonised education, which means we want the decommodification of education and knowledge production. We want different pedagogies at the university and an institution that is decolonised, which would mean that knowledge production and pedagogies are centred in decolonial theory and praxis. We are also calling for liberation, challenging racism, patriarchy, misogyny and sexism within the university and outside. Those are very big calls and very big challenges that have faced much resistance at the institution but also outside of it. (Hotz, 2017: 125)

In an editorial to the special issue of feminist journal *Agenda*, Ndelu *et al.* (2017: 1) argue that 'the RMF and then the FMF student movements irrevocably chang[ed] the political and cultural landscapes of university campuses', and they draw attention to the extensive role of 'cyber activism that deployed social media on a scale heretofore unseen in the national political arena' (Ndelu *et al.*, 2017: 1). RMF went on to inspire protest action at a number of UK universities, including Oriel College at Oxford where 'Rhodes Must Fall Oxford' (RMFO) was born, as well as the 'Royal Must Fall Movement' at Harvard Law School in the USA.

Educating Teachers in Conditions of Coloniality: Ethical-epistemological Projects

The conversations on which this book is based explored how we as teacher educators might respond ethically to the complex demands of contested and polarised times of protests and closures. A necessary first step was and is to acknowledge our own situatedness at an elite English-medium university which charges high fees. Historically, when teacher education was restructured after apartheid and colleges of education were closed, UCT was one of only two universities in the country that did not incorporate a college. The new national qualification system provides for four years of initial teacher education, either offered as a single four-year Bachelor of Education (BEd) degree, or a three-year Bachelor's degree followed by a one-year Post Graduate Certificate in Education (PGCE). All of the universities that incorporated colleges during the restructuring offer four-year BEd degrees, but UCT does not. Teacher education students come into our programmes with degrees, many from other institutions. The racial demographics of our one-year certificate class have changed over the last five years from majority white students to majority black students. The dominant languages of our context are English, Afrikaans and isiXhosa.

Having attended schools in South Africa, we ourselves embody the multiple segmentations of apartheid's history. Although we abhor the assumption that 'race' exists as a category of being, we cannot escape the structures of racism, nor can we erase our historical positionality even as we push against it. Moreover, given that apartheid was a form of racial capitalism and that the post-apartheid government has embraced global neoliberalism, we also need to acknowledge that entangled class inequalities have shaped our educational opportunities and experiences. Chapter authors were educated in different sections of the unequal apartheid schooling system, divided by its racial classification system, its spatial segregation and its colonialist language policies. As individuals we attended a range of different apartheid schools: separate English- and Afrikaans-medium 'white' schools; lesser resourced 'coloured' schools; poorly resourced black 'African' schools; and elite private schools. Being educated under the South African curriculum, most of us are formally bilingual in English and Afrikaans – although this does not necessarily translate into language fluency. Some of us have African home language backgrounds and several have communicative capacity in an African language, but others of us do not. All of us have experienced apartheid but were positioned differently in its power relations. We bear these histories, even if unwillingly or unwittingly, as embodied, experiential differences. As teacher educators, all of us by dint of our histories engage with schools that are different from those that we ourselves attended. And, specifically, as the editors of this book, we are cognisant both of our privileged positions in whiteness, as speakers of English, and as a tenured university professor (Carolyn) and a retired tenured professor (Pam) in elite institutions, albeit in the Global South, as well as the limitations of knowing and experiencing this brings.

Given that teacher education straddles both universities and schooling systems, and that both systems struggle with entangled inequalities as mentioned earlier, we felt acutely aware that the challenges of teacher education could neither be sidestepped, nor easily resolved, in times of protest. Even a cursory glance at the corpus of international literature on teacher education shows that there are inherent problems and persistent uncertainties across the field. These include debates about: the knowledge base for teaching; what is entailed in teaching for learning, particularly in a range of different classroom contexts; the need to engage with existing schooling systems which may be far from 'ideal'; the role of the practicum (placements, aims, length, assessment); how to teach for recognition of cultural and linguistic diversity; how research might inform teaching, and so on. Although commonly occurring across different places, these points of debate need to be engaged with in situated ways. In South Africa, the challenge may be starkly put as follows: How might initial teacher education programmes best prepare students to work for social justice in one of the most unequal societies in the world, with a divided and variably performing schooling system of which they themselves are products? How, in times of crisis and polarisation, might the professional requirements of qualifications be met, and students from different backgrounds and with different beliefs be supported to build their knowledge for teaching and to be prepared to teach in the complex and unequal schooling system?

Debates on coloniality highlight the fraught relationship between Western canonical knowledge forms and other knowledges. On the one hand, the externally imposed requirements of the professional teaching qualification as well as the formal curriculum of schools mean that students need to have a level of proficiency in canonical and disciplinary knowledge. This is particularly important in terms of their competence and confidence to teach in formal classroom contexts. On the other hand, student protests highlight the coloniality of these same knowledge forms, and the linguistic and epistemological violence associated with university achievement under these conditions. In short, protests highlight an uncomfortable tension between the necessity of canonical knowledge in the university and its simultaneous symbolic violence. In our conversations, we came to recognise that there would be no simple resolutions, and that these tensions must be held to explore possibilities of thinking and acting within their complex entanglements. Acknowledging our situatedness in these knowledge practices is a necessary starting point, but it cannot suffice as an end point – as is shown by the work of education scholars such as Vanessa Andreotti (2016). The chapters of this book reflect our moves to work with these conditions of knowledge production that we must engage with as ethical-epistemological projects.

Coloniality of language

A related curriculum issue that we grapple with in teacher education is the prevalence of Anglonormativity (McKinney, 2017: 80), the normative 'expectation that people will be or should be proficient in English, and are deficient, even deviant, if they are not', in the face of linguistic diversity across the country. Without a doubt, one of the most powerful expressions of coloniality is the continuing denigration of the language practices and resources of black speakers around the globe. In an interview, Ngũgĩ wa Thiongo reflects as follows on the destructive effects of language suppression under colonialism:

> When people or anybody alienates you from your own language, it's a kind of alienation really from many things. First, from the knowledge carried by that language – so the knowledge of the area, the trees, the rivers, whatever, gone. Second, from the history of the community that made that language, gone. For a language it takes many years, hundreds of years to be where it is. So, that external power completely whips out, like a hurricane, like a bomb that comes and clears everything that was there and it tries to plant something else on this terrain or contaminated ground, that's how I call it. (Barison *et al.*, 2018: 276)

As Ngũgĩ points out, language is much more than a means of communication; it also constructs culture and knowledge: 'mediating between me and my own self; between my own self and other selves; between me and nature' (Ngũgĩ wa Thiongo, 1986: 15). In an observation that would apply to post-apartheid education for students speaking African languages, he states:

> Colonial alienation ... starts with a deliberate disassociation of the language of conceptualisation, of thinking, of formal education, of mental development, from the language of daily interaction in the home and in the community. It is like separating the mind from the body so that they are occupying two unrelated linguistic spheres in the same person. (Ngũgĩ wa Thiongo, 1986: 28)

It is interesting to note that Ngũgĩ was imprisoned when he wrote in Kikuyu to make his ideas accessible to local people rather than an English-reading audience – an indication of the political importance of language for communication. Monolingual language of instruction in English, a colonial language, is a major and unresolved issue in South African education. Several of the chapters of this book grapple with how to disrupt monolingualism in English and use students' full language repertoires as resources for learning.

Third space and pluriversality

Not only are the majority of learners' languages excluded from education, but the divides in provisioning are profound, and they are also spatially variable. While many former white-only schools in suburbs and towns are desegregated and those in wealthier communities are able to charge substantial fees to supplement state allocations, the majority of schools are no-fee black schools located in townships and rural areas, and receiving woefully inadequate state funding. Given the very poor performance of the majority of schools and their location in contexts of poverty and disadvantage, how do we meet ethical responsibilities as teacher educators both to work critically within structural constraints and also to shift them? The teaching practicum highlights the general challenges we face in working with schools, particularly where there are differences in functionality. What schools should students be allocated to for school experience? How do we support students who experience racism and sexism at practicum schools? What are the consequences when a privileged former white-only school offers our top graduate a traineeship rather than a full position because she is a black woman? How do we respond to students' concerns about corporal punishment, outlawed but widely practised in schools? What do we do when students and staff are held up at gunpoint at school gates or have their cars hijacked? Daily life in South Africa and its schools is often brutal and confronting, and we cannot sidestep this.

For many of us, the concept of third space (as discussed in the work of Bhabha, Anzaldúa and Gutierrez) and of creating and working within pedagogical third spaces has been generative. Gutierrez (2008: 152) defines third space as 'a transformative space where the potential for an expanded form of learning and the development of new knowledge are heightened'. Significant for several of the chapters in this book, Gutierrez argues for the importance of collaborative or collective third space as 'interactionally constituted'. Most of the chapters in this book grapple with the kinds of spaces that are and that can be constituted through embodied, multimodal and multilingual interaction, taking cognisance of the fact that interaction involves the resources of language, gesture and the body, artefacts and affect, all of which are shaped by our lived experiences and aspirations for the future. As we are using it here, third space is filled with intentionality to create and describe something new, to grapple productively with difference and to shift dominant ideologies. Contact zones (Pratt, 1991) and borderlands (Anzaldúa, 2012 [1987]) are constituted by the clash and conflict of culture, and different ways of knowing and being that are hierarchical following the logic of coloniality, at times producing weeping wounds (Anzaldúa). Although transformative, third space is not a utopia and is characterised both by discomfort and by pleasure.

During periods of shutdown at the university, we had to learn how to constitute spaces for learning that were not undermining of protest but that enabled us as teachers and students to learn together from and within the current sociopolitical moment. The political moment challenged us to recognise the constitutive nature of physical space for formalised teaching and learning, while exploring how to work in different spaces to build interactionally constituted pedagogic practices in ways that are sustainable, or at least potentially sustainable. The visual essay at the beginning of Part 2 of the book gives a sense of the different spaces of contestation and learning during the protests. Contributions to the book also show the opportunities for learning in spaces outside of the traditional lecture halls and classrooms such as the atrium of our building and the open-air amphitheatre outside it, the university plaza and the forecourt of parliament in the city, an interactive science centre, as well as the spaces of semi-rural and urban under-resourced schools. As well as showing different places of learning, contributions also explore how the spaces inside lecture halls and seminar rooms can be transformed by changing:

- what and how we teach and learn
- what languages are used
- who participates, and
- what kinds of participation are enabled.

In short, what we learnt was that breaking the formal transmission mode in different ways opened up expanded and unanticipated learning opportunities for students and ourselves. Points of rupture that required us to 'leave the script' and open ourselves to uncertainty together with students brought unplanned and unpredictable opportunities for knowledge work – work that could extend (and at times disrupt and replace) conventional canonical knowledge without surrendering to an 'anything goes' relativism. In conditions of complex coloniality, moments such as these offered opportunities to question assumptions about normative language practices, about constructing disadvantage as deficit, and about the emphasis on individual, cognitive approaches to learning at the expense of collective, embodied, multimodal and multilingual learning. Reflecting on these as moments of 'interactionally constituted' learning, we do not regard them as stable achievements or moments of triumph in a decolonial struggle. Rather, they are moments – short or more extended, improvisational or planned – that surface the contradictions of our context as teacher educators and enable us to engage or confront them.

In our conversations from border positions, we grapple in particular with Mignolo's conception of pluriversality – with the challenges of thinking *within* the border and not simply *about* the border. In Mignolo's words:

> Pluriversality is not cultural relativism, but entanglement of several cosmologies connected today in a power differential. That power differential is the logic of coloniality covered up by the rhetorical narrative of modernity. ... If a pluriverse is not a world of independent units (cultural relativism) but a world entangled through and by the colonial matrix of power, then, a way of thinking and understanding that dwells in the entanglement, in the borders, is needed. (Mignolo, 2013)

Our aim is for the chapters and conversations in the book to demonstrate how we work pluriversally, providing examples of how we as teacher educators, learners at schools and student teachers dwell within the borders of, and of how we work within, across and outside disciplinary boundaries and formal spaces in our daily practice. To this end, chapters take different forms including traditional research genres, a photo-essay, use of cartoon conventions to represent video-recorded/visual data and the development of an academic argument through an interview, i.e. a hybrid of oral and literate forms. Visual data are especially important in representing the multimodal and embodied nature of participation in knowledge-making, in teaching and learning. Chapters are also interspersed with unconventional genres for academic writing such as poetry, personal reflective pieces and extracts of transcribed conversations among authors. This is our attempt to work with pluriversality in form, where the expected norms of an academic genre can sit alongside a photo-essay and an interview, although not necessarily comfortably. As such it is part of our enactment of dwelling within the borders. The effect is discontinuous, an interruption in the seamless flow of argument we might expect from edited books. It might be experienced as disruptive, or irritating, but we believe it has helped us to expand the ways in which knowledge is made and (re)presented to readers. It also helps us to make visible different practices of participation in knowledge-making that are often hidden, and we actively invite readers to engage in this space.

Outline of the Book

The contributions in this book are divided into three parts. **Part 1** focuses on the continuing coloniality and spaces for decoloniality in schooling, beginning with poetry and drawing on fieldwork in three very different sites. All three sites/spaces provide schooling for the majority of African language speaking children who are marginalised in the current system. Part 1 opens with a poem by our much-admired late colleague, Professor Harry Garuba, which captures his own experience of schooling in conditions of coloniality in Nigeria. Collectively, the opening poem by Harry Garuba and the chapters by Xolisa Guzula, Pinky Makoe and Robyn Tyler provide insights into the ways in which coloniality continues to shape schooling, particularly through the use of English as a language of teaching and learning and current language policy implementation. But Xolisa's and Robyn's research also show us possibilities for delinking from colonial language ideologies. Xolisa's chapter begins by giving us an account of the historical development of the post-apartheid language in education policy and its implementation that is the heartbeat of coloniality in the schooling system. She then provides us with an inspiring case study of a third space: an after-school literacy club which goes beyond artificial language boundaries and enables bilingual and emergent bilingual isiXhosa-English speaking children to work with their full linguistic and semiotic repertoires.

Pinky Makoe's research on children's oral storytelling in a Year 1 class is a disturbing account of how classroom practice is sculpted by 'Eurocentric historical ideologies of superiority and inferiority emanating from the colonial project'. The exclusive valuing of Western folkloric narratives in this space effectively seals off the children's life worlds and experiences from what counts in the classroom. Here the classroom resembles a contact zone (Pratt) where the children's voices are asserted, but not necessarily heard. Robyn Tyler's research with bilingual isiXhosa/English speaking Grade 9 science students focuses on language and identity in learning chemistry. Here the learning space becomes a productive borderland with the meshing of multiple language and semiotic resources, discourses and identity positions. Robyn focuses on the heteroglossic practices that students use, subverting and disrupting the imposed monolingual colonial language ideology of English-only textbooks and assessments in a process of 'identity meshing'. This case study has important implications for decolonial pedagogy and teacher education. Like Xolisa's literacy club, the learning space created here is expansive, experimenting with how we can delink from coloniality in pedagogical practices. All three of these chapters have significant implications for teacher education: student teachers need to confront the ways in which coloniality continues to shape practices in our schools as well as to see how they might be able to work against this.

Part 2 of the book focuses on spaces of learning in teacher education, and on experiences of doing teacher education in a context of coloniality. We begin this part with a photo-essay by Kate Angier, Carolyn McKinney and Catherine Kell, curating images from the student protests on our campus beginning in 2015 and moving through to the protests against gender-based violence of 2019. The curated images are an attempt to represent some of the learning and teaching that took place outside the walls of the formal lecture theatre and seminar rooms, such as in the atrium/courtyard of our building, outside on the plaza on the campus and in the forecourt of parliament in the city centre. The images are interwoven with reflections on our learning in these moments of crisis and tension-filled spaces. In Chapters 6 and 7 that follow, Annemarie Hattingh and Rochelle Kapp take us into student teachers' learning experiences during their school-based teaching practice. Both chapters draw attention to how much can be learned from student practice teaching in under-resourced schools: Annemarie's in semi-rural areas and Rochelle's in urban working-class schools. Annemarie reflects on how to do socially just science teacher education in a context of coloniality, where student teachers must work both within and against the systemic inequalities. She shows us how the village schools can be a productive third space for teacher education. Rochelle's research draws our attention to a number of different borderland spaces within which the student teachers have to dwell: they are both students and teachers in the school space; they bring with them their own experiences of well-resourced or elite schooling into the urban working-class schools where they will practise teaching. Rochelle shows how the student teachers grapple with inhabiting the borderlands through reflective journal writing, highlighting how three students 'located themselves within the borders, simultaneously placing themselves in learning positions and enacting considerable agency in order to counter deficit constructions of black working-class learners'.

Chapters 8 and 9 by Soraya Abdulatief and Carolyn McKinney take us into case studies of teacher education practice within the student teachers' coursework. Soraya shares her research on an intervention conducted with four multilingual science teacher education students who expressed an interest in receiving additional support to succeed in the PGCE. Against the background of the students' own constrained schooling and undergraduate experiences, Soraya shows the power of participation in an interactive science centre, a space outside the university classroom, for students' learning, and for the expansion of their repertoires of practice.

She argues that third space which offers a 'radical openness' is productive theoretically and practically for enacting decolonial science teacher education. Carolyn shares a case study of teaching and learning in a literacy methodology course for early years teachers (reception to Grade 3) which aimed to prepare them for multilingual classrooms and to unlearn colonial language ideologies. The course enabled students to confront the colonially shaped, and thus racialised, hierarchies of multilingualism. In such hierarchies, proficiency in multiple European languages is valorised while proficiency in Indigenous languages is rendered invisible, an ideology not unique to South Africa (García & Lin, 2018). Carolyn shows how the lecturer constructed a translingual space where the African language resources of students that are usually invisible became central to successful participation in the class and where ways of knowing usually excluded from the English canon were valorised.

Part 2 concludes in Chapter 10 with reflections from a senior literacy studies scholar, Catherine Kell, who is interviewed by language and literacy studies scholars Xolisa Guzula and Carolyn McKinney about her work with in-service teachers of literacy enrolled in postgraduate study. Catherine argues that, in order for teachers to be able to approach literacy education in a decolonial way, they are required to unlearn colonial and racialised ideologies of orality, literacy and the written word. Literacy teachers need to understand the invention of schooled literacy and the need for its reinvention. This creates a contact zone of another kind, where teachers have to confront their complicity in the coloniality of the curriculum, language and literacy pedagogies and recover their sense of agency to resist these.

Part 3 of the book offers reflections and dialogue from teacher educators grappling with coloniality and education in a range of geopolitical contexts, including perspectives from the Global South: Brazil, Canada and Chile. In Chapter 11, Cloris Porto Torquato engages in dialogue with us from her position as a language teacher educator and researcher in Brazil. Cloris highlights the parallels between Brazil and South Africa in terms of racialised participation in, and exclusion from, education, especially during the shift to 'online' learning in pandemic times. She points to 'the separation of mind, body, emotions and spirit' inherent in modernity/coloniality and, in congruence with our experience, highlights the part played by language in 'hierarchising people and their knowledges, world views and practices'. Recognising the differences between our contexts, Cloris draws attention to the continued working of centralising (colonial) and decentralising (decolonial) forces in contemporary Brazil, and stresses the need to hear marginalised and excluded voices as we engage in heterogeneous decolonial critiques, projects and praxis.

In Chapter 12, Vanessa Andreotti and Sharon Stein take up the invitation to offer an outsider perspective on our work, drawing on work with their collective on Gesturing Towards Decolonial Futures. They give a strong and important warning that critiques of modernity/coloniality may easily reproduce modernity's grammar and 'harmful traits', even when intended as acts of resistance. As an alternative to 'education for mastery' which is characteristic of modernity/colonialism, Vanessa and Sharon propose 'education for depth', where learning is understood as happening 'through a nested system where an intellectual layer is embedded in an affective layer that is embedded in a relational layer that is embedded in a "metabolic" layer', the latter being learning with and through the earth itself. Education for depth seeks to prepare learners with the 'stamina and dispositions' to hold complexities, contradictions and uncertainties without repressing them or seeking immediate resolution. 'Not knowing', they suggest, can be a generative starting place for diving deeper.

Finally, in Chapter 13, Natalia Ávila Reyes offers a transnational reflection on the reading of this book from her position of teaching and researching writing in higher education in Chile. In her account, Natalia highlights striking and important similarities between higher education in Chile and South Africa, as places located in the Global South. One is the 'implicit deficit thinking' that operates when societies and universities are predominantly monolingual, and consequently the need to build bridges between academic literacy and the richness students bring in their 'interests, ethical commitments, expressive repertoires, and agency'. The other is the historical role that student movements have played in both countries in reshaping education. In Chile, the student movement showed the capacity 'to frame and communicate educational grievances' and highlighted struggles against patriarchy – also features of #RMF in South Africa. Natalia's reflection resonates with our own: 'Ultimately, the students are the ones who have confronted us, educational researchers and teacher educators, with ethical and educational imperatives'.

Reflection

We prepare this manuscript for publication in the midst of the COVID-19 global pandemic. As happened periodically during times of student protest over 2015–2017 and in 2019, our campus is again closed for 'face-to-face' teaching and learning, and we are engaged in a process of 'Emergency Remote Teaching'. We have not seen our students in a physical classroom for over six months. Yet again as teacher educators we find ourselves contemplating how best to prepare our students to become agentic teachers in a context that is anything but 'textbook' and of even further widening inequality. Although the cause of closure is different, the experience of teaching in a time of crisis is not and our experience over the past five years has taught us that we need to prepare our students and ourselves as educators for teaching and learning in turbulent times. To suggest that uncertainty and insecurity are the 'new normal' as some are doing at

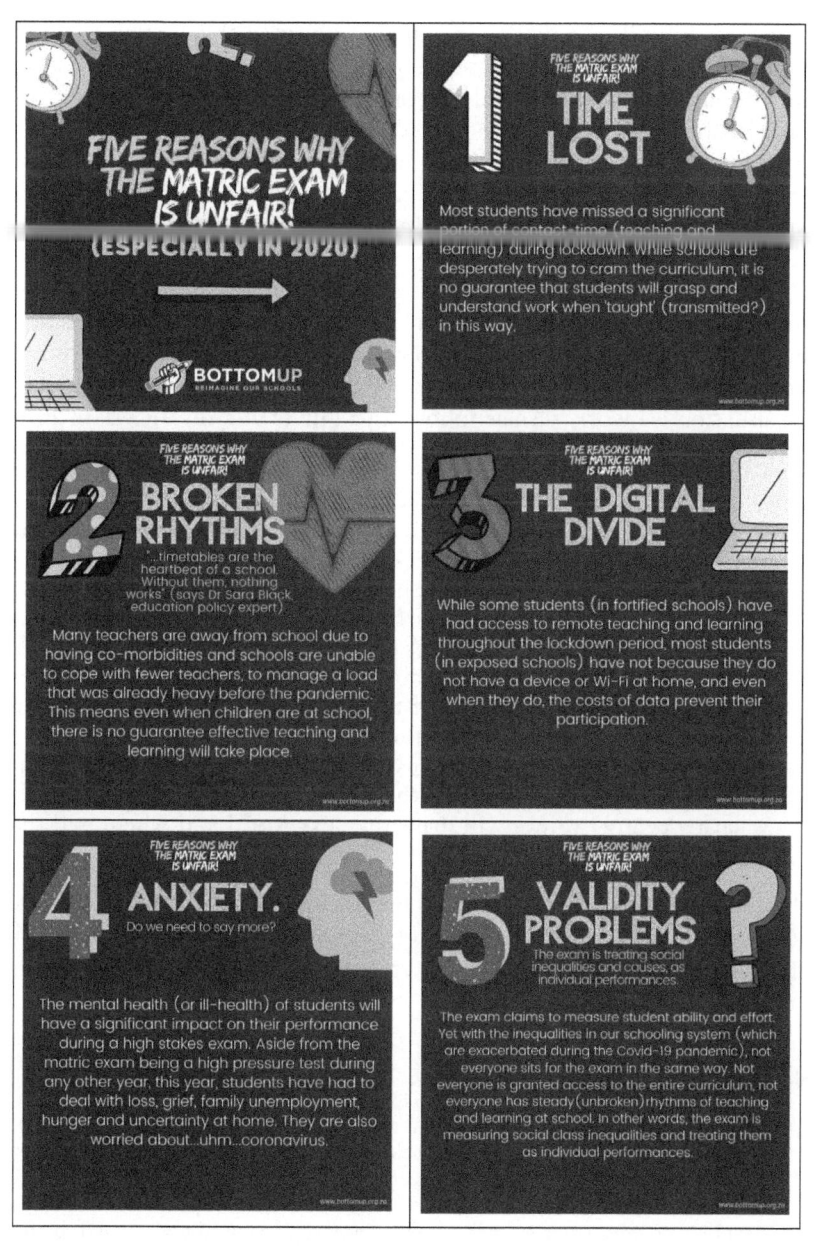

Figure 1.1 Five reasons why the matric exam is unfair! (Especially in 2020)
Source: Bottomup.

present is, however, to reveal the privileged position within the colonial matrix of power from which that statement is made.

There is nothing normal about 80% of our school students having no access to formal teaching and learning for over five months when schools were closed, while a minority in elite schools were able to continue with online learning using their personal or family devices and home access to the internet. And there should be nothing normal about students across the schooling system having to proceed with the end-of-school matriculation examinations in conditions of pandemic, as though all have had equal access to the curriculum. The creative campaign by alternative education NGO, *bottomup*, crystallises the inequality reproduced by the matric examinations (Figure 1.1).

Current educational injustice is an exacerbation of an increasingly unequal education system which continues to constitute the darker side of modernity. The need to engage and dwell within the borderlands is ever more urgent. Njabulo Ndebele, former Vice Chancellor of UCT, presented the situation we work with as follows in a public talk on #RMF in 2021:

> The garnish of excrement on Rhodes's statue, never a visual part of the celebration of western achievement, was at the time brought into full global view, as was to be the more recent knee of white American police officer Derek Chauvin, on the neck of George Floyd. That knee, which today takes on the look of vaccine nationalisms, the very displays of technological achievement in a horribly unequal world, has been on the throats of two-thirds of the world's population beyond Euro-America, for some five hundred years of world history. South Africa and the continent it belongs to feel the pressures of that global knee daily. It has become manifestly clear that the global values that have driven humanity and our shared world up to now, have led us all to a dead end. A new value system has to take its place. And that is the heraldic part of the Fall of Rhodes. What redeeming values will drive the next world and where will they come from? (Ndebele, 2021)

He concludes: 'The world I want to breathe in is the one many of us have been unable to create until perhaps this moment, now, when the conditions have arisen for me and you to create it. I want to breathe in a world that we now have to create.'

Notes

(1) We recognise 'race' as a social construct with profound material effects. Despite our recognition of the ways in which apartheid racial terminology reifies and essentialises race, we continue to use the apartheid categories of black African, white, Indian and 'coloured' in the book chapters as these categories are currently used for the implementation of redress policies such as employment equity and admissions and continue to describe the fault-lines and social positioning of South Africans. At some points the term 'black' is used inclusively for black African, coloured and Indian. The term 'coloured' refers to people who trace their blended ancestries largely to Africa, Asia and Europe. As a racial category created during the apartheid era, it is contested, both embraced and rejected by different people (see Antia & Dyers, 2019).
(2) There is a growing literature on the Rhodes Must Fall and Fees Must Fall movements. For student-produced accounts of RMF at UCT, see the *Johannesburg Salon* special edition edited by RMF students (2015); for student accounts of Fees Must

Fall at the University of Witwatersrand, see Editorial Collective (2017); for feminist student accounts across RMF and FMF, see the special issue of *Agenda* (2017). Academics Gillespie and Naidoo (2019) have guest edited an 'Against the Day' section of *South Atlantic Quarterly* on #MustFall. For a controversial account of FMF at the University of Witwatersrand from the perspective of the Vice-Chancellor, Adam Habib, see his monograph *Rebels and Rage* (2019). For insights into Black, working-class students' experiences in a historically white university, see the longitudinal research of Bangeni and Kapp (2017). For perspectives of a 'coconut', see Chikane (2010). On Oxford Rhodes Must Fall and allied movements in universities in the UK and Harvard, USA, see Chantiluke *et al.* (2018). There is a large literature on the post-apartheid restructuring of education. For overviews of changes in teacher education, see Chisholm (2019), Kruss (2008), Robinson (2003) and Sayed *et al.* (2018).

References

Andreotti, V. (2016) The educational challenges of imagining the world differently. *Canadian Journal of Development Studies* 37 (1), 101–112.

Antia, B. and Dyers, C. (2019) De-alienating the academy: Multilingual teaching as decolonial pedagogy. *Linguistics and Education* 51, 91–100.

Anzaldúa, G. (2012 [1987]) *Borderlands/La Frontera: The New Mestiza*. San Francisco, CA: Aunt Lute Books.

Bangeni, B. and Kapp, R. (2017) *Negotiating Learning and Identity in Higher Education: Access, Persistence and Retention*. London: Bloomsbury Academic.

Barison, G., Carmello, B., El Hansali, A. and Pratali Maffei, D. (2018) Ngũgĩ wa Thiong'o: An interview. *Il Tolomeo* 20 (December).

Chantiluke, R., Kwoba, B. and Nkopo, A. (eds) (2018) *Rhodes Must Fall: The Struggle to Decolonise the Racist Heart of Empire*. London: Zed Books.

Chikane, R. (2018) *Breaking a Rainbow, Building a Nation: The Politics Behind the #MustFall Movements*. Johannesburg: Picador Africa.

Chisholm, L. (2019) *Teacher Preparation in South Africa: History, Policy and Future Directions*. Bingley: Emerald Publishing.

Christie, P. (2020) *Decolonising Schools in South Africa: The Impossible Dream?* London and New York: Routledge.

Christie, P. and McKinney, C. (2017) Decoloniality and 'Model C' schools: Ethos, language and the protests of 2016. *Education as Change* 21 (3), 160–180.

Council on Higher Education (2013), A Proposal for Undergraduate Curriculum Reform in South Africa: The Case for a Flexible Curriculum Structure, http://www.che.ac.za/sites/default/files/publications/ (accessed 28 November 2013).

Editorial Collective (2017) *Rioting and Writing: Diaries of the Wits Fallists*. Johannesburg: SWOP, University of the Witwatersrand.

García, O. and Lin, A.M.Y. (2018) English and multilingualism: A contested history. In P. Seargeant, A. Hewings and S. Pihlaja (eds) *Routledge Handbook of English Language Studies* (pp. 77–92). London & New York: Routledge.

Gillespie, K. and Naidoo, L. (2019) #MustFall: The South African student movement and the politics of time. *South Atlantic Quarterly: Against the Day* 118 (1), 191–194.

Gramling, D. (2016) *The Invention of Monolingualism*. New York: Bloomsbury Academic.

Gutierrez, K. (2008) Developing a sociocritical literacy in the third space. *Reading Research Quarterly* 43 (2), 148–164.

Habib, A. (2019) *Rebels and Rage: Reflecting on #Fees Must Fall*. Johannesburg: Jonathan Ball.

Hotz, A. (2017) Interview with Fallist organiser Alex Hotz. *Agenda* 31 (3–4), 122–126.

Kruss, G. (2008) *Teacher Education and Institutional Change in South Africa*. Cape Town: HSRC Press.

Maldonado Torres, N. (2007) On the coloniality of being: Contributions to the development of a concept. *Cultural Studies* 21 (2–3), 240–270.

McKinney, C. (2017) *Language and Power in Postcolonial Schooling: Ideologies in Practice*. London and New York: Routledge.

Mignolo, W. (2011) *The Darker Side of Western Modernity: Global Futures, Decolonial Options*. Durham, NC: Duke University Press.

Mignolo, W. (2013) *On Pluriversality*. See http://waltermignolo.com/on-pluriversality/ (accessed 19 October 2017).

Mlachila, M. and Moeletsi, T. (2019) Struggling to make the grade: A review of the causes and consequences of the weak outcomes of South Africa's education system. IMF Working Paper No. 19/47. New York: International Monetary Fund.

Mzileni, P. and Mkhize, N. (2019) Decolonisation as a spatial question: The student accommodation crisis and higher education transformation. *South African Review of Sociology* 50 (3–4), 104–115.

Ndebele, N. (2021) What will rise after the fall of Rhodes Falls? University of Cape Town Inaugural #RhodesMustFall Scholarship Public Lecture. See https://www.uct.ac.za/register-inaugural-rhodesmustfall-scholarship-open-lecture?utm_source=VC-Desk&utm_medium=Link&utm_campaign=RMF-Open-Lecture&utm_content=Register-Now.

Ndelu, S., Dlakavu, S. and Boswell, B. (2017) Womxn's and nonbinary activists' contribution to the RhodesMustFall and FeesMustFall student movements: 2015 and 2016. *Agenda* 31 (3–4), 1–4.

Ngũgĩ wa Thiongo (1986) *Decolonising the Mind: The Language of African Literature*. London: James Currey.

Pratt, M. (1991) Arts of the contact zone. *Profession* 91, 33–40.

RMF, Writing & Education Subcommittees (2015) *Johannesburg Salon Special Edition 9*.

Robinson, M. (2003) Teacher education policy in South Africa: The voice of teacher educators. *Journal of Education for Teaching* 29 (1), 19–34.

Sayed, Y., Carrim, N., Badroodien, A., McDonald, Z. and Singh, M. (2018) *Learning to Teach in Post-apartheid South Africa*. Stellenbosch: Sun Press.

Xaba, W. (2017) Challenging Fanon: A Black radical feminist perspective on violence and the Fees Must Fall movement. *Agenda* 31 (3–4), 96–104.

Part 1

De/coloniality in Schooling

Leaving Home at 10

It was an old Peugeot 403
They don't make them anymore

Tyres inspected, engine oiled, brakes checked
All in order as only an old Peugeot can be.
Its creaking body held together by care,
My father drove me to the boarding school
In a small town one hour away from home …

My tears and the car held through the journey
Through the pothole in my heart and the tear on the road
Through the window, I watched the world rush past

The houses and the trees and the streets and the names
I had known and loved, all running backwards, with
No time to pause for a goodbye, no time to wave
To the departing son leaving the embrace of home and hearth

We arrived over an hour later, father and son,
driving through the school gate to the dormitory
that was to be my home for the next five years.
Then my father left … and, averting my eyes, I cried.

On initiation night I recited the prescribed words:
'I am a fag, a rotten green toad. I promise
to give up all my rustic and outlandish ways
and to become a true student of Government College, Ughelli.'

Soon after I lost the language of guavas and spirits
And ever since I have been boarded up in a new home,
A new language with neither spice nor bite.

I miss all the coarse and colourful words I can no longer use
The power and potency of the curse uttered with a gob of spittle
Let loose in the language of the body and the spirit

I miss the language that once lived in my body.

Harry Garuba
Animist Chants and Memorials,
Kraftgriots/Kraft Books Limited, 2017

2 De/coloniality in South African Language in Education Policy: Resisting the Marginalisation of African Language Speaking Children

Xolisa Guzula

Introduction

Post-1994, language debates in South Africa have tended to focus exclusively on Black African language speaking children rather than White English and Afrikaans speaking children. These debates construct Black African children as learners with deficits and fail to acknowledge their language resources. At the same time, policymakers, academics, educators and parents fail to critique the unjust system to which they are subjected and of which they are victims. There have been no debates in the Language in Education Policy (LiEP) about medium of instruction for English and Afrikaans speaking children: it is assumed that they must be educated in English or Afrikaans, 'their languages'. These languages are not even referred to as mother tongues because English, and to some extent Afrikaans as well as monolingualism, are an invisible norm. In this chapter, I present a case study of children belonging to the Stars of Today Literacy Club# to show the possibilities and ways in which these children can be positioned as competent multilinguals and, in so doing, can resist the prevailing deficit view. This chapter has three key aims. First, I aim to bring to light the coloniality of, and racist ideology behind, the current implementation of language policy in schooling, showing how it constructs Black African language speaking children as inherently different from White English and Afrikaans speaking children. Second, I aim to describe how inequality is thus created and entrenched through undifferentiated language in education policies, curriculum, textbooks and assessments, all of which are based on the normative idea of the child being middle class and English speaking. Third, I aim to demonstrate how bilingual children can be positioned as capable, rather than deficient, through the creation of third spaces (Anzaldúa, 1987) that transcend language and literacy borders. Such spaces, I argue, move us towards decolonising language and literacy pedagogies.

I begin by tracing the history of language policy and medium of instruction in South African schooling from 1907 to 1994 in some detail, considering it important to provide a comprehensive context for what is essentially a policy based on colonial ideologies, and to show clearly the historical interconnectedness of current language policy with apartheid ideology. Second, I review the current position of language policy (1994 to date) in practice to show how it continues to discriminate against Black African language speaking children by constructing them as emergent bilinguals with a deficit while continuing to advantage White English and Afrikaans speakers, constructing them as competent monolinguals. I then proceed to analyse and discuss the ideologies behind the language policy implementation, relating this to the historical context. Finally, I present a case study of the third space created in the Stars of Today Literacy Club#, to demonstrate how dynamic bilingualism can be used to challenge the monolingual norm and the English bias, and ultimately to delink from colonial language ideologies in policy and practice.

Historical Overview of Language in Education Policy

State policies on the education of Black African language speaking children were designed to ensure their perpetual failure in education and this has its roots in the construction of their childhoods by colonial and apartheid governments. This dates from the colonisation of Southern Africa by the Dutch and the English and, more recently, the ushering in by the apartheid government of Bantu education in 1953. The marginalisation, exclusion and erasure of these children from South African citizenship, the denial of their basic right to education and their positioning as inferior to whites and as servants of whites was evident in the way discussions about education dating from the early 19th century focused solely on Dutch and English speaking children (Alexander, 1989; Christie, 1991). From the mid- to late 1800s right through to 1948, education discussions included language of instruction and focused on whether Dutch, later Afrikaans, and English speaking children were to be taught through dual or single medium (Malherbe, 1943). In these debates the existence of the Black African language speaking child was rendered invisible in the ongoing struggle for state power between English and Afrikaner. The British victory in the Anglo-Boer War of 1899–1902 was a crucial moment in the history of language policy and debates in South Africa. First, it ushered in the Anglicisation policy of the British imperialists which discriminated against the Dutch/Afrikaans speaking people (Christie, 1991; Heugh, 2001; Malherbe, 1943). Second, it created opportunities for debates about the education of African language speaking children and the languages through which they ought to be taught. At the start of these discussions, Junod (1905) of the Transvaal Swiss Mission presented a paper at a missionary conference, titled 'The role of Native Language in Native Education'. He suggested two polarised methods for educating the 'Native' child, one 'through 'English only' and the other 'through vernacular at the base and English at the top' (Junod, 1905: 3). However, such discussions were soon abandoned as the Dutch citizens of the Transvaal focused on resisting Milner's Anglicisation policy through the Dutch Reformed Church, which established schools in the Transvaal in 1907 and in the Free State in 1908. These schools introduced education in two languages (Heugh, 2001; Malherbe, 1943). This opened a pathway to dual medium education as a practical way of showing cooperation between the Afrikaners and the English after the Union of 1910. During this period, a significant number of African language speaking children lived in the reserves where there was no compulsory education (Christie, 1991). While English and Afrikaans speaking children were constructed as equals by the Union of South Africa government at this time, with compulsory schooling, and their languages unquestioned as mediums of instruction in a dual medium education system, African language speaking children were seen as not needing to be educated or taught in their own language. This inequality was one of the key principles on which apartheid ideology was founded.

By the 1940s, the rise of Afrikaner nationalism saw the end of dual medium education and the adoption of parallel medium and single medium education. Dual medium education was perceived to be against the principle of mother tongue education by the Afrikaans nationalists at the time (Malherbe, 1943). In 1951 pronouncements by UNESCO on the value of teaching children in the mother tongue served to intensify the push for single or parallel medium education (Heugh, 2001). This became an opportune moment for the Afrikaner Nationalist government, which came into power in 1948, to combine the use of African languages with the formation of Bantustans, and the ushering in of Bantu education for African language speaking children to consolidate its racialised policy of Separate Development (Heugh, 2001; Maake, 1991). Through Bantu education, African language speaking children were to experience inferior education, positioned as only able to serve their own communities, with no place in the European community except as a future poorly paid and exploited labour force (Maake, 1991).

The apartheid government's policy on dual medium English-Afrikaans education in high schools for African language speaking children led to the Soweto uprisings in 1976. The revolt against Afrikaans came to include both the rejection of Bantu education and of African languages that had been used as vehicles for making Bantu education possible and for entrenching apartheid. The result of this revolt was the passing of Act 90 in 1979, which reduced the number of years during which African language speaking learners were to be exposed to mother tongue education from eight to four, with an abrupt transition to English medium taking place in Grade 5, and later in Grade 4 (Heugh, 2000; MacDonald & Burroughs, 1991). Since then, many African language speaking children have experienced a form of subtractive bilingual education, even after the passing of the national LiEP in 1997 which promotes additive bilingualism, what Alexander (2003) calls Mother Tongue Based Bilingual Education (MTBBE). Additive bilingualism, or MTBBE, according to Alexander, means starting education with mother tongue as medium of instruction in the foundation phase and maintaining it in the intermediate phase while adding English as a second medium. Both during apartheid and in the post-apartheid period, single medium, and in a few cases parallel medium, schooling became normalised for English and Afrikaans speaking children, while the switch to English medium education from Grade 4, and the expectation of using the same curriculum, textbooks and assessment, became normalised for most African language speaking children. This situation has in fact reinforced apartheid's idea that African language speaking children do not need to enjoy the same conditions for learning as do English and Afrikaans speaking children.

Current Language in Education Policy in Practice and the Construction of the African Language Speaking Child

Twenty-five years into democracy, African language speaking children continue to experience racism, as well as an inferior education. Although the LiEP of 1997 looks good on paper, *in practice* the official curriculum and assessment policies, and the pronouncements by the national department of basic education (DBE), education researchers and policymakers about the poor performance of African language speaking children in local and international assessments, all continue to construct African language speaking children as deficient English monolinguals (McKinney, 2017). The subtractive bilingualism that replaces African languages of instruction with monolingual English instruction from Grade 4 means that African language children experience significant discontinuities between the foundation phase and the intermediate phase, and between home and school. The combination of language medium switch, the increase in subjects, the fact that all books and learning materials are provided in English only, low literacy in the mother tongue and poor proficiency in English sets the African language speaking child up for failure while English-speaking children continue their education seamlessly, without any change to their language of instruction from Grades 3–4.

The switch from monolingual African language instruction to monolingual English has led to the children being constructed as with a deficit, as passive/agentless, as failures, as having low levels of comprehension, as unable to decode, as needing remedial assistance, as non-readers and as non-producers of meaning. They are referred to by educators as children with 'no language' (Makoe, 2007: 66), signalling that these children are not proficient in any of the languages they speak, read or write. This view has resulted in the push for English from earlier on as set out in the current Curriculum and Assessment Policy Statement (DBE, 2011). In fact, CAPS presents itself as a policy that normalises and entrenches the abrupt switch to English medium immediately after foundation phase, thus rewriting the LiEP through the back door (McKinney, 2017). CAPS supports neither home language education nor bilingual education. It is biased towards English from Grade 4 and it has the support of many parents who are under the impression that learning through English is best. Blommaert (2005: 77) argues that inequality occurs whenever there is 'a difference between capacity to produce function and the expected or normative function'. Simply put, the gap between ability to make meaning and proficiency in English for African language speaking children, together with the lack of educational materials and literature to support and valorise the use of African languages as mediums of instruction, creates and perpetuates deep inequalities in our education system.

It is therefore not uncommon for people to argue that learning materials have never been developed in African languages, or that African languages do not possess the capacity/vocabulary for teaching content subjects, even though historically these languages were used to teach content subjects up to Grade 8 (Heugh, 2000). The continued absence of reading materials in children's home languages, written by African language speaking writers, means that children continue to be exposed to a form of colonial and apartheid education. Readers written by missionaries during colonial times and apartheid, and currently by English speaking writers, continue to be impoverished in terms of relevant content, and fail to reflect children's lived experiences in township and rural settings (Maake, 1991). These writers conceptualised/conceptualise the material through white, English speaking and middle-class lenses. As a result, translation of this material is based on English source texts as determinants even for how African languages should be written, and which ideas are normalised. Mkhize (2016) argues that, in many cases where African language literature exists, 'textual production (fiction and non-fiction) has historically been heavily bent towards conservative themes, in which cultural pride, propriety and identity take centre stage – that is, a literature that speaks to "Good Bantus"' (Mkhize, 2016: 147).

Thus, instead of supporting instruction in children's home languages, together with bilingual education, with the materials for this purpose, the misguided CAPS' conception of equality as monolingual and monoglossic English elects to solve educational inequality by offering all children of South Africa the same curriculum, materials, teacher training and language of teaching and learning, regardless of the sociocultural context within which children live and with which they engage daily. The switch to English medium continues despite the well-documented challenges that African language speaking children experienced during apartheid when switching in Grade 5 (MacDonald & Burroughs, 1991). The fact that African language speaking children from Grade 4 are forced to use the same textbooks as English home language children clearly advantages English speakers and disadvantages emergent bilinguals.

Language Ideologies and the Construction of Deficient Monolinguals

It is important to make visible and to analyse the history and the mechanisms that construct African emergent bilinguals as deficient monolinguals, and that construct their language resources as problematic. McKinney (2017: 18) argues that who makes policies and the curriculum, as well as their language ideologies, matters. Monolingual middle-class English speakers who continue to be entrusted with the responsibility of crafting the curriculum and education policies, and with writing textbooks, often with no consultation with teachers and learners, 'are often unable to see beyond their own limited language experiences' and tend to calibrate the curriculum based on their sociocultural and linguistic experiences and practices (bua-lit, 2018; Reed, 2006). The construction of African language speaking children as English monolinguals in LiEPs, in curriculum and assessment policies, in learning materials and in pedagogy is largely informed by policymakers' beliefs about what counts as good language use, and what counts as best in terms of languages for teaching and learning (Blackledge, 2000; Makoe & McKinney, 2009; McKinney, 2017). Since policymakers currently belong to the dominant classes in society, and thus to the classes that control the country's economy, their beliefs and ideas about what is good language use tend to be imposed on the rest of society (Nomlomo, 1993). Alexander (1989) and Makalela (2015) argue that the views of this dominant class about what languages should be used in education, and what counts as good language and literacy learning, are largely influenced by Eurocentric and colonial ideologies that came with the formation of nation-states in Europe. According to this historical perspective, the diverse regional varieties of language were homogenised by missionary linguists in favour of one 'pure' – and fixed – single standard language (Makalela, 2015; Makoni, 1999).

Although single medium or parallel medium schools uphold the principle of mother tongue education, and can be described as bilingual schools because two languages are taught as subjects in the schools, they offer a weak form of bilingual education in comparison to dual medium education, which exposes children to two mediums of education (Heugh, 2000; Malherbe, 1943). However, despite dual medium education being a stronger form of bilingual education, historically it tended – and continues – to apply only in classrooms where there were equal numbers of learners speaking Afrikaans and English, and this required teachers to code-switch from one language to another to expose each group of children to their own mother tongue as well as to give them access to the other language (Malherbe, 1943). The notion of dual medium education, however, evolved and informed ideas about an additive bilingualism approach in the LiEP of 1997, or Mother Tongue Based Bilingual Education (Alexander, 2003; Heugh, 2001) for schools attended by many Black African language speaking children.

Although the principle of the mother tongue at the base is noble in both single medium, parallel medium and dual medium education, it still fails to account for multilingualism and multilinguality (Pluddemann, 2010) in primary schools, where children speak different languages, or varieties of the named languages, and where they are expected to develop bilingual competence in home languages and English in order at a later stage to learn through English. Malherbe's (1943) study accounted for many bilingual children in Afrikaans and English speaking families and demonstrated that, with mother tongue at the base and dual medium at the top, the principle of mother tongue could still be honoured, while at the same time children could get exposed to two languages. The fact that African language speaking children continue to transition to English medium in Grade 4 assumes the continued hegemony of the English language and Anglonormativity – 'the expectation that everybody should speak English and if they don't, they are deviant or even deficient' (McKinney, 2017: 80). While bilingual education for African language speaking children means learning in their home language and in English, multilinguality usually involves children speaking in the varieties of the named languages in which they learn (Pluddemann, 2010). For isiXhosa speaking children, for example, these varieties include dialects such as isiBhaca, isiHlubi and isiMpondo, as well as urban varieties of isiXhosa and English (Nomlomo, 1993). Schools, however, insist, for example, on standard isiXhosa and standard English varieties and look less favourably on the non-standard varieties (Nomlomo, 1993). In their efforts to give children access to standard languages, schools often undermine and devalue children's non-standard varieties. This works to maintain dominant monoglossic language ideologies and the use of the principle of mother tongue or non-standard varieties to get to the standard form of the language or to get to English proficiency.

Language practices of bilingual or multilingual learners in daily life are much more heteroglossic than would be expected in formal learning situations, or within the curriculum, and in assessment policies. As a result, many children engaging in heteroglossic language practices are viewed as linguistically deficient. Thus, the questions to be asked are: How do we then legitimise all languages and all varieties without giving more power to one language or variety? How do we align language policies, the curriculum, texts and assessments with everyday practices and uses of language, and succeed in calibrating education to the needs of African multilinguals? How do we view children's multilingualism and multilinguality as a resource rather than a problem? How do we disrupt the coloniality of language in our current schooling system?

Third Spaces and Multiliteracies for African Language Speaking Children's Literacy Learning

Working within a sociocultural perspective, I draw on the concepts of third spaces and multiliteracies to demonstrate how I began to challenge the deficit positioning of African language children in an after-school literacy club. Third spaces are spaces 'in between' and beyond two binaries, conceptualisations and discourses that are often thought as separate and uncombinable (Anzaldúa, 1987; Bhabha, 1990; Gutièrrez et al., 1999). These spaces are characterised by hybridity, and dynamic and shifting perspectives that also transcend traditional binaries of first spaces or second spaces (Bhabha, 1990). Because third spaces allow for multiple perspectives, inhabitants of these spaces often encounter ambivalence, assuming multiple identities, including being monolingual, bilingual or multilingual, speaking a patois, and being in a state of perpetual transition (Anzaldúa, 1987). The purpose of hybridity is not about being able to trace two original moments from which third space emerges; rather, hybridity is a third space that enables different positions to emerge (Bhabha, 1990). The mixing of different perspectives and ideologies in one space should be viewed positively as it leads to a 'third element', 'a new understanding or a new consciousness' which transcends our differences (Anzaldúa, 1987; Gutièrrez et al., 1999). Thus, bilingual or multilingual children do not operate as separate monolinguals but occupy a linguistic third space with one linguistic repertoire consisting of all the languages they speak (Cummins, 2008; Flores & García, 2014). The space they occupy is known as a translanguaging space (Li, 2018). García (2009) defines translanguaging as 'the act performed by bilinguals of accessing different linguistic features or various modes of what are described as autonomous languages' (García, 2009: 141).

I also draw on the concept of multiliteracies which challenges written language as a sole means of communication, and which encourages plurality of languages in learning spaces (New London Group, 2000). Scholars in multiliteracies propose multimodality as a mode of communication, plurality of languages, and a multiliteracies framework for pedagogy. Multimodality refers to the integration or orchestration of the many ways in which children make meaning. These include linguistic, audio-visual and performative meaning-making (Bock, 2016; Kress, 2007; Newfield, 2011; Stein, 2004).

I draw on the four aspects of the multiliteracies framework for pedagogy, namely, situated practice, overt instruction, critical framing and transformative practice. Situated practice means that we teach children by drawing on their lived experience, including language practices, recognising that this needs to be extended and enhanced. Overt instruction allows learners to gain explicit information, encourages collaborative efforts between teachers and learners, develops conscious awareness of what is being learned, and gives learners metalanguages to talk about their learning (New London Group, 2000). Although Cummins (cited in Baker, 2006: 186) provides a conceptual distinction between Basic Interpersonal Communication Skills (BICS) and Cognitive Academic Language Proficiency (CALP), which is useful for understanding a variety of repertoires that children might have, this distinction tends to be applied in binary ways in practice, where teachers delay the teaching of academic concepts until children have acquired proficiency in the language. Thus, I argue that by exposing children to both BICS and CALP simultaneously we might transcend this binary application. In addition to situated practice and overt instruction, the New London Group (2000) proposes a pedagogy that values critical framing, arguing that it enables learners to develop their ability to be critical and to recognise injustice based on unequal power, and ideology. This then forms the basis of the fourth aspect of the multiliteracies framework: 'transformative practice', a reflective practice which develops from critical framing and results in learners producing new practices embedded in their own goals and values (New London Group, 2000). Below I discuss a case study of an established third space in the form of a literacy club called Stars of Today Literacy Club#. I draw on the data I collected as part of the club's three-day holiday programme to show how multilingual children made use of their semiotic resources to display capabilities that are often made invisible.

Methodology

This brief case study discusses a literacy club where I worked with emergent bilinguals to build a culture of literacy. Using a sociocultural perspective on language and literacy, through which I seek to understand children's uses of language and literacy in their daily lives and then calibrate their literacy learning to these, I established a literacy club which the children named the 'Stars of Today Literacy Club# (STLC#)'. The club was conceptualised and set up as an established physical, social, linguistic and conceptual third space (Canagarajah, 2017; Flores & García, 2014; Gutièrrez *et al.*, 1999) encouraging dynamic, shifting and hybrid language practices and activities. Thus, the club normalised children's multilingualism and multimodality as legitimate language and literacy practices. It comprised between 30 and 60 children from a primary school in Khayelitsha (a sprawling urban township on the periphery of Cape Town). Children were recruited from Grades 3–6 (9–12 year-olds) because I was interested in how age boundaries could be transcended, thus creating a third space for learning in recognition of the children's sociocultural lives where young children learn from their older peers. I recruited fellow facilitators through Facebook and word of mouth. These facilitators are also a hybrid of multilingual visual artists, storytellers, teacher trainers, teachers, and university students studying language and literacy or early childhood development, who contributed their skills and expertise, thus making the vision of multiliteracies possible by integrating song, stories, art, performance, reading and writing and heteroglossic language practices (see Figures 2.1 and 2.2).

The children and the facilitators attended the club on a voluntary basis every Saturday from 10am to 12pm over 2015–2017. Initially my role was that of founder and lead facilitator of the literacy club, a role that included leading the planning for Saturday bilingual and multimodal literacy sessions with fellow facilitators. I sought donations of children's literature and stationery, and trained literacy club facilitators by modelling heteroglossic practices and multiliteracies practices to both the facilitators and the children.

In researching children's language and literacy practices at the STLC#, I draw on methodological tools of linguistic ethnography. Copland and

Figure 2.1 A group of STLC# participants playing in a ring

Figure 2.2 A STLC# group writing outside

Creese (2015: 13) define linguistic ethnography '... as an interpretive approach which studies the local and immediate actions of actors from their point of view and considers how these interactions are embedded in wider social contexts and structures'. Linguistic ethnography makes visible those mechanisms in which everyday linguistic practices relate to social life and shows how these reproduce each other through everyday activities (Copland & Creese, 2015). At the STLC# I collected data using ethnographic data-collection tools which included participant observation, field notes, audio- and video-recording, still photographs, and a collection of visual and textual artefacts made collaboratively by the children and facilitators. For the purposes of this chapter, I elected to analyse data from an audio- and video-recording as they clearly illustrate the children's capability using multilingual and multimodal practices. I analyse the discourses and practices produced at the STLC# by drawing on the theoretical concepts of linguistic third spaces (Flores & García, 2014), third space (Gutièrrez *et al.*, 1999) as well as multiliteracies (New London Group, 2000).

Changing Deficit Stereotypes of Multilingual Learners: A Case Study

In this case study I illustrate the ways in which children's play and language are powerful pedagogical resources for learning language and literacy, and how these have been drawn on for meaning-making, thus constructing and positioning the children as competent bilinguals. The case study demands that we shift our theoretical and pedagogical lenses from viewing African language speaking children as monolinguals with a deficit to children who are critical thinkers, competent and creative language users, translators and interpreters, and creative bilingual composers, among other roles and identities. The Grade 3–6 children participating at STLC#, and the rest of the children in the school, experience subtractive bilingualism. They learn English as a first additional language from Grade 1, and then transition to English medium in Grade 4. The curriculum expects them to learn two languages separately from Grade 1 and constructs them as multilinguals with separate monolingualisms in their heads. Although their teachers code-switch at least in oral language to explain concepts to them, children are not allowed to mix languages or speak in any of the varieties of those languages or write in two languages. Teachers do not regard code-switching as a legitimate practice and often reprimand children for drawing on their own linguistic resources (Nomlomo, 1993). Later, in Grade 4, the children are exposed to, and experience, an Anglonormative ideology as they are expected to become English monolinguals.

The STLC# draws on hybridity as a resource, and facilitators model dynamic bilingualism (García, 2009), drawing on the situated practice aspect of the multiliteracies framework to legitimise the children's linguistic resources and to encourage languaging for learning (Guzula et al., 2016). They also draw on children's translation and interpreting skills as forms of translanguaging that position the children as competent multilinguals.

The data analysed demonstrate that African language speaking children are most often translingual and will draw on their full semiotic repertoire for meaning-making when this is allowed. The data show STLC# members as embodied bilinguals, who are competent users of an expanded repertoire and competent and creative translators.

Construction of the Stars of Today Literacy Club# (STLC#) as third space

As a way of drawing on children's sociocultural resources and their conceptualisation of language and literacy, facilitators organise activities based on the children's expectations of the literacy club (see Figure 2.3).

At the first meeting of the club, the children expressed that they wanted to sing, play, read and write, tell stories, dance, do art, learn spelling and make videos and audio-recordings together, as captured by the facilitator in Figure 2.3. Their expectations were in sync with the multiliteracies conceptualisation of literacy that combines plurality of language use and multimodality (New London Group, 2000). They were also in

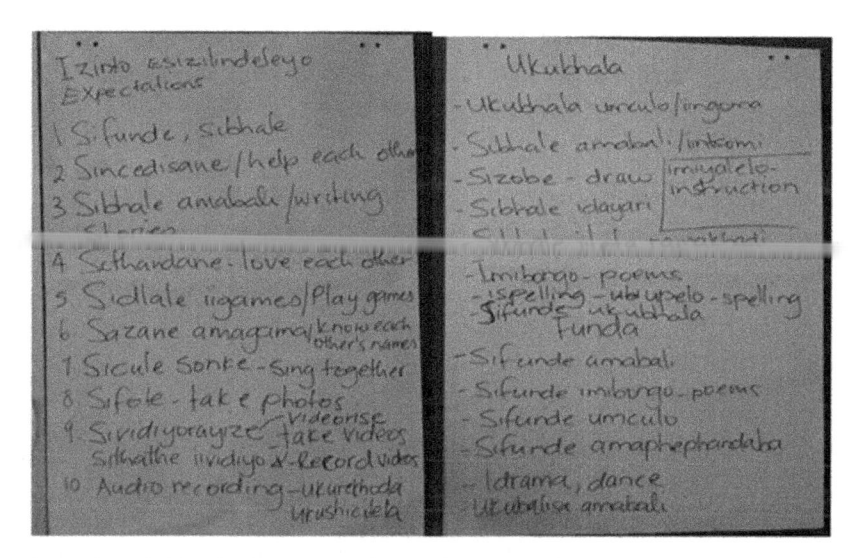

Figure 2.3 Children's expectations for the literacy club

sync with third space theory in that they are inclusive of print literacy and multimodal literacies, and skills approaches as well as social practices, because they expected to be taught spelling alongside social literacies. In this case study, I analyse the creation of STLC# as a third space through play or games.

It has been argued that many adults, including teachers, do not pay attention to children's games. While teachers might supervise children in the playground, they do not necessarily participate in games, nor do they use them for teaching in the classroom. This can create a dislocation between children's daily life and classroom life (Harrop-Allin, 2014). Harrop-Allin argues that the diminishing of play between first- and third-generation adults and the children she studied means that both adults and children in the family were being increasingly robbed of spaces for co-creation of shared play engagements, and of maintaining the rhetoric of play as identity. One of the radical ways in which the playground as occupied by STLC# members challenges binaries in education is the fact that play involves the participation of children of different ages, and adult facilitators with different knowledges, skills and experiences that can be harnessed to enhance and shape children's learning.

A literacy club day usually begins with game songs or musical games (Harrop-Allin, 2014), played indoors or outdoors depending on the weather, followed by activities which include reading, writing, art, storytelling and drama. Young bi/multilingual children observe and engage with the games together with older and developing bilinguals of the upper grades and get presented with opportunities for informal language acquisition in the playground. They experience formal language learning once the games are brought into the classroom for overt instruction. The literacy club's facilitators also challenge the notion that knowledge only lies with the teacher. The multi-age composition of play challenges ageism and encourages intergenerational interaction and transmission of values, knowledge and sociocultural resources. It closes the binary between children and adults and enables adults to travel to the child's world to recognise the child in them, to realise that they can inhabit both the adult and the child in them. Inhabiting both worlds creates a 'third space that does away with totalisation of oneself and makes one ambivalent because of the recognition of that otherness in themselves [for example, an adult recognises a child in herself] and helps in one shifting her/himself through identifying with the other' (Bhabha, 1990: 211; Lugones, 1987). It also helps teachers and adults to observe children at play, with the understanding that children learn informally through play, and with the aim of harnessing play as a pedagogical tool, thus creating a pedagogical third space.

Thus, by insisting, in their expectations, on the incorporation of play and games into the literacy club, the children were challenging the adults to listen to them, to get to know what interests them, and to build literacy learning on their interests rather than imposing what adults think is appropriate for them. They were asking facilitators to reckon with play more than they have ever done, thus disrupting not only the literacy pedagogy that is solely based on books and written language, but also positioning themselves as knowers and active participants in the co-creation of the literacy club programme.

The use of the playground and the classroom as sites for playing games also creates a physical third space that values out-of-school literacies and school literacies, as well as informal and formal learning. It integrates and connects children's engagement and experiences with literacy across different physical spaces, such as the classroom and the playground. It positions these different spaces not as hierarchical in terms of first and second spaces, but instead shows how learners can navigate these spaces flexibly while making connections between the learning they achieve in these spaces. The use of classroom space for the club not only creates bridges between the first and second spaces of the classroom and the playground, but offers something more – a third element which combines and transcends the boundaries between these. The dynamic and flexible shifts within and between learning spaces highlight the values and affordances, and the constraints, of each physical space for children's meaning-making processes. The shifts between indoors and outdoors capitalise on the different learning experiences being generated in each of the spaces. They also offer different tools that can be used strategically for teaching and learning purposes.

By integrating the children's sociocultural resources in the form of game songs in the playground and the classroom, for example, the facilitators create third space practices that bring about different knowledges and discourses. This is a political act for ensuring cultural, social and epistemological change, where the competing knowledges of the school, home and community challenge and reshape both academic and everyday knowledge (Barton *et al.*, 2008). In fact, the shifts between and within different learning spaces challenge what are currently designated as legitimate places and spaces for learning, and generate new heterogeneous and hybrid knowledges, practices and experiences. I argue that the creation of third spaces is a political, social and practical act that centres the typical African language speaking child who has for so long been invisible in South African educational policy.

Play itself also creates an affective, linguistic and social third space that considers affect as an important aspect in learning, and that challenges the individual conceptualisation of language and literacy learning by legitimising collaborative work and constructing children as bi-multilinguals through repeated linguistic practices that draw on their full linguistic repertoire. During play, games are introduced either by children or by facilitators (see Figure 2.1).

Children as competent bilinguals with embodied communicative competence

As a lead facilitator, I sometimes played a role in introducing new games and concepts and demonstrating how they work to both the children and facilitators, because the facilitators were reserved in the beginning. I demonstrated to the facilitators how to use songs and games for teaching, and how to draw and build from these sociocultural and semiotic resources for meaning-making. Drawing on the critical aspect of the multiliteracies framework, I introduced a game called the 'Lion Hunt' as a text to work from to help children to develop a critical perspective of texts. (the Lion Hunt draws on the rhyming text of David Axtell's (2007) children's book, *We're Going on a Lion Hunt* and Michael Rosen & Helen Oxenbury's (1997) well-known children's picture book, *We're Going on a Bear Hunt*). The Lion Hunt game below is controversial, in that it mentions guns, bullets and hunting, which some might not consider appropriate. It is exactly for this reason that the facilitators at the STLC# felt it productive to use the game as it can be used to teach children critical literacy skills through getting them to consider the reasons why the game would or would not be considered appropriate. This enables children to identify the inappropriateness themselves, and then redesign the game, rather than the facilitator or teacher telling them that they should not play it. The first part of the game goes like this:

We're going on a lion hunt
I'm not scared
Got a gun by my side (touching hips)

Bullets, two (showing two fingers)
We come to some grass
Some tall grass (bending and raising hand to high above the head)
We can't go over it, (showing with hands)
We can't go under it
We can't go around it
We have to through it
Let's go … swish, swish, swish (moving the grass to the side with hands)

This gets repeated in the second and third parts, with grass being replaced with mud and a cave.

After playing the game, I introduced critical framing to the children by explaining to them that sometimes communication, verbal and non-verbal, gets interpreted differently by different people. I explained that even the games we play, such as the Lion Hunt, can be heard positively or negatively by different people. I made two columns on the board and wrote 'good' on one side and 'bad' on the other. I asked the children to think about and mention all the things they liked about the game, and to suggest things they thought people could potentially find problematic about the game, and why. I wrote on the board all the things that the children thought were positive or negative about the game, using the affordances of the classroom space with the chalk board which enabled us to record children's responses, something that would have been harder to achieve in the playground. As can be seen in Figure 2.4, for the positives, the children said the game is fun, it helps them to see how to walk through the grass, mud and cave, and it teaches English in an

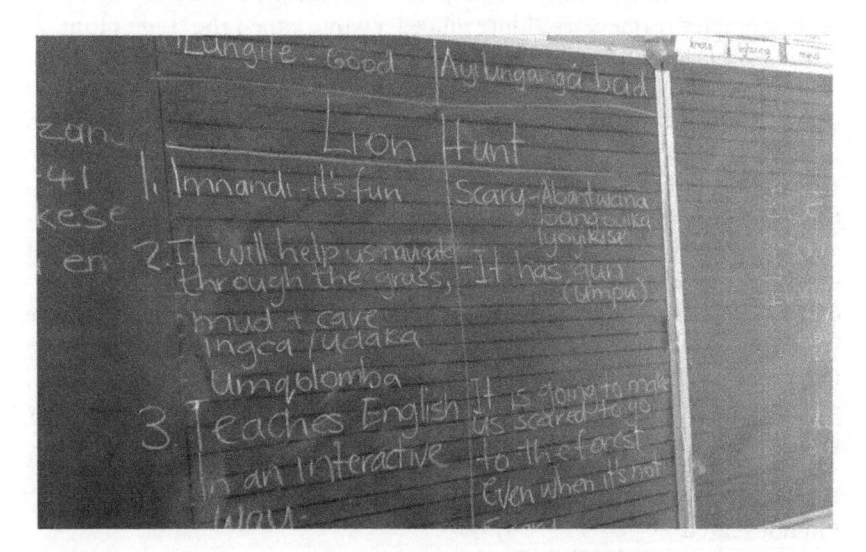

Figure 2.4 Discussion of advantages and disadvantages of the Lion Hunt game

interactive way, something that the playground enables more than the classroom. Thus the use of both the playground and the classroom also created a pedagogical third space, which draws on both these spaces to offer children opportunities for learning that include performative aspects of play as well as integrating talk and writing about children's ideas. On the negative side, they said the game is scary, it has guns, and it would make them fear going to the forest even when it's not that scary.

In the session that followed this on the following Saturday, the aim was to work with the children to transform the game to make it acceptable to all people. I started off by reviewing the work they had done the previous week. We usually did this to help those children who had been absent to understand what had happened before moving on. Although in this example I focus on one child, Noni's, full linguistic repertoire, at the club we also raise an awareness about mechanisms in which educational inequality is produced (Delpit, 1988; Janks, 2010) by exposing children to an expanded repertoire that includes powerful standard language use in isiXhosa and English. I asked Noni to summarise what we thought was good about the game. Noni started off by talking about what was 'good', and in her talk she drew on the semiotic resources afforded by the game to make her point (Table 2.1).

In the Lion Hunt game described above, not only were the facilitators playing the game in English in the playground, but they were also extending the children's English and isiXhosa repertoire by implicitly creating opportunities for languaging through both verbal and non-verbal communication (Swain, 2006). The explicit discussion and writing of both English and isiXhosa terms for guns/imipu, cave/umqolomba and mud/udaka also helped to develop bilingual vocabulary, adding to their knowledge. As Noni and I discuss the 'good' aspects of the game, Noni demonstrates that she cannot make her point without using both English and isiXhosa. She begins her response in isiXhosa but draws on specific English vocabulary to make her point about the game's semiotic affordances and educational value: 'Ngoba ukuba umntu akayazi ukuba ukuhamba **over it** mhlawumbi njengoba sithetha ngeEnglish uyabona ngezandla ba **we can't go over it**' ['Because if a person doesn't know what walking **over it** means, maybe because we speak **English** s/he can see through the use of hands that '**we can't go over it**']. Noni is drawing on her full semiotic repertoire for participation and for making a particularly important conceptual point about the affordances that the game provides for languaging, participation and inclusivity (Guzula *et al.*, 2016). It has been argued by multiliteracies scholars that there are limitations to the exclusive use of language as sole means of communication (Kress, 1997; Newfield, 2011; New London Group, 2000; Stein, 2004). Noni's competent argument about people's ability to draw on their full semiotic repertoire in meaning-making positions her as intellectually and linguistically

Table 2.1 Noni conceptualises the semiotic repertoire

Original	Translation
Xoli: …Okay, ngubani okhumbulayo? Siye sathi zintoni ezigood ngala game? Sithe zintoni esizithandayo ngayo? Zintoni ezilungileyo ngayo? Hayi kaloku siyathetha tyhini abantu bandijongile nje, bandijongile nje abantu balibele ngoku. Sithe la game igood ngoba kutheni? Noni?	**Xoli:** …Okay, who remembers? What things did we say are good about that game? What did we say we like about it? What are the good things about it? No, we have to speak hey, people are just looking at me, they have forgotten now. Why did we say that game is good? Noni?
Noni: Ngoba ukuba umntu akayazi ukuba ukuhamba over it mhlawumbi njengoba sithetha ngeEnglish uyabona ngezandla ba we can't go over it, we can't go under it, we can't go around it uyabona okay uover nguntoni, u-under yintoni, uaround yintoni and then… (inaudible)	**Noni:** Because if a person doesn't know what walking over it means, maybe because we speak English s/he can see through the use of hands that 'we can't go over it', 'we can't go under it', 'we can't go around it' and see what 'over' means, what 'under' means and what 'around' means and then… (inaudible)
Xoli: Ukuba ngaba… umntu… akamazi… uover it nhe, uyabona ngezandla nhe… ngezandla, naxa usithi under… under it nhe? Utshilo nhe?	**Xoli:** That if… a person… doesn't know… what 'over it' means, hey, s/he can see through the hands, hey… and when you say 'under'… under it, hey? You said so, hey?
Noni: E-e **Xoli:** Nobani omnye?	**Noni:** Ewe, Yes **Xoli:** And what else?
Noni: noaround it	**Noni:** And around it
Xoli: noaround it… noaround it, nhe? Uyabona ngezandla naxa usithi… ngezandla. Sathi igood loo nto nhe? Iyasifundisa loo nto ukuba kuthethwa ukuthwani andithi? I think uyibeke kakuhle kakhulu uNoni, ngendlela ecacileyo. Wonke umntu ucacelwe nhe? (Audio recording: 5 March 2016, 04:00–05:33)	**Xoli:** and around it… and around it, hey? You can see through the hands when and when you… through the hands. We said that is good, hey? That teaches us what is meant by spoken words, isn't it? I think Noni expressed it so well, so clearly hey? Everybody is clear, hey? (Audio recording: 5 March 2016, 04:00–05:33)

competent. Through her argument she defies the negative or deficit stereotypes that teachers in many classrooms associate with children who have a multilingual repertoire and participates freely without fear of judgement for using resources from two languages. Although she is still a child in primary school, she makes similar arguments about communication as multimodal and multisensory to those arguments made by theorists of communication.

By bringing the game into the classroom, and by doing overt instruction of the kind that focuses on critical literacy, I demonstrated to the rest of the facilitators how to capitalise on both implicit and explicit pedagogical strategies to shape and enhance children's meaning-making. My use of overt instruction and writing down word for word Noni's response on the newsprint recognised, acknowledged and affirmed her linguistic repertoire. I also demonstrated to her, and to the other children, what a bilingual text looks like and created a linguistic third space that affirmed her linguistic resources. I did this deliberately to disrupt monoglossia, to valorise Noni's sociocultural resources and to encourage all the children to draw on all of their linguistic resources for meaning-making.

The value of the Lion Hunt game for literacy learning cannot be underestimated. The game has huge potential for helping to build the children's background knowledge (as the game was introduced the previous week and has become part of what they know) and vocabulary, and they can use these in reading new texts. Thus, the game is not merely energising for play; it is necessary for building children's schema for further learning. The children can make text to self connections (as in 'I know this game, we play it at the club') and between the books they read (*We're Going on a Lion Hunt* and *We're Going on a Bear Hunt*) when the books are read at the literacy club or in class. Earlier I mentioned that the children were learning English vocabulary through the Lion Hunt game by making use of verbal and non-verbal communication, thus showing how games are sites for multimodal communication and for languaging where children move their bodies as well as talk or sing, and where they can also make use of objects, such as stones and shoes, as part of their play (Harrop-Allin, 2014; Swain, 2006). In doing this, they engage in language learning using many modes at once.

Conclusion

Noni's case study above shows an instance of a multilingual child – and children – as being competent users of their full linguistic repertoire. It demonstrates how teachers can recognise, acknowledge, affirm and build lessons from children's sociocultural resources. Through her use of her full linguistic repertoire, Noni showed herself able to express a highly sophisticated conceptual point about the affordances of the game of the Lion Hunt: through translanguaging she explained how the actions and gestures mediated the English words. This example shows that, by moving beyond the false binary of mother tongue or English medium instruction and by teaching bilingually, we can pay attention to issues of power and marginalisation. This contributes to the view of an African child, not as a monolingual, but as a child having a multilingual identity. By allowing children to draw on their full semiotic repertoire, we begin to open pathways for meaningful learning, self-conception, identity, representation of what exists and what it means to be an African language speaking child, a concept that goes beyond colonial representations and even 'traditional' representations, both of which wish to freeze the growth and creativity of the children. The case study of STLC# as a third space, linguistically, physically and pedagogically, shows how we can re-position African language speaking children as resourceful and capable learners.

References

Alexander, N. (1989) *Language Policy and National Unity in South Africa/Azania*. Cape Town: Buchu Books.

Alexander, N. (2003) Multilingual education – a training of trainers' programme. *LEAP News* 5, 3–4.

Anzaldúa, G. (1987) *Borderlands/La Frontera: The New Mestiza*. San Francisco, CA: Aunt Lute Books.

Axtell, D. (2007) *We're Going on a Lion Hunt*. Square Fish. UK

Baker, C. (2006) Theories of bilingualism and the curriculum. In *Foundations of Bilingual Education and Bilingualism* (4th edn). Clevedon: Multilingual Matters.

Barton, A.C., Tan, E. and Rivet, A. (2008) Creating hybrid spaces for engaging school science among urban middle school girls. *American Educational Research Journal* 45 (1), 68–103.

Bhabha, H. (1990) The third space. Interview with Homi Bhabha. In J. Rutherford (ed.) *Identity: Community, Culture, Difference* (pp. 207–221). London: Lawrence & Wishart.

Blackledge, A. (2000) Monolingual ideologies in multilingual states: Language hegemony and social justice in Western liberal democracies. *Estudios de Sociolinguistica* 1 (2), 25–45.

Blommaert, J. (2005) *Discourse: A Critical Introduction*. Cambridge: Cambridge University Press.

Bock, Z. (2016) Multimodality, creativity, and children's meaning-making: Drawings, writings, imaginings. *Stellenbosch Papers in Linguistics Plus* 49, 1–21.

bua-lit Language and Literacy Collective (2018) *How Are We Failing Our Children? Reconceptualising Language and Literacy Education*. See https://bua-lit.org.za/.

Canagarajah, S. (2018) Translingual practice as spatial repertoires: Expanding the paradigm beyond structuralist orientations. *Applied Linguistics* 39 (1), 31–54.

Christie, P. (1991) *The Right to Learn*. Johannesburg: Raven Press.

Copland, F. and Creese, A. (2015) *Linguistic Ethnography: Collecting, Analysing and Presenting Data*. Los Angeles, CA: Sage.

Cummins, J. (2008) Teaching for transfer: Challenging the two solitudes assumption in bilingual education. In J. Cummins and N. Hornberger (eds) *Encyclopedia of Language and Education, Vol. 5: Bilingual Education* (2nd edn) (pp. 65–75). New York: Springer Science + Business Media.

Department of Basic Education (2011) *Curriculum Assessment Policy Statement. Department of Basic Education*. https://doi.org/10.4324/9781315067070

Delpit, L. (1988) The silenced dialogue: Power and pedagogy in educating other people's children. *Harvard Educational Review* 58 (3), 280–298.

Flores, N. and García, O. (2014) Linguistic third spaces in education: Teachers' translanguaging across the bilingual continuum. In D. Little, C. Leung and P. Van Avermaet (eds) *Managing Diversity in Education: Languages, Policies and Pedagogies* (pp. 243–256). Bristol: Multilingual Matters.

García, O. (2009) *Bilingual Education in the 21st Century: A Global Perspective*. Malden, MA and Oxford: Wiley Blackwell.

Gutièrrez, K., Baquedano-López, P., Alvarez, H. and Chiu, M. (1999) Building a culture of collaboration through hybrid language practices. *Theory into Practice* 38 (2), 87–93.

Guzula, X., McKinney, C. and Tyler, R. (2016) Languaging for learning: Legitimising translanguaging and enabling multimodal practices in third spaces. *Southern African Linguistics and Applied Language Studies* 34 (3), 211–226.

Harrop-Allin, S. (2014) Bana etlong retlobapala: Examining children's musical games on a Soweto playground. *Journal of Musical Arts in Africa* 11 (1), 1–20.

Heugh, K. (2000) The case against bilingual and multilingual education in South Africa. Occasional Paper No. 6. Cape Town: Praesa.

Heugh, K. (2001) A history of mother-tongue and bilingual education in South Africa. In T. Beckett (ed.) *Reports on Mother-tongue Education.* Cape Town: Praesa.
Janks, H. (2010) *Literacy and Power.* New York: Routledge.
Junod, H.A. (1905) The native language and native education. *Journal of the African Society* 5 (17), 1–14.
Kress, G. (1997) *Before Writing.* London: Routledge.
Li, W. (2018) Translanguaging as a practical theory of language. *Applied Linguistics* 39 (1), 9–30.
Lugones, M. (1987) Playfulness, world-travelling, and loving perception. *Hypatia* 2 (2), 13–19.
Maake, N.P. (1991) Language and politics in South Africa with reference to the dominance of the Nguni languages. *English Studies* 34 (2), 55–64.
MacDonald, C. and Burroughs, E. (1991) *Eager to Talk and Learn and Think: Bilingual Primary Education in South Africa.* Cape Town: Maskew Miller Longman.
Makalela, L. (2015) Moving out of linguistic boxes: The effects of translanguaging strategies for multilingual classrooms. *Language and Education* 19 (3), 200–215.
Makoe, P. (2007) Language discourses and identity construction in a multilingual South African primary school. *English Academy Review* 24 (2), 55–70.
Makoe, P. and McKinney, C. (2009) Hybrid discursive practices in a South African multilingual primary classroom: A case study. *English Teaching and Critique* 8 (2), 80–85.
Makoni, S. (1999) African languages as colonial scripts. In C. Coetzee and S. Nuttall (eds) *Negotiating the Past* (pp. 242–248). Cape Town: Oxford University Press.
Malherbe, E.G. (1943) *The Bilingual School: A Study of Bilingualism in South Africa.* Johannesburg: Central News Agency.
McKinney, C. (2017) *Language and Power in Postcolonial Schooling: Ideologies in Practice.* New York and London: Routledge.
Mkhize, N. (2016) Away with Good Bantus: De-linking African language literature from culture, 'tribe' and propriety. *Arts and Humanities in Higher Education* 15 (1), 146–152.
Newfield, D. (2011) Multimodality and children's participation in classrooms: Instances of research. *Perspectives in Education* 29 (1), 27–35.
New London Group (2000) A pedagogy of multiliteracies: Designing social futures. In B. Cope and M. Kalantzis (eds) *Multiliteracies: Literacy Learning and the Design of Social Futures* (pp. 9–37). London and New York: Routledge.
Nomlomo, V. (1993) Language variation in the Transkeian Xhosa speech community and its impact on children's education. Master's dissertation, University of Cape Town.
Pluddemann, P. (2010) Home language based bilingual education: Towards a learner-centred language typology in primary schools in South Africa. Occasional Paper No. 32. Cape Town: Praesa.
Reed, Y. (2006) Imagining the subject: Designing and producing English textbooks for South African schools. *Journal of English Studies in Africa* 49 (1), 139–162.
Rosen, M and Oxenbury, H. (1997) *We're Going on a Bear Hunt.* Little Simon. UK
Stein, P. (2004) Representation, rights, and resources: Multimodal pedagogies in the language and literacy classroom. In B. Norton and K. Toohey (eds) *Critical Pedagogies and Language Learning* (pp. 95–113). Cambridge: Cambridge University Press.
Swain M. (2006) Languaging, agency and collaboration in advanced second language proficiency. In H. Byrnes (ed.) *Advanced Language Learning: The Contribution of Halliday and Vygotsky* (pp. 95–108). London: Continuum.

Making Connections/Entanglements

My home linguistic repertoire and the monolingual bias of the school

As a rural child growing up kwilali yakuZwelitsha, kwisithili saseMhlanga, huddled in a triangle between three small towns of Cacadu, eLadyfreyi (former Lady Frere), eNdwe (Indwe) naseDodrerha, eDododolorho (Dordrecht) as well as close to farms, I knew no other language before I attended school, except for isiXhosa. It was easy for people to assume that we were all coming from the same speech community, meaning that we all spoke the same variety of isiXhosa and that we all knew and had similar conventions of speaking. Kodwa isiXhosa sam siboleke a lot from Afrikaans, especially because of the influence from Afrikaners living in Indwe and Dordrecht and from the village workers who commuted to and from the farms or did seasonal migrant labour kwiifama zaseFreyistati. Elalini yam, ixhaphakile into yokubiza indlu enkulu sithi lihesi from Afrikaans huis; flat house as iplati from Afrikaans plat, fence-idrati from Afrikaans draat and many other words. The school and isiXhosa books however used words like uxande for ihesi (big house) and ucingo for idrati (fence). However, behind our house we had abamelwane who are amaHlubi, who did things a little bit differently from those of us who are abaThembu, from ceremonies and from ways of speaking. Abamelwane spoke with a different variety and had a different pronunciation for some of the words we used, which are spelt the same, such as amalongwe, ubulongwe, for cow dung example. This was not a problem; we spoke our varieties and understood one another.

It was not until I went to high school in Cofimvaba that I realised that I had a repertoire, indlela eyahlukileyo yokuthetha from my school mates. I became self-conscious and had to adjust my ways of speaking to fit with those of my schoolmates. That alerted me that, though we lived in the same village, and in the Transkei, we had different ways of speaking and to the fact that there are no stable speech communities, but ndandiziva ndinyanzelekile ukuba ndithethe the same way my school mates. Slowly, Afrikaans vocabulary started to be replaced by English vocabulary in my repertoire. At the beginning of high school, in Grade 8 many of us spoke mainly isiXhosa amongst ourselves. However, there were a

Annotations:
- In Zwelitsha Village, in the Mhlanga Region
- Children called it eDodrerha. My grandfather called it eDodolorho
- But my isiXhosa borrowed
- From farms in the Free State.
- In my village, it is common for us, for example, to refer to a big house as ihesi.
- neighbours
- a different way of speaking
- but I felt compelled to speak the same way as my schoolmates.

few learners who had gone to boarding schools much earlier than us and had been taught by English speaking nuns and became more proficient in English than us. These learners were comfortable in speaking both isiXhosa and English. In an effort by abaphathi besikolo to force all of us to speak English, we were told to police each other for speaking isiXhosa. The punishment was the literal plastering of our mouths to silence us followed by the unceremonious removal of the tape, which pulled the hairs on our skin so hard ukuze kube buhlungu. But this attempt was unsuccessful because as learners, we carried on speaking our languages and thought it was a futile exercise to police each other. [*The school management*] [*That it hurt*]

However, the fact that there were mainly English-speaking teachers from Ghana, Uganda and teachers of Indian and Austrian origins, more than local isiXhosa speaking teachers can be seen as another strategy for entrenching English dominance, even though it had other positive aspects to it. They spoke English only and refused to respond to us when we spoke isiXhosa. UNoGhana, my Ghanaian teacher laughed at us xa siqwabaza uJoji, when we broke 'King George', as we referred to English, despite her husband struggling to say 'railway'. He pronounced 'railway' as 'lairway'. For that reason, zange ndathetha eklasini. All my teachers saw my performance in written form. I was doing well in written English, so, babengenanto yokuthetha. I could see how impressed my English teacher was with my bookish English when I was finally selected for matric oral examinations to talk about farming. Given an unprepared topic and being caught on the spot, I quickly remembered izifundo zam zeJiyografi on subsistence farming and commercial farming and the commercial businesses we learnt about in business economics. That day, ndariyelayiza for the first time how speaking English earned one respect, not only of the teachers but also of the classmates. [*I never spoke in class*] [*They had nothing much to say*] [*My Geography lessons*]

Imobile layibhrari only circulated English books and nothing in isiXhosa. Slowly we saqalisa ukufunda kakhulu ngesiNgesi because it was the only available language. Learners also brought mainly English literature from home. This is how isiXhosa literature or reading habits were slowly being eradicated, zapheliswa, nya. [*The mobile library*] [*We started reading more in English*]

3 Navigating Hegemonic Knowledge and Ideologies at School: Children's Oral Storytelling as Acts of Agency and Positioning

Pinky Makoe

Introduction and Background

Formal schooling may be regarded as an attempt to level the playing field so that all children in the modern state will have the same educational opportunities regardless of race, ethnicity, class or socioeconomic background. However, schooling remains the main institutional mediator (beyond family background) for social, cultural and linguistic reproduction and this includes the 'imposition of systems of symbolism and meaning (i.e. culture) upon groups or classes in such a way that they are experienced as legitimate' (Jenkins, 2002: 104). Most schools tend to operate as primary sites of in/exclusion wherein higher value and privilege are attributed to language, literacy and identity activities that reproduce dominant institutional practices, while different complexes of repertoires (ways of speaking, being, knowing, doing) are constructed as 'benignly deviant' (in Foucault's (1979) terms) and inferior. In the face of increasing diversity, ideologies that foster and reinforce linguistic, cultural and behavioural homogeneity remain normalised, and heterogeneity is seen as a problem, or at best an exception.

Present-day multilingual settings are often characterised by actions of acculturation and assimilation, reflecting how schools act as institutions of social stratification, of erasure of difference and exclusion. In these settings, discourse practices are still entrenched in historical, political, ideological processes – usually Western or European perspectives premised on the nation-state philosophy of cultural and linguistic homogeneity. Monoglossic and monolingual ideology permeate schooling and re/produce the hegemony of the language of power in a nation-state. For example, García and

Torres-Guevara (2009: 182) show that despite the presence of bilingual programmes in US Latinas/o education, 'the language of schooling is and has been, English. Spanish ... is only considered a "foreign" language, and taught as such. It is English that is used as the medium of instruction, and it is English literacy and language arts that are emphasized and assessed'. Writing in the Australian context, French (2016) notes that the inculcation of a monolingual ideology reflects legacies of colonialism in that 'curriculum texts, assessment practices, and instructional practices were founded on historical assumptions of a culturally homogenous and monolingual English-speaking student body' (French, 2016: 290) – this is in spite of the presence of Indigenous and other-than-English immigrant languages.

There is still a tendency in classrooms in diverse settings to underestimate and silence those sociocultural experiences that typify students' participation in 'communities of practice' (Lave & Wenger, 1991) or 'discourse communities' (Gee, 1989) outside of the ideological norm. However, local and international research advocating for the transformation of pedagogical approaches in diverse settings increasingly continues to validate the wealth of multilingual repertoires or 'funds of knowledge' (Moll et al., 1992) that learners bring into their schools as resources to be cultivated rather than problems to be overcome. Employing different theoretical/conceptual prisms including heteroglossia (Bailey, 2007; Blackledge & Creese, 2014; Busch, 2010), hybridity (Gutiérrez et al., 1999a, 1999b; Makoe & McKinney, 2009), multimodality (Kendrick et al., 2006; Kress & Bezemer, 2009; Stein, 2008), multiliteracies (New London Group, 1996, 2000), third space (Gutiérrez et al., 1999b; Guzula et al., 2016; Moje et al., 2004), translanguaging (García, 2009; Makalela, 2015; Makoe, 2018), to name only a few examples, these bodies of literature elucidate pedagogies of the possible in which the leveraging of children's rich background of knowledge and linguistic/cultural toolkits serves as a resource for social and cognitive accomplishments, ultimately mediating epistemic access.

Recent scholarship in postcolonial African settings stresses that opening up education spaces for languages, literacies, cultures and identities that have traditionally been neglected and ignored serves as 'a springboard for learning' (Gregory, 1997: 6), because 'when children possess the cultural repertoires upon which school depends, all goes well' (Blackledge, 2000: 8). Exploring literacy activities in multilingual under-resourced South African township schools, Stein (2008) draws attention to ways in which teachers employed pedagogies that foster inclusive learning environments by giving learners opportunities to draw on local/Indigenous forms of knowledge and representation previously marginalised and devalued by the apartheid regime. The acts of re-appropriation of cultural practices (e.g. words, gestures, genres, portrayals, metaphors from their respective home languages and cultures) connected to learners' lives enabled them to use multiple semiotic resources to express their own meanings, fostered learner autonomy and increased classroom participation.[1] Using a translanguaging lens, Makoe (2018) has shown how children in a monoglot context mobilised and (re)positioned their multilingual repertoires as resources for learning in a Grade 3 South African classroom, and in the process disrupted the English-only dictates of the school and made their multilingual identities, all too often silenced, visible. She concludes that 'the emergence of translanguaging practices in the public space of the classroom demonstrates children's agentive (re)positioning of themselves as meaning-makers, knowledge creators and linguistically resourceful and competent' (Makoe, 2018: 13). Kiramba (2016) explores heteroglossic practices in a multilingual fourth grade science classroom, situated in rural Kenya, wherein learners' proficiency in written and spoken English (LoLT) is low but they are competent in one or more local languages. She demonstrates that the use of available multilingual/multicultural resources by the teacher and learners to mediate and contextualise subject knowledge 'creates a space for pedagogy of integration and dialogue, which liberates historically omitted languages and asserts the fluid linguistic identities of multilingual learners' (Kiramba, 2016: 11).

This chapter focuses on pedagogic activities and practices into which learners from diverse backgrounds are socialised inside their first grade classroom in an English-medium South African school. Drawing on theoretical concepts of decoloniality, language ideology and new literacy studies, I seek to describe and examine oral storytelling performances of multilingual learners to illustrate ways in which common knowledge and values get established at school on the one hand, and how learners themselves embed and appropriate experiences typifying their sociocultural worlds in the process of learning, on the other hand. Focusing on learners' narrative accounts that exemplified their lived experiences and that are saturated with everyday sociocultural questions, e.g. violence, punishment, criminality, this chapter shows continuities and discontinuities between out-of-school knowledge and formal school knowledge (knowledge taught at school). The taken-for-granted notions of what counts as legitimate forms of knowledge, including forms of language use and delegitimation of non-dominant ways of engaging with classroom activities, recreate patterns of inclusion and exclusion in schooling. My analysis reveals learners' capacity to navigate the highly regulated learning context entrenched with complex dynamics of power and inequality. I argue that students are able to challenge and/or transform essentialist conceptions of what counts and does not count in the classroom by drawing on and appropriating their out-of-school experiences into the classroom space where sanctioned practices and script are at odds with that of the learners who inhabit it. Through this act of recovery of their unheard voices, not only are these learners making themselves visible, asserting their agency, and proclaiming their heterogeneous identities; they are also carving out for themselves a space in dominant classroom discourses.

Theoretical framing

In framing this study, I draw upon the notions of decoloniality, ideology and sociocultural approaches to literacy/knowledge, in particular new literacy studies (NLS). These lenses help to uncover particular means by which learners become socialised into institutionally valued identities, and simultaneously show how these learners are able to navigate the official script to incorporate as well as reposition community knowledge and experiences enveloping their lives as academic capital. By adopting decoloniality and ideology as complementary theoretical lenses, I aim to provide a window into conditions that give rise to and maintain Western linguistic/cultural orthodoxies in schooling, commonly framed in a philosophy of uniformity and homogeneity. Decoloniality and ideology are useful concepts through which to view cultural and material dynamics of colonial power structures historically instituted and reproduced in different domains such as education, if we are to extricate the ex-colonised peoples from the effects of coloniality that sustain asymmetrical relations of power globally and locally. The term colonialism differs from coloniality: the withdrawal of European countries from many colonies represented the end of colonialism, but coloniality (i.e. hegemonic ways of thinking, knowing, doing and being) remained. That is, 'we have come out of a period of global colonialism to enter a period of global coloniality' (Grosfoguel, 2011: 14). In this sense, colonialism refers to political and economic structures established by the coloniser to dominate and exploit the colonised. Regarding this logic engineered through colonialism, Lander (2005, in Borelli *et al.*, 2020: 304) argues that by constructing the notion of universality from the particular (or parochial) experience of European history and interpreting the totality of the time and space of human experience from the point of view of this particularity, a radically excluding universality is instituted.

In contrast to colonialism, coloniality refers to the establishment of a colonial matrix of power that continues to be reproduced even in the absence of direct colonial administrations. According to Maldonado-Torres (2007: 243), coloniality entails 'long-standing patterns of power that emerged as a result of colonialism, but that define culture, labor, intersubjective relations, and knowledge production well beyond the strict limits of colonial administrations'. In this way, 'coloniality survives colonialism' and exists as 'an embedded logic that enforces control, domination, and exploitation disguised in the language of salvation, progress, modernization, and being good for everyone' (Mignolo, 2005: 6, 8). Based on this context, the nexus of decoloniality and ideology not only provides valuable insights into schools as sites of colonial reproduction where Eurocentric pedagogies and epistemologies are the imposed and natural order, but enables us to problematise the privileging of European knowledge, language, subjectivity and the invisibilisation of non-European forms of knowing.

Commenting on the role of education, Ndlovu-Gatsheni (2013: 10) warns us that 'what Africans must be vigilant against is the trap of ending up normalizing and universalising coloniality as a natural state of the world' because 'endogenous and Indigenous knowledges have been pushed to the margins of society. Africa is today saddled with irrelevant knowledge that disempowers rather than empowers individuals and communities'. Decolonial thinking advocates for the change of unequal relations of power, conceptions of knowledge and the place of the person who produces this knowledge, so as to 'transcend western epistemology and canon' (Grosfoguel, 2010, in Borelli *et al.*, 2020: 307), 'to delink, to escape from the iron cage of imperial absolute knowledge' (Mignolo, 2012: xiv) by 'making visible the invisible' (Maldonado-Torres, 2007: 262). This openness will allow us not only to confront the Western episteme's universalising of hegemonic knowledge including the interests it serves, but also to recognise the silenced and marginalised ways of knowing.

Consistent with decolonial transformation intent, NLS (e.g. Gee, 2008; Street, 1995, 2012) sets aside the idea that literacy involves technical skills learned only in mainstream schooling and stresses the importance of literacy knowledge embedded in out-of-school social settings such as home, communities and churches. Essentially, the traditional view of literacy as the ability to read and write rips literacy out of its sociocultural contexts and treats it as an asocial cognitive skill with little or nothing to do with human relationships. It cloaks literacy's connections to power, to social identity and to ideologies, often in the service of privileging certain types of literacy and certain types of people (Gee, 2008: 67).

Distinguishing between autonomous and ideological models, Street (1995) argues that the former assumes a universal-skills basis to literacy while the latter sees literacy as situated social and cultural practice, the plurality of which is reflected in the use of the term literacies. Following the sociocultural perspective, I contend that literacy is always situated, multiple and meanings contextual as opposed to being something static and devoid of context. In other words, 'beyond the technical skill to read or function within social contexts, literacy includes the ability to think and reason, a way of living, a means of looking at the world and the behavior in the world' (Makalela, 2018: 829–830). This said, the positioning of different literacy practices in South African schools is inherently ideological and mired in power relations of superiority and inferiority. Referring to language practices and the curriculum in post-apartheid South Africa, Christie and McKinney (2017: 12, 8) posit that schools, 'whether for the privileged or poor, operate firmly within the logic of coloniality' and the curriculum is deeply embedded 'in the trope of powerful knowledge in the Western episteme'. As the analysis will demonstrate, by excluding or devaluing non-dominant ways of engaging with knowledge and literacy that epitomise learners' sociocultural worlds, I will argue that the education system is complicit in past and present inequities because 'there is much to be gained in better understanding the literacies students bring to the classroom ... as well as for making literacy-learning in school pertinent to students' everyday lives and therefore more compelling and motivating' (Au & Raphel, 2000: 173).

Research Setting and Data Collection

The research reported on here was conducted in the only Grade 1 classroom of a private[2] primary school situated in the metropolis of Johannesburg, where the language of instruction is English and yet for the majority of the learners it is a second or third language. Except for the teacher who is of Coloured[3] background and an Afrikaans home language speaker, all learners in this classroom are African with a small number coming from surrounding suburban areas and most from townships in and around Johannesburg. Many of the learners are multilingual and speak a range of Indigenous South African languages such as isiZulu, Setswana, Sesotho, Tshitsonga and isiXhosa. Furthermore, there are a few foreign learners from other parts of the African continent, including Zimbabwe, Lesotho and Rwanda. This classroom consisted of 33 learners in total, 19 girls and 14 boys, with ages ranging from seven to nine years old. As reported by the teacher, nearly all of these learners had not had the opportunity to attend Grade R (i.e. reception year) or kindergarten and attending Grade 1 represented their first year of formal schooling experience. In line with the policy and practice of the school, no language other than English is to be used on the school grounds, meaning that all communication, be it for social, teaching or learning purposes, must take place in English. This choice of English-only schooling indexes many parents' attitudes and conceptions of what constitutes good quality education, what facilitates access to future economic or employment opportunities as well as what type of schools are well-positioned to proffer quality. As Granville *et al.* (1998: 258) put it, 'South African parents believe correctly, however unfortunate this may be, that English also has material power. It provides entry to the middle class, to middle class jobs and to middle class pay packets'.

In addition, a large proportion of these learners from townships travel long distances to access quality education or better schools in the city and suburbia, as perceived by parents. This increased daily movement for good schools/education characterises continued patterns of inequality in post-apartheid schooling as a result of racially, linguistically and spatially planned education systems aimed at keeping differently racialised groups separate. Fataar's (2009) research on subjectivities associated with the changing schooling landscape in the city of Cape Town shows how 'the rigid, racialized apartheid city grid has been fundamentally rearranged by children and families' school choices. While people by and large still live in racialized pockets in the city, their school choices have been transacted across the city' (Fataar, 2009: 14). This is so because coloured and black learners who can do so opt for schools outside their immediate township neighbourhoods since access to city suburban education is seen as an investment equated with middle-class aspirations and lifestyles. This dynamic of migration in democratic South Africa draws attention to social justice questions about levelling the education field for all. It also accentuates the divide between the students' out-of-school sociocultural worlds and their in-school experiences.

The data for the present study were gathered over a five-month period from the multilingual Grade 1 classroom, using ethnographic methods aligned with traditions of school/classroom ethnography (e.g. Kenner & Ruby, 2012; Kiramba, 2016; Makoe & McKinney, 2009, 2014). The database is made up of field notes of classroom observations and experiences, video-recordings of learners' oral storytelling texts and audio-recordings of interviews with the teacher. School visits and classroom observations were done twice a week, for a maximum of one hour per visit, pending the teacher's availability. Children's presentation of oral stories was done voluntarily and a total of 53 stories were recorded during the fieldwork. The substance of and emphasis in each story was unique, and the length was variable, with some of these being short, taking three minutes, while others were longer, lasting about 10–15 minutes. Direction and guidance provided about the classroom activity were open-ended: learners were given the option of remaining seated at their respective desks or standing in front of the classroom during storytelling; they could tell any story of their choice about/involving family members, preschool teacher/s or friends, or stories that a community member could have read or told to them. Moreover, learners were told that they could use languages other than English in this activity. This change of practice is an interesting one considering the English-only policy that permeated school life. Throughout my classroom visits, I only ever observed learners openly invited to draw on their linguistic resources during the storytelling activity. However, this opportunity was not fully taken up by learners, because oral stories were mainly communicated in English, and an insignificant number of about three in Indigenous languages. Based on the teacher's instructions, there was no direct indication of any limitations in terms of time/duration, length of story, themes, kinds of content or structure. On the face of it, learners were free to share with the rest of the classroom community those narratives that exemplified their sociocultural worlds outside the classroom. In practice, however, the teacher had specific assumptions about what storytelling should look like in her classroom, as the extracts from my research data will show.

Findings and Discussion

My analysis of Grade 1 classroom storytelling begins with a number of interrelated extracts. Extract 1(a) is an abridged version of Belinda's (a learner's) storytelling, including the teacher's remarks in Extract 1(b), and the four extracts that follow are drawn from an interview between the researcher and the teacher. To give perspective, learners' uncorrected extracts mirror their use of English, their conceptions of oral narration, and the gestures they used. This illustrates meanings and messages embedded in and out of their school experiences. The teacher's reflections are important in illustrating her pedagogical and methodological approach to knowledge and literacy. More broadly, her reflections also provide a window into the modus operandi and culture of this school classroom, particularly in terms of how discourses, as systematically organised sets of statements, give expression to the meanings, practices and values of an institution, including what it is possible to say and not to say (see Kress, 1989).

Belinda's story

Extract 1(a) 'Once upon a time'

Belinda's original storytelling	*Belinda's story as mediated by researcher*
Once upon a time there was a hen, cat and the dog. Diana you wake up early in the morning (*twittering her fingers*). Go to the shops go and buy, go and buy the food. He cook, cook, cook (*rolling her hands to show that she is cooking*) the cat and the dog come in and he wake up and they eat, eat and mm and that hen he goes with that food at his friends (*pointing the direction of the hen*) he say knock, knock (*using her hands to show that someone is knocking*). Come in. Hey you guys where are you going? Home. I am going at my mother.	Once upon a time there was a hen, cat and the dog. Diana woke up early one morning and went to the shops to buy some food. Upon her return she cooked/prepared that food, and was later joined by the cat, dog and hen that had just woken up from sleep. To everyone's surprise the hen stole some of the food with the intention to share with friends. The hen ran to friends' house and knocked very hard (hoping not to get caught in its tracks). **At the friends' house** The hen finds a fight brewing and asked the siblings (his friends) whether their mother was home or not. Hen asks: where is your mother? One of the friends responds: She is gone to work. Hen: There is no need to fight. Stop it. **Diana catches up with the hen, at friends' house**

Where is your mother here? He is gone at work. No stop fighting. He said you go. You go there. (*pointing*) To go and Diana and say. You Diana I have I have to kill you. Hey Diana why are you staying here now, you want to go at my home and kill my friends there, I'll kill you next time. That is the end of the story.	Hen: Do not even think of taking back the food otherwise I will kill you. Do not trouble my friends. Go back home. Note: This mediated re-telling is inspired by Gee's (2008) transcription of children's oral storytelling and Blommaert's (2006) approach to narrative analysis described as ethno-poetics. Extract 1(a) is mediated to exemplify the focus and essence of the story, and in particular how the setting, characters and theme introduced contribute to the meaning of the story.

The teacher's response to Belinda's story in class

Extract 1(b) 'Tell us a nice story' (T: Teacher)

2 T: You said you are going to tell us about mm… and the hen… and now you are telling us about something… You forgot! Oh Shame! *(shaking her head)* Right the next one. Okay tell us Vinolia, stand up. Tell us a nice story, a short one. Stand there Vinolia and speak up.

Belinda's opening sentence in Line 1 '*once upon a time there was a hen, cat and the dog*' displays awareness and grasp of the genre and trajectory or plot structure of conventional storytelling that she has been exposed to at school. From the utterance '*Diana you wake up early in the morning*', however, she switches to a different storytelling genre as well as different content, reflective of her lived experience outside of school. To bring life to the storyline and ultimately persuade listeners, she uses oral strategies such as gesture, repetition and tone of voice to complement her performance. However, the teacher's response negates both the genre and the content of Belinda's story. Both the form of the text Belinda produced and its subject matter are seen as nonconforming and Belinda's conduct is treated as 'benignly deviant' (Foucault, 1979). The teacher's response in Extract 1(b) '*you said you are going to tell us about… the hen and now you are telling us about something…*' shows clearly that deviation from, or adaptation of, the official original classroom script becomes constructed in deficit terms '*You forgot! Oh Shame!*'. On one level, 'You forgot!' suggests that the teacher thinks Belinda does not remember what her story was supposed to be about, while on another level, the teacher might think that Belinda has 'forgotten' the classroom conventions of storytelling that the teacher expected her to demonstrate.

The teacher's interview reflections on the classroom moment (Extracts 2, 3, 4 and 5 below) provide further insights into her pedagogical approach and her assumptions about knowledge and literacy.

The teacher's reflections on Belinda's story

Extract 2 'That is not a story, it is something' (R: Researcher; T: Teacher)

3   R: Why did you say that Belinda was telling you something not the story about the hen, dog and cat?
4   T: I read them a story, a comprehension-like story about the dog and the hen. It was from one reader [graded reading book] at school. What is the name by the way mm, mm, mm I forgot the name. I will remember it just now.
5   R: Okay, you will tell me as soon as you remember it.
6   T: Okay, I read the story to them and that is why I said she was telling us something.
7   T: You see that is not a story, it is something.
8   R: If you do not mind can you tell me about the story of the hen and the dog.
9   T: I do not remember very well. I have read a lot of these stories. You know at foundation phase that's mainly what you do.
10   R: I do not really mind, tell me what you remember.
11   T: It is about the hen and the dog. It is something like the dog threatening to eat the hens, chickens and eggs. You see what I mean?

The teacher herself has forgotten the actual story '*I do not remember very well. I have read a lot of these stories.*' (Line 9). This suggests that the genre of school storytelling is of more concern to her than the actual content of this story. Her statement '*I read them a story, a comprehension-like story*' (Line 4) suggests that, pedagogically, she expects students to reproduce her format without giving them explicit instructions to do so at the start of the activity. (This is further illustrated in Extract 3 below.) Beyond saying '*it is something*' (Line 7), the teacher has no name for what Belinda has presented, suggesting that she does not recognise storytelling in its non-school form.

The interview extract portrays the mismatch between school as an institution and learners who inhabit this space. The teacher's assertion '… *that is not a story, it is something*' (Line 7) provides an example of pedagogic processes and practices by which linguistically and culturally diverse learners become socialised into the dominant culture and ethos of the school. The othering of Belinda's story as '*something*' simply because it does not find resonance with the '*comprehension-like*' prototype as modelled by the teacher is illuminating. These utterances reveal ideologies of acculturation at work, simultaneously privileging hegemonic ways of knowing while pathologising non-hegemonic forms of knowledge. As

Moll (2001: 13) points out, 'this dual strategy of exclusion and condemnation of one's language and culture, fostering disdain for what one knows and who one is, has critical consequence in terms of schooling – it influences children's attitudes towards their knowledge and personal competence. That is, it creates a social distance between themselves and the world of school knowledge'.

For the teacher, the classroom story has only one format, and Extracts 3, 4 and 5 below show clearly that she expects the content to be drawn from the repertoire of Western fairy tales rather than students' everyday lives out of school. There is also an implicit assumption that school stories are told in English.

The teacher's expectations of a 'school story'

Extract 3 'Things which are not stories'

12 T: … You know Vinolia?
13 R: Yes
14 T: Every time I read stories to them, she tells the story exactly as I have told them. She does not mix things. She is a very clever girl. If she had told us that story about the hen and the dog, it would have been the same like the one in the reader. So some of these kids just tell things which are not stories. Like Megan that day she said she was going to tell us a story about Little Red Riding Hood but then she told us about people in the township trying to kill a tsotsi which stole a TV. You see that is not a story. It is something.

Extract 4 'School is "the first time they hear stories"'

15 R: Mm, do they sometimes tell their own stories?
16 T: Only those who know stories. Otherwise they just don't do it correctly. It's their first year at school and some is the first time they hear stories. Those who know these stories attended pre-school and it's only a few. That's why we have a pre-school at our school from this year. They come to school not prepared. They cannot speak English. The school is an English medium.

In Extract 1b earlier, the teacher had invited Vinolia to *'tell us a nice story'* (Line 2). In Extract 3, Vinolia is judged to be *'a very clever girl'* (Line 14) because she is able to reproduce the form and content of a Western fairy tale: *'the same like the one in the reader'* (Extract 2, Line 4). I argue that this illustrates that the teacher reinforces homogeneity at the expense of heterogeneity; acts of regurgitation are cultivated, and creativity of the sort shown by Belinda is inhibited. Thus, the juxtaposition between Belinda's version as immaterial and Vinolia's version as exemplary practice perpetuates the divide between in and out of school lived experiences. Furthermore, the teacher's dismissal of Megan's story shows clearly that students are not permitted to adapt storylines to include their everyday worlds, despite her initial, seemingly open-ended instructions. The fact that the teacher does not explore why Megan adapted Little Red Riding Hood as she did suggests that she is more interested in children's memorisation than in their meaning-making. Extract 4 confirms that there is only one way to tell a story at school. The teacher is clear that *'only those who know stories'* are able to *'do it correctly'*, and the assumption is that storytelling is learnt in school settings, and in English. And Extract 5 below shows that there is only one version of Little Red Riding Hood, and that is the teacher's version.

Furthermore, the teacher's affirmation of Vinolia's story in contrast to her dismissal of Belinda's shows the value that is placed on the ability to execute dominant mainstream activities (say, narrative as taught at school) and how this is reinforced to enable learners to claim the most valued classroom identities and participate in particular practices. At the same time, not validating the performance of alternative activities confines learners to trivial identities and restricts their legitimacy to participate in other practices. Ultimately, this affects their access to meaningful learning and quality education.

Developing the theme of inclusion and exclusion, Extract 5 sheds further light on the teacher's own conception of what constitutes a story, the kinds of stories she teaches or exposes children to, as well as which genres of story are validated or not validated. Her response to *'what kind of stories do you encourage your children to tell?'* explicitly gives background and context about the philosophy that guides her classroom practice.

Extract 5 'The stories I know and teach'

17 R: What kind of stories do you encourage your children to tell?
18 T: Stories like Little Red Riding Hood. Yes, those are the stories that I know and teach. Some of the new ones you get from the readings that we do at school.

Reference to *'Little Red Riding Hood'* in Line 18 delineates the operative and epistemic framework the teacher draws on in facilitating teaching and learning. In other words, the story tales are a part of European Western epistemology that is foreign to most of the children in this setting. This is positioned as absolute, universal knowledge at the expense of local knowledge practices. The fact that learners from contexts of diversity are mainly exposed to Western traditional folktales that are taught and learned in English reflects the continuing legacy of colonial dynamics of power, inequalities of knowledge and epistemic monoculture. The role of schooling as a site of reproduction is noticeable here – learners are guided to fit into and to replicate privileged models of literacy or 'curriculum ... firmly anchored in the trope of "powerful knowledge" in the Western episteme' (Christie & McKinney, 2017: 8) while other ways of knowing become relegated to the periphery. This is an example of how schools, as sites of social reproduction, 'impose the legitimate forms of discourse and the idea that discourse should be recognised if and only if it conforms to legitimate norms' (Bourdieu, 1977: 650).

That said, reproduction does not happen without contestation. Amid the strictures of the classroom, I consider Belinda's performance in Extract 1(a) as an act of transformation, although limited, and the teacher's comment about Megan's story in Extract 3 also invites this interpretation. Belinda's ability to navigate discursive practices inculcated in this classroom and her *'telling us something'* (Extract 2, Line 6) that is considered illegitimate demonstrates her agentive role. By producing a text at odds with tradition and/or institutionally recognised script, Belinda not only locates her sociocultural world and lived experiences as resources for learning, but also re-positions herself as a knower and meaning-maker. In this sense, she challenges what counts and does not count in this classroom, and in the process asserts her voice and agency. Similarly, Megan's adaptation of Little Red Riding Hood mentioned in Extract 3 suggests an agentive role and meaning-making. This shows that learners are not simply passive recipients in socialisation processes of the school but have the capacity to take up positions within activities and proclaim their multiple identities.

In line with NLS, I contend that knowledge and literacy as situated and hybrid narrative texts such as Belinda's incorporate learners' representations of reality, in particular the dynamic movement across and within various communities. Because learners participate in multiple domains and communities, it is important that classrooms adopt a more dynamic/multiple lens on literacy with a view to capitalising on learners' diversity as well as giving space for the use of their full repertoires (language, literacy, knowledge) in the service of meaning-making, purposeful learning.

Pratt's (1991) notion of contact zones provides a useful lens for understanding the complex relationship between in and out of school ways of knowing, as conceptualised by the teacher. This term refers to 'social spaces where cultures meet, clash, and grapple with each other, often in highly asymmetrical relations of power, such as colonialism, slavery or their aftermath lived on in many parts of the world' (Pratt, 1991: 34). The imposition of Western ways of knowing as normal, on the one hand, and the positioning of learners' lived experiences as somewhat abnormal, on the other, shows the extent to which cultures are not given space to grapple with each other in this classroom. Not only are these learners being subjected to knowledge production conceived elsewhere; they are regularly expected to construct knowledge and make meaning in a foreign colonial language. Accordingly, Prah (2018: 17) argues that 'the maintenance and use of the colonial languages in education and social intercourse' inevitably 'leads to one destination, the terminus of assimilation;

estrangement from our African cultural character and moorings; and alienation from precisely what we need to build on'.

This said, the teacher's own conception of narratives '*yes those are the stories that I know and teach*' (Line 14) explicates her academic value system underpinned by Eurocentrism as well as how she operates or confines herself within her comfort zone of what she knows and teaches. Implicit in her explanations is the relationship between 'self' and 'history'. Indirect references to her own academic experience/background, identity as a teacher and modus operandi show that her participation in multiple domains and communities has a bearing on how she engages with and mediates classroom activities. In other words, she may be teaching as she was taught or how she was taught to teach. It may be argued that her professional socialisation and disposition are shaped by complex historical dynamics of superiority and inferiority that persist after colonialism. Arguably, she has internalised dominant language and literacy practices as resources to be normalised or reproduced while others are a liability. The problem with this approach to education is that '[t]he success of the modern/colonial world-system consists precisely in making subjects that are socially located on the oppressed side of the colonial difference think epistemically like the ones in dominant positions' (Grosfoguel, 2011: 6). Following decolonial thinking there is a need to delink from colonial matrix of power to enable the 'unfreezing of the subaltern's potential for thinking otherwise' (Kumaravadivelu, 2016: 79).

Conclusion

Using decoloniality, ideology and NLS as theoretical lenses, the data in this chapter illustrate how, at the micro-level of classroom practice, South African education remains deeply rooted in Eurocentric philosophy as a result of the colonial history of the country and its education system, where superiority is synonymous with forms of knowledge and knowing from the Global North, while forms from the Global South are constructed as inferior and deliberately excluded. Focusing on learners' narrative accounts, my analysis reveals that the teacher's conception and explicit valuing of traditional Western folkloric narratives as cultural capital, while simultaneously prohibiting and/or obscuring learners' specific histories, backgrounds these and undermines students' ability to be heard. The setting up of school-based knowledge and literacy as insulated and sealed off from learners' ways of knowing, as mediated by the teacher, underscores the complex relationship between learners' worlds outside the classroom and what they encounter inside the classroom. This said, my research shows one learner's ability to navigate the highly regulated context, embedding alternative voices and making visible her outside worlds (in production of texts) within the classroom. I argue that this demonstrates learners' agency in relation to socialisation processes or ways of knowing, being, talking and doing constructed by the teacher. This re-ordering of the classroom space to bring in different realities, frames of reference and 'economies of meaning' (Kerfoot & Tatah, 2017) somewhat changes or disrupts hegemonic power/knowledge. However, these disruptions are not without tension. Nonconforming conduct may be treated as 'benignly deviant' (Foucault, 1979), and dismissed as failure on the students' part.

Notes

(1) Kendrick *et al.*'s (2006) work in two Ugandan sites, like Stein (2008), shows how the incorporation of multimodal activities involving drawing, photography and drama enabled English language learners to produce material depicting their own local textual, cultural and linguistic meanings. This pedagogic approach created a transformative curriculum to support learning, and afforded teachers new and expanded ways to validate learners' forms of communication, representation, engagement and knowledge.
(2) This is a private school; however, the fees are lower compared to traditional wealthy private schools, often situated in affluent suburban neighbourhoods. The movement of learners from township schools in search of better education in cities or suburban areas, and importantly offered through the medium of English, resulted in the mushrooming of low-cost schooling in post-apartheid South Africa.
(3) The contested term 'Coloured' refers to people who trace their blended ancestries largely to Africa, Asia and Europe. As a racial category created during the apartheid era, it is rejected by many (see Antia & Dyers, 2019).

References

Antia, B. and Dyers, C. (2019) De-alienating the academy: Multilingual teaching as decolonial pedagogy. *Linguistics and Education* 51, 91–100.
Au, K. and Raphel, T. (2000) Equity and literacy in the next millennium. *Reading Research Quarterly* 35 (1), 170–188.
Bailey, B. (2007) Heteroglossia and boundaries. In M. Heller (ed.) *Bilingualism: A Social Approach* (pp. 257–274). Basingstoke: Palgrave Macmillan.
Blackledge, A. (2000) *Literacy, Power and Social Justice*. Staffordshire: Stoke-on-Trent: Trentham Books.
Blackledge, A. and Creese, A. (2014) Heteroglossia as practice and pedagogy. In A. Blackledge and A. Creese (eds) *Heteroglossia as Practice and Pedagogy* (pp. 1–20). Dordrecht: Springer.
Blommaert, J. (2006) Applied ethnopoetics. *Narrative Inquiry* 16 (1), 181–190.
Borelli, J.D.V.P., Silvestre, V.P. and Pessoa, R.R. (2020) Towards a decolonial language teacher education. *Revista Brasileira de Linguística Aplicada* 20 (2), 301–324.
Bourdieu, P. (1977) The economics of linguistic exchanges. *Social Science Information* 16 (6), 645–668.
Busch, B. (2010) School language profiles: Valorizing linguistic resources in heteroglossic situations in South Africa. *Language and Education* 24 (2), 283–294.
Christie, P. and McKinney, C. (2017) Decoloniality and 'Model C' schools: Ethos, language and the protests of 2016. *Education as Change* 21 (3), 160–180.
Fataar, A. (2009) Schooling subjectivities across the post-apartheid city. *Africa Education Review* 6 (1), 1–18.
Foucault, M. (1979) *Discipline and Punish: The Birth of the Prison* (A. Sheridan, trans.). New York: Vintage Books.

French, M. (2016) Students' multilingual resources and policy-in-action: An Australian case study. *Language and Education* 30 (4), 298–316.

García, O. (2009) *Bilingual Education in the 21st Century: A Global Perspective*. Oxford: Wiley-Blackwell.

García, O. and Torres-Guevara, R. (2009) Monoglossic ideologies and language policies in the education of U.S. Latinas/os. In E.G. Murillo Jr., S. Villenas, R.T. Galván, J.S. Muñoz, C. Martínez and M. Machado-Casas (eds) *Handbook of Latinos and Education: Theory, Research and Practice* (pp. 182–193). Abingdon: Routledge.

Gee, J.P. (1989) Literacy, discourse, and linguistics: Introduction. *Journal of Education* 171 (1), 5–17.

Gee, J.P. (2008) *Social Linguistics and Literacies: Ideology in Discourses* (3rd edn). London and New Yok: Routledge.

Granville, S., Janks, H., Mphahlele, M., Reed, Y., Watson, P., Joseph, M. and Ramani, E. (1998) English with or without g(u)ilt: A position paper on language in education policy for South Africa. *Language and Education* 12 (4), 254–272.

Gregory, E. (1997) *One Child, Many Worlds: Early Learning in Multicultural Communities*. London: David Fulton.

Grosfoguel, R. (2011) Decolonizing post-colonial studies and paradigms of political-economy: Transmodernity, decolonial thinking, and global coloniality. *TRANSMODERNITY: Journal of Peripheral Cultural Production of the Luso-Hispanic World* 1 (1), 1–37.

Gutiérrez, K., Baquedano-López, P., Alvarez, H.H. and Chiu, M.M. (1999a) Building a culture of collaboration through hybrid language practices. *Theory in Practice* 28 (2), 87–93.

Gutiérrez, K., Baquedano-López, P. and Tejeda, C. (1999b) Rethinking diversity: Hybridity and hybrid language practices in the third space. *Mind, Culture and Activity* 6 (4), 286–303.

Guzula, X., McKinney, C. and Tyler, R. (2016) Languaging-for-learning: Legitimising translanguaging and enabling multimodal practices in third spaces. *Southern African Linguistics and Applied Language Studies* 34 (3), 211–226.

Jenkins, R. (2002) *Pierre Bourdieu* (2nd edn). London and New York: Routledge.

Kendrick, M., Jones, S., Mutonyi, H. and Norton, B. (2006) Multimodality and English education in Ugandan schools. *English Studies in Africa* 49 (1), 95–114.

Kenner, C. and Ruby, M. (2012) Connecting children's worlds: Creating a multilingual syncretic curriculum through partnership between complementary and mainstream schools. *Journal of Early Childhood Literacy* 13 (3), 395–417.

Kerfoot, C. and Tatah, G. (2017) Constructing invisibility: The interdiscursive erasure of a Cameroonian immigrant learner in two South African primary schools. In C. Kerfoot and K. Hyltenstam (eds) *Entangled Discourses: South-North Orders of Visibility* (pp. 35–58). New York and London: Routledge.

Kiramba, L.K. (2016) Heteroglossic practices in a multilingual science classroom. *International Journal of Bilingual Education and Bilingualism* 22 (4), 445–458.

Kress, G. (1989) *Linguistic Processes in Sociocultural Practice* (2nd edn). Oxford: Oxford University Press.

Kress, G. and Bezemer, J. (2009) Knowledge, creativity and communication in education: Multimodal design. *Beyond Current Horizons: Technology, Children, Schools and Families Project*. London: Futurela.

Kumaravadivelu, B. (2016) The decolonial option in English teaching: Can the subaltern act? *TESOL Quarterly* 50 (1), 66–85.

Lave, J. and Wenger, E. (1991) *Situated Learning: Legitimate Peripheral Participation*. Cambridge: Cambridge University Press.

Makalela, L. (2015) Translanguaging practices in complex multilingual spaces: A discontinuous continuity in post-independent South Africa. *International Journal of the Sociology of Language* 234, 115–132.

Makalela, L. (2018) Community elders' narrative accounts of ubuntu translanguaging: Learning and teaching in African education. *International Review of Education* 64 (1), 823–843.

Makoe, P. (2018) Translanguaging in a monoglot context: Children mobilising and repositioning their multilingual resources for learning. In G. Mazzaferro (ed.) *Translanguaging as Everyday Practice* (pp. 13–30). Cham: Springer.

Makoe, P. and McKinney, C. (2009) Hybrid discursive practices in a South African multilingual primary classroom: A case study. *English Teaching: Practices and Critique* 8 (2), 8–95.

Makoe, P. and McKinney, C. (2014) Linguistic ideologies in multilingual South African suburban schools. *Journal of Multilingual and Multicultural Development* 35 (7), 658–673.

Maldonado-Torres, N. (2007) On the coloniality of being: Contributions to the development of a concept. *Cultural Studies* 21 (2–3), 240–270.

Mignolo, W.D. (2005) *The Idea of Latin America*. Malden, MA: Blackwell.

Mignolo, W.D. (2012) *Local Histories/Global Designs: Coloniality, Subaltern Knowledges and Border Thinking*. Princeton, NJ: Princeton University Press.

Moje, E.B., Ciechanowski, K.M., Kramer, K., Ellis, L., Carrillo, R. and Collazo, T. (2004) Working toward third space in content area literacy: An examination of everyday funds of knowledge and discourse. *Reading Research Quarterly* 39 (1), 40–70.

Moll, L.C. (2001) Diversity in schooling: A cultural-historical approach. In M. de la Luz Reyes and J.J. Halcon (eds) *The Best for Our Children: Critical Perspectives on Literacy for Latino Students* (pp. 13–28). New York: Teachers College Press.

Moll, L., Amanti, C., Neff, D. and González, N. (1992) Funds of knowledge for teaching: Using a qualitative approach to connect homes to classrooms. *Theory into Practice* 31 (2), 131–141.

Ndlovu-Gatsheni, S.J. (2013) Why decoloniality in the 21st century? *The Thinker for Thought Leaders* 8, 10–15.

New London Group (1996) A pedagogy of multiliteracies: Designing social futures. *Harvard Educational Review* 66 (1), 60–92.

New London Group (2000) *Multiliteracies: Literacy Learning and the Design of Social Futures*. London: Routledge.

Prah, K.K. (2018) Discourse on language and literacy for African development. In L. Makalela (ed.) *Shifting Lenses: Multilanguaging, Decolonisation and Education in the Global South* (pp. 9–20). Cape Town: CASAS.

Pratt, M.L. (1991) Arts of the contact zone. *Profession* 91, 33–40.

Stein, P. (2008) *Multimodal Pedagogies in Diverse Classrooms: Representation, Rights and Resources*. London and New York: Routledge.

Street, B.V. (1995) *Social Literacies: Critical Approaches to Literacy in Development, Ethnography and Education*. London: Longman.

Street, B.V. (2012) Society reschooling. *Reading Research Quarterly* 47 (2), 216–227.

4 Identity Meshing in Learning Science Bilingually: Tales of a 'Coconuty Nerd'

Robyn Tyler

Research Participants as Border-crossers

The fieldwork I undertook for my PhD project involved crossing linguistic and disciplinary borders. Two anecdotes are illustrative in this regard. A linguistic border was crossed daily as I journeyed to and from my research site. The middle-class suburb of Cape Town in which I live is English dominant and the township in which I carried out my fieldwork is isiXhosa dominant. On the way into school in the mornings, I tuned in to the isiXhosa-language radio station in my car and switched to an English-language station in the afternoon. Listening to isiXhosa radio also facilitated my language learning which was so crucial to my fieldwork: I needed to inhabit the identity of a learner and I needed growing isiXhosa-language knowledge in order to be able to interact with fellow participants and analyse my data.

Embarking on research into language in science learning necessitated a disciplinary border crossing for me. My first professional training was as a high school English teacher and so studying meaning-making in Grade 9 Natural Science required me to acquire some very basic chemistry quickly. I went about this by purchasing the Grade 9 textbook in use in the school and drawing on my social network which included a university chemistry professor who tutored me briefly. Significant to both of these actions is that I was able to utilise resources that were available to me in order to accomplish the learning I desired. These resources were highly valuable in my border-crossing endeavours: independent transport, my prior isiXhosa learning at school, access to a university professor in the subject I wanted to learn, disposable income to spend on a textbook. Having this variety of resources at my disposal connects me to the research participant who is the focus of this chapter.

Khethiwe was the top student in her natural science class at the time of my study. She is a highly proficient speaker of isiXhosa and English and used these daily at school for a variety of functions, as did her peers. She was a curious science learner and, supported by her high proficiency in English, was the learner who engaged most in talk with me about science. Despite utilising these resources which enable border crossing for Khethiwe and me, we were both, on at least one recorded occasion during the study, positioned as illegitimate holders of some of these resources. Khethiwe recorded on a questionnaire being called a 'coconuty nerd' by her cousins and friends – an insult arising from her enjoyment of using English as a black isiXhosa speaker. The term 'coconut' accuses her of affiliating too closely with white culture, while 'nerd' accuses her of identifying too closely with academic knowledge. I was positioned as an illegitimate holder of isiXhosa resources by Khethiwe who, during our first study group meeting, responded to my isiXhosa greeting with a surprised cry of 'weird!', which was followed by a chorus of giggles from the other 15-year-olds in the room. While Khethiwe expressed this as 'weird', she was merely echoing a societal expectation that white South Africans do not speak an African language. The positioning of Khethiwe and me as taking on illegitimate identities occurs as a result of monoglossic language ideologies which link race and language in simple, linear ways, assuming clear boundaries between named languages such as 'English' and 'isiXhosa'. We both needed to mesh our 'legitimate' and 'illegitimate' identities in socially risky ways – although Khethiwe had far more to lose than I did – in order to get science learning done in this context.

Introduction

For South African teenagers, learning science in high school involves negotiating multiple, and often disparate, languages and identity positions. The science classroom is a borderland (Anzaldúa, 2012 [1987]) where these resources interact and grate against each other, often being meshed to produce a new voice. Heteroglossic (Bakhtin, 1981), or multivoiced, practice of this nature stands in contrast to a curriculum and language policy framework which proceeds from an orientation to learning that favours the use of English only (Guzula, this volume). This chapter examines the meaning-making practices of isiXhosa-English bilingual teenagers learning science in a township school in Cape Town. Using the analytical tools of linguistic ethnography, the chapter provides a case study of one high-achieving learner, Khethiwe, to show how language registers and other modes of meaning-making are meshed in a learning episode in science. Khethiwe's skilful use of linguistic registers and modes such as gesture allows her to perform different identity positions simultaneously, both for learning science and for maintaining a good social standing among her peers. I argue that it is this simultaneity and fluidity of meaning-making practices which makes Khethiwe – self-identified as a 'coconuty nerd' – a successful science learner in her context.

The chapter proceeds as follows. First, I outline how the science classroom in South Africa constitutes a borderland in which English, African languages and other semiotic modes are employed as meaning-making tools. This context is discussed from a decolonial perspective. Then, I discuss how learning in science is quintessentially an identity project and how theories of bilingual languaging help us understand how this works to enable appropriation of a new discourse. Next, through a close analysis of an episode of interaction in a science study group, the multiple registers and modes used in meaning-making are identified and I discuss how they produce what I describe as *identity meshing*. The episode is presented as a comic strip which, I argue, offers new insights into identity meshing in classroom discourse. Elsewhere (Tyler, 2021) I have argued that the comic strip as transcript facilitates a decolonial understanding of classroom interaction. I argue that Khethiwe's language and identity meshing enables appropriation of science discourse and the development of her social identity simultaneously. I conclude with implications for decolonial pedagogies and teacher education.

The Position of African Languages and English in Science Classrooms in South Africa

The debate about how to use language for learning science and other content subjects for black South Africans has become unhelpfully stuck in a tug-of-war between two named languages: English – considered a 'world language' – on the one hand; and whichever African language is the 'home language' of the learners in question on the other (McKinney, 2017). The imperative implicit in the curriculum that all African language speaking children will switch from their home language as the medium of instruction to English after three years of formal schooling is underpinned by strongly held language ideologies (McKinney, 2017). Language ideologies comprise attitudes, beliefs and values related to language which circulate in society through discourses about language. A monoglossic language ideology holds that natural language can be separated into silos and named as 'English' or 'isiXhosa' – autonomous entities that have definable boundaries. An Anglonormative language ideology assumes the English monolingual speaker as the norm and positions the ability to speak English as imperative and those who do not speak English as deficient or even deviant (McKinney, 2017). The position of English in current South African society is a result of colonisation and therefore Anglonormativity is described as a colonial ideology (Christie & McKinney, 2017). Added to these strong language ideologies, the dominance of the English-only view is shored up by a resistance to 'mother tongue education' because of a history in which African language speakers were denied access to English and at the same time were subject to an impoverished curriculum as part of Bantu Education – a system of planned under-education for black African children under apartheid (Christie & McKinney, 2017; Guzula, this volume). Our current curriculum documents favour the side of the debate that teaching content subjects in English only is the best way forward for all South African learners (Tyler, 2018). Departmental communiques warn of the detrimental impact of 'code-switching' and implore teachers to use only English in subject teaching from Grade 4 (Western Cape Education Department, 2014). Followed religiously, this instruction would result in the exclusion of learners' most familiar linguistic resources from the classroom and restrict their access to science and other academic subject content and discourse. In reality, however, teachers and learners engage in heteroglossic practices, often guiltily (Probyn, 2009), to get learning done.

Therefore, science learning in South Africa is significantly shaped by coloniality, while there are also examples of learning practices that are indicative of decoloniality (Maldonado-Torres, 2007; Mignolo, 2011; Ndlovu-Gatsheni, 2015) at work in the borderlands. A key tenet of decolonial thinking is pluriversality, or the acceptance of the entanglement of cosmologies within a power differential (Mignolo, 2007). Pluriversality in the present context refers to the entanglements of different languages, registers and other modes for learning science and, I will argue, is epitomised in Khethiwe's performance in this chapter. Taking a 'border thinking' (Mignolo, 2007) perspective on learners' meaning-making in science requires accepting and describing the pluriversality of meaning-making in a South African science classroom.

Science Learning as Discourse Appropriation

The relationship between language and identity and the role of both in learning has long been a preoccupation of education researchers. Sociocultural theories of learning have recognised that students of particular content knowledge need to participate in the practices of the discipline or field under study in order to be successful. This involves acquiring (Gee, 2004), or appropriating (Bakhtin, 1981), the discourses associated with the new content. These processes of acquisition and appropriation involve identity negotiation and transformation and are mediated through meaning systems, the best understood of which is natural language.

Scholars of science discourse, such as James Gee, have argued that embracing a new academic discourse involves 'participat[ing] in another identity' which represents some loss (Gee, 2004: 18). This loss, he argues, is particularly sharply felt for those whose 'lifeworlds are not the type of middle-class ones that historically have built up a sense of shared interests and values with some academic specialist domains' (Gee, 2004: 18). Brown (2006) echoes Gee in discussing the 'cultural conflict' involved in learning science for minorities in the United States and found that students need to 'balance the tension between their academic and personal identities' (Brown, 2006: 96). While it is important to recognise the loss and conflict, these metaphors run the risk of oversimplifying the process of appropriation and offer a gloomy picture for the minoritised majority of multilingual South African science learners. In focusing only on loss of identity, we can miss the opportunities for decolonising science learning offered by a vision of identity and language meshing. Another aspect of decolonising science learning is exemplified in Hattingh's chapter in this volume, where Indigenous community knowledge and language resources related to the science curriculum are positioned as central.

Poststructuralist scholars have proposed that identity is multiple and fluid (Blommaert, 2008; Weedon, 1987) and a site of negotiation and contestation during learning (Ballenger, 1997; Brown, 2006; Makalela, 2014; McKinney & Norton, 2008). Mikhail Bakhtin, in his discussion of the processes of appropriation of particular discourses, draws our attention to the struggle inherent in making a new discourse one's own:

> Language is not a neutral medium that passes freely and easily into the private property of the speaker's intentions; it is populated – overpopulated – with the intentions of others. Expropriating it, forcing it to submit to one's own intentions and accents, is a difficult and complicated process. (Bakhtin, 1981: 293–294)

Other scholars of the learning accomplished by multilinguals suggest the potential for learning that drawing on a full language/identity repertoire involves. For example, Ballenger describes the scientific argumentation of bilinguals in the United States as follows:

> Because they did so in ways which did not place these ways of talking and thinking in stark opposition to their out-of-school discourse, they were able to explore the content area (in this case, the growth of mould) in a way that led them well beyond the fairly simple and unproblematic explanations typically developed in school. (Ballenger, 1997: 2)

Canagarajah (2004) and Makalela (2014) hold that constructing hybrid identities is integral to the language acquisition process. The data analysis presented in this chapter aims to offer an example of how bilingual science learners in South Africa today draw on different resources in their semiotic repertoires in order to appropriate science for their own intentions, even when these resources have been ideologically positioned as being in conflict with science learning. In so doing, learners move through different identity positions, even performing them simultaneously.

Science Learning as Bilingual Meaning-making

Meaning-making is conceptualised in social semiotics as human action in which resources for sign making are used and transformed through social interaction according to the interest of the sign maker (Kress *et al.*, 2014), and is taken up as a core concept in studies that emphasise multimodality in learning. Studying meaning-making, rather than the use of named languages, also allows a non-binary lens on the linguistic mode. Integral to the current scholarship on meaning-making in multilingual contexts is the theoretical work in applied linguistics on languaging which takes the multilingual speaker as the norm (May, 2014). The concept of *translanguaging*, first developed in Wales by Cen Williams (1996) and now re-invigorated and expanded by scholars around the world working in multilingual education and sociolinguistics, has been central to the multilingual turn. A view of bi/multilingual communication as translanguaging conceives of bi/multilinguals as having one integrated linguistic repertoire, rather than two or more separate named languages as cognitive linguistics would posit, from which they draw in any interaction (García & Li, 2014). In recent years the use of the term 'translanguaging' has been extended to include the fluid use of different features of varieties or registers of languages in interaction, leading to the proposition that monolingual people can also translanguage (Otheguy *et al.*, 2015). A term that points specifically to how registers interact in languaging for learning, register-meshing, was proposed by Gibbons (2006) in her study of primary science classrooms in Australia. Although Gibbons looked only at the English features of classroom languaging, the idea of 'meshing' is easy to apply to multilingual discourse. Helpfully, 'translanguaging' has also been extended to incorporate the use of different semiotic modes in meaning-making (García & Li, 2014). This broader application of the term is expressed in the coining of a new term to carry this meaning: trans-semiotising (Lin, 2015). Lin's work in content teaching and learning (focused on science) has pointed to:

> the key role played by trans/languaging and trans-semiotizing practices in the dialogic construal of content meaning. (Lin, 2019: 5)

Lin's phrase 'the dialogic construal of content meaning' captures what is at the heart of research into translingual and transmodal practices in learning: rather than a focus on reified objects of study such as named languages, the process of making-meaning is most important. *Process* is also central to Kusters *et al.*'s argument as they posit that all forms of meaning-making should be included in an analysis of 'co-constructed meaning in communication':

> Extending our inventories of the semiotic resources that people use to communicate, offer(s) a more sophisticated understanding of the relationship across and between modalities and shedding new light into the processes, dynamics and principles of co-constructed meaning in communication beyond the boundaries of codified 'modalities' and 'languages'. (Kusters *et al.*, 2017: 228)

This approach of considering the semiotic resources, or semiotic repertoire (Kusters *et al.*, 2017), involved in learning new content allows us to see which practices are occurring in the borderlands of South African science classrooms. These are the borders between 'scientific registers' and 'everyday registers', 'English' and 'home language' (i.e. an African language), linguistic and 'paralinguistic' modes, writing and speaking (Tyler, 2018: 52). Khethiwe, the key actor in the data, must disinvent colonial notions of appropriate language for learning science (Makoni & Pennycook, 2005; McKinney & Tyler, 2019) in order to make meaning in this instance. I will argue that this perspective reveals a complex and meshed use of semiotic resources to accomplish identity development in the service of science learning and care for the social standing of the self (Ballenger, 1997). Building upon Gibbons' (2006) concept of register meshing, I introduce the concept of identity meshing, i.e. drawing together two or more identity positions previously considered to be distinct and enacting these simultaneously in order to create a new voice to move learning forward.

Khethiwe in the Borderlands

This chapter draws on a broader case study of bilingual meaning-making in a high school science setting in Cape Town. The study considered meaning-making in ten science class lessons and eight study group meetings (Tyler, 2018). The overarching methodological framework I used was linguistic ethnography (Copland & Creese, 2015; Rampton *et al.*, 2004). Linguistic ethnography is an approach to the study of language in use which maintains that gaining an understanding of the small linguistic details of discourse in a particular place and time will illuminate wider social and ideological constructs operating in that place and time, and equally that understanding the context and other present texts of any language event will inform the reading of the specifics of the discourse. In linguistic ethnography, interactional data often form the core data set.

The classroom lessons were dominated by communication constrained by the school language policy, which designates only English as the language of learning and teaching. The class activities comprised mostly written textbook exercises and the review of these through whole-class triadic discourse. The study group, from which the present data are drawn, is described as an 'established translanguaging space' (García & Li, 2014) or a 'third space' (Gutiérrez, 2008), as it was designed to enable translingual activities, drawing on learners' full semiotic repertoires. The study group was thus a transgressive, or marginal, space in the context of the school, due to the power of Anglonormativity (McKinney, 2017) expressed through the school language policy and language ideologies held by staff. Activities in the study group, which I facilitated, were often inquiry based and proceeded from topics raised by the learners.

Khethiwe, the central actor in the episode to be presented, is the top-scoring science learner in her class. She was also the only member of the Grade 9 Natural Science class to respond to my invitation for further comments at the end of the language questionnaire that I circulated (Figure 4.1).

Khethiwe's response on the questionnaire echoes and illuminates her performance in the study group. It employs different modes and voices to make her point: academic formulations of English ('hense') and quotation marks, but also a playful emoji to illustrate her response to the name-calling – 'coconut' being a derogatory metaphor to describe someone who has brown skin on the outside, but who displays aspects of white culture and is therefore 'white on the inside'. She creates a meshed register here in which her feelings of love and sadness around her use of English are juxtaposed. It is this meshed register that expresses her life in the borderlands where her academic and social identities meet.

The comic strip in Figure 4.2 represents a moment in the study group, just before we closed the meeting one Thursday afternoon, when Siphosethu became interested in a box of coloured pencils lying on the shared table. Having read the text on the back of the box ('wood-free coloured pencils'), Siphosethu was puzzled about the raw materials used to make the pencils. I challenged the group to find out more about what the pencils were made of by 'writing down the question'. The challenge was given impetus by my offering them all 'a prize if you give me a good answer'. It was soon after this challenge was made that the action in Frame 1 ensued. Phumeza sought help from her peers in interpreting my

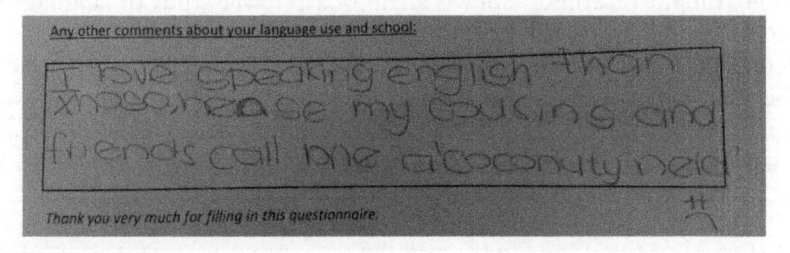

Figure 4.1 Khethiwe's questionnaire response
Transcription: I love speaking English than xhosa, hense my cousins and friends call me a 'coconuty nerd' ☹.

Identity Meshing in Learning Science Bilingually 71

Figure 4.2 Comic strip representing Khethiwe's language and identity meshing
Note: Frame 1 Siphendule ngoku? 'Must we answer now?'

instruction by asking whether she was correct in assuming that the task at hand was to answer the question about the composition of the pencils. Khethiwe then identifies her error in Frame 2 and poses an alternative task in Frame 3 – finding the aim of the investigation – which the group take up in Frame 4.

The comic strip (Figure 4.2) was co-created by myself and an artist who drew the frames from video stills I sent her in a move intended to break the conventional academic genre used for presenting classroom discourse – a linguistic transcript. By disrupting the conventions of classroom discourse research writing in this way, I am signalling a dissatisfaction with the traditional genres and inviting us to look at new ways of thinking about discourse in science classrooms, particularly in classrooms where learners recruit the resources of languages other than the sanctioned English to make meaning.

In these contexts, it is often the named languages that are the focus of analysis, identified in transcripts through translation, separated from each other by being presented in different font styles or in separate columns. This is often because the imagined audience is English monolingual, or the focus of the research is on the functions of different languages

(Tyler, 2021). The comic strip genre introduces a narrative element to the meaning-making and represents movement in space and time. It avoids the hierarchy of modes created by a transcript in a table where whatever is on the left is given priority due to European norms of literacy (Ochs, 1979). In a comic strip, the modes of gesture, facial expression and verbal expression are represented simultaneously and laminated on top of each other. An element of drama is attained through the use of different cinematographic 'shots': medium close-up, long shot, to tell the story of the episode. In representations of classroom discourse this helps the researcher to recreate the drama of a learning moment and to show how learners achieve identity meshing as they appropriate the science discourse. It assumes a bilingual isiXhosa/English reader-viewer by leaving the oral mode uncluttered by translation, thereby centring this language in an academic text. The comic strip is intentionally subjective and partial, which Ochs argues cannot be avoided in a transcript, but should be made explicit (Ochs, 1979). Khethiwe is in focus in this transcript which foregrounds the visual mode and backgrounds the linguistic mode.

Accomplishing Appropriation through Language and Identity Meshing

Figure 4.2 represents a moment of interaction in which multiple semiotic modes come together to create meaning. Frame by frame the interaction shifts from the uncertainty of which activity the participants are involved in (Frame 1) through a period in which a new activity is suggested by Khethiwe (Frames 2 and 3) to a place of settling upon an activity (Frame 4). It is through this process that Khethiwe appropriates science discourse.

At least eight modes of Khethiwe's meaning-making are discernible in the moment captured by Frame 3, relying on the audio- and video–recordings and my memory of it: facial movement (eyebrows raised, eyes wide, smiling), gesture (fingers forming 'o'), body positioning (leaning forward), gaze (at the friend who asked the question), a meshed lexical mode[1] (Esengingqi, or local language, and Scientific English), voice volume (increased), vowel length (extended), intonation (rising tone). These modes combine in a powerful meshed identity performance to realise a complex and nuanced meaning. Through the simultaneous use of these multiple modes, or trans-semiotising, Khethiwe brings different identities into play which could be seen as incompatible by virtue of, for example, the school language policy which holds that science should be taught and learned in English.

In Frame 3, Khethiwe continues to situate the current task within the investigation genre which she introduced in Frame 2 by pointing to a specific investigation activity: finding the *aim* of the investigation and articulating it. However, the lexical features she uses do not conform to the notions of scientific English espoused by the textbook or curriculum documents. It is a meshed register that she utters, employing features of the familiar register in use among the youth of Khayelitsha: 'de' and 'we-', and features of scientific English: 'aim' and 'investigation'. She layers her lexical meaning-making with other modes in order to: (a) draw attention to her skill at applying a science genre to a task which the teacher/facilitator has not framed as such; (b) distance herself from an academic identity position to which she does not want to appear attached in order to maintain good social standing among her peers; and (c) create a moment of playfulness.

Her raised volume and extended vowel sound as she utters the word 'aim' are enough to draw attention to her skill at recruiting this academic discourse into the informal task of finding out about pencils for a prize. Adding stress to the word 'aim' in Frame 3, where 'investigation' in Frame 2 received no stress, is listed by Lemke as a common 'thematic development strategy' (Lemke, 1990: 226) that teachers employ to build up a network of meaning relationships across a topic of science. Like a skilled teacher, Khethiwe has used vocal stress to highlight a significant scientific unit of meaning which facilitates her peers' understanding here. The action modes, such as gesture, facial movement and change in body position go further. Because they are so exaggerated when compared to the other actions in the group immediately prior to Frame 3, I argue that Khethiwe is seeking distance from the performance of an academic/scientist/teacher identity position in this moment.

Owing to the censure Khethiwe has received for her use of English and her academic prowess – being a 'coconuty nerd' – she utters scientific discourse in an informal learning moment at her peril. She risks identifying too closely with the predispositions and value systems of science that science words carry. Drawing on Bakhtin, McKinney and Norton recognise that

> the appropriation of the words of others is a complex and conflictual process in which words are not neutral but express particular predispositions and value systems. (McKinney & Norton, 2008: 193)

Kapp (2004) found similar risk management in her study of English in a high school in Cape Town where she concluded that 'to be seen to be investing in English ... is to risk humiliation and derision' (Kapp, 2004: 258). Even when the named language of the students and the science discourse is the same, the appropriation of the register of science can pose identity risks for students. In his study of African American Vernacular English speaking youth in science classes in the United States, Brown (2006) found that the black students struggled to appropriate the discursive practices of science and had to 'balance the tension between their academic and personal identit(ies)' (Brown, 2006: 96). The students in Brown's study actively resisted using 'slang' or features from their familiar registers in talking about science, as they argued, 'It isn't no slang that can be said about this stuff' (Brown, 2006: 96).

In order to mitigate the conflict of appropriation, Khethiwe folds the science discourse into her social discourse through trans-semiotising. The message that I argue Khethiwe intends through her performance in Frame 3 is, to repurpose the words of Goffman (1975), 'whatever I am, I am not just someone who can only speak scientific English'.[2] Goffman's phrase 'whatever I am' poignantly captures the tender stage of identity flux and experimentation in which a 15-year-old such as Khethiwe finds herself.

Khethiwe's performance is supported by her peers in Frame 3, particularly Siphosethu (out of frame) and Phumeza, who respond through uninterrupted gaze directed at Khethiwe, smiling and positioning their bodies to face her. The responses of Khethiwe's peers in Frame 4 – smiles and the validating action of taking up her discourse in echoes and beginning to write – are also indicative of this support. In this way Khethiwe sets in motion a flow of meaning-making (Lin, 2019) in which many of the members of the study group participate, so that the translanguaging that is achieved is a communal endeavour. In Frame 4 we see participants picking up the scientific term 'aim' and it echoes around the group. The flow of meaning-making results at the end of the episode with one of the learners, Thandile, co-uttering the question, 'What do wood-free coloured pencils made of?', as he inscribes the words into his exercise book. The result of the joint trans-semiotising is the phrasing of a question for scientific investigation. The group have functioned as 'game-changers' (Kerfoot & Bello-Nonjengele, 2016: 20) by 'challenging existing economies of meaning' through trans-semiotising.

Another motivator of Khethiwe's utterance is her human interest in joy and humour, or what Huizinga (2014) describes as 'the playful character of many social, cultural and political practices' (as cited in Blommaert, 2017: 3). This motivator is in evidence in her catching her friend's eye as she looks on in Frame 3. Having not asked the participants about their laughter during this episode, I can only speculate that it is due to their delight in their own cunning at having linked a seemingly social activity of working towards a potential prize to an academic genre used in class lessons and the fun they are having in simultaneously playing and ridiculing 'the academic'.

Discussion and Conclusion

Research beyond the boundaries between 'everyday' and 'scientific' registers, between 'isiXhosa' and 'English', between 'linguistic' and 'paralinguistic' modes, brings into focus the identity work that meshed registers and trans-semiotising achieves. Meaning-making in the borderlands enables the necessary identity meshing involved in learning new content in school. Appropriating science discourse is about trying out new identity positions, meshing them with currently held positions and creating something new with which to pursue your own intentions in the discourse.

For Khethiwe and her peers, participation in the practices of school science is desirable and aspirational, but an autonomous academic identity is unpalatable and so the distance from this position enacted by Khethiwe is a productive tactic for successful science appropriation. She is not only on the way to acquiring 'full scientific English', but she is performing something complete here which would not be possible in only full scientific English. Her performance succeeds because she does not speak exclusively in English or isiXhosa: she is selecting and mixing from her repertoire these particular features for a purpose.

There was no planning involved in the investigation task that precipitated Khethiwe's identity meshing. It arose spontaneously from a learner's interest. From there it was formulated collaboratively with learners and their facilitator. As Ballenger (1997) found, the combination of the inquiry-based 'design' of the task and an established translanguaging space created good conditions for appropriation. This is an important check to the assumption that employing learners' home language resources, or translanguaging, will necessarily enhance meaning-making (critiqued by Jaspers, 2018). Planned use of learners' semiotic resources should go hand-in-hand with approaches, such as inquiry-based learning, which enable science appropriation, beyond acquisition or simple parroting of the discourse.

Meshed practices such as Khethiwe's should lead researchers and educators to:

- interrogate the language ideologies that underpin current normative practices;
- define the goal of science education (or any content subject) as an expanded repertoire (Lin, 2015) which makes space for meshed registers as well as strict discipline-specific registers;
- pay attention to, and draw upon, learners' full semiotic repertoire in learning; and
- recognise the risks involved in appropriating science discourse for learners and allow play and identity meshing to form part of this appropriation.

The kind of identity meshing that Khethiwe has modelled serves as an example of what it might mean to decolonise the practice of learning science at school. Khethiwe thrives in the borderlands where new learning possibilities emerge, and perhaps even where new science can emerge.

Notes

(1) 'Lexical mode' is taken here to be the meaning of the lexemes without references to the intonation, accent, volume, etc., of the spoken utterance.

(2) Writing about a five-year-old's irreverent actions while riding a merry-go-round horse, Goffman reflects: 'To be a merry-go-round horse rider is now apparently not enough, and this fact must be demonstrated out of dutiful regard for one's own character. ... The child says by his actions: "Whatever I am, I am not just someone who can barely manage to stay on a wooden horse"' (Goffman, 1975: 124).

References

Anzaldúa, G. (2012 [1987]) *Borderlands/La Frontera: The New Mestiza*. San Francisco, CA: Aunt Lute Books.

Bakhtin, M.M. (1981) Discourse in the novel. In M. Holquist (ed.) *The Dialogic Imagination: Four Essays*. Austin, TX: University of Texas Press.

Ballenger, C. (1997) Social identities, moral narratives, scientific argumentation: Science talk in a bilingual classroom. *Language and Education* 11 (1), 1–14.

Blommaert, J. (2008) *Grassroots Literacy: Writing, Identity and Voice in Africa*. New York: Routledge.

Blommaert, J. (2017) Ludic membership and orthopractic mobilization: On slacktivism and all that. Tilburg Papers in Culture Studies No. 193. See https://www.tilburguniversity.edu/upload/6cfbdfee-2f05-40c6-9617-d6930a811edf_TPCS_193_Blommaert.pdf (accessed 24 October 2020).

Brown, B.A. (2006) 'It isn't no slang that can be said about this stuff': Language, identity, and appropriating science discourse. *Journal of Research in Science Teaching* 43 (1), 96–126.

Canagarajah, S. (2004) Subversive identities, pedagogical safe houses, and critical learning. In B. Norton and K. Toohey (eds) *Critical Pedagogies and Language Learning* (pp. 116–137). Cambridge: Cambridge University Press.

Christie, P. and McKinney, C. (2017) Decoloniality and 'Model C' schools: Ethos, language and the protests of 2016. *Education as Change* 21 (3), 160–180.

Copland, F. and Creese, A. (2015) *Linguistic Ethnography: Collecting, Analysing and Presenting Data*. London: Sage.

García, O. and Li, W. (2014) *Translanguaging: Language, Bilingualism and Education*. Basingstoke: Palgrave Macmillan.

Gee, J.P. (2004) Language in the science classroom: Academic social languages as the heart of school-based literacy. In E.W. Saul (ed.) *Crossing Borders in Literacy and Science Instruction: Perspectives on Theory and Practice* (pp. 13–32). Newark, DE: International Reading Association.

Gibbons, P. (2006) *Bridging Discourses in the ESL Classroom*. London: Continuum.

Goffman, E. (1975) Role distance. In D. Brissett and C. Edgley (eds) *Life as Theatre* (pp. 123–133). New York: Aldine de Gruyter.

Gutiérrez, K.D. (2008) Developing a sociocritical literacy in the third space. *Reading Research Quarterly* 43 (2), 148–164.

Jaspers, J. (2018) The transformative limits of translanguaging. *Language and Communication* 58, 1–10.

Kapp, R. (2004) 'Reading on the line': An analysis of literacy practices in ESL classes in a South African township school. *Language and Education* 18 (3), 246–263.

Kerfoot, C. and Bello-Nonjengele, B.O. (2016) Game changers? Multilingual learners in a Cape Town primary school. *Applied Linguistics* 37 (4), 451–473.

Kress, G., Jewitt, C., Ogborn, J. and Tsatsarelis, C. (2014) *Multimodal Teaching and Learning: The Rhetorics of the Science Classroom* (2nd edn). London and New York: Continuum.

Kusters, A., Spotti, M., Swanwick, R. and Tapio, E. (2017) Beyond languages, beyond modalities: Transforming the study of semiotic repertoires. *International Journal of Multilingualism* 14 (3), 219–232.

Lemke, J. (1990) *Talking Science: Language, Learning and Values*. Norwood, NJ: Ablex.
Lin, A.M.Y. (2015) Egalitarian bi/multilingualism and trans-semiotizing in a global world. In W.E. Wright, S. Boun and O. García (eds) *Handbook of Bilingual and Multilingual Education* (pp. 19–37). Hoboken, NJ: Wiley-Blackwell.
Lin, A.M.Y. (2019) Theories of trans/languaging and trans-semiotizing: Implications for content-based education classrooms. *International Journal of Bilingual Education and Bilingualism* 22 (1), 5–16.
Makalela, L. (2014) Fluid identity construction in language contact zones: Metacognitive reflections on Kasi-taal languaging practices. *International Journal of Bilingual Education and Bilingualism* 17 (6), 668–682.
Makoni, S. and Pennycook, A. (2005) Disinventing and (re)constituting languages. *Critical Inquiry in Language Studies: An International Journal* 2 (3), 137–156.
Maldonado Torres, N. (2007) On the coloniality of being: Contributions to the development of a concept. *Cultural Studies* 21 (2–3), 240.
May, S. (2014) *The Multilingual Turn: Implications for SLA, TESOL and Bilingual Education* (2nd edn). New York: Routledge.
McKinney, C. (2017) *Language and Power in Post-colonial Schooling: Ideologies in Practice*. New York: Routledge.
McKinney, C. and Norton, B. (2008) Identity in language and literacy education. In B. Spolsky and F.M. Hult (eds) *The Handbook of Educational Linguistics* (pp. 192–205). Oxford: Blackwell.
McKinney, C. and Tyler, R. (2019) Disinventing and reconstituting language for learning in school Science. *Language and Education* 33 (2), 141–158.
Mignolo, W. (2007) Delinking: The rhetoric of modernity, the logic of coloniality and the grammar of de-coloniality. *Cultural Studies* 21 (2–3), 449–514.
Mignolo, W. (2011) *The Darker Side of Western Modernity: Global Futures, Decolonial Options*. Durham, NC: Duke University Press.
Ndlovu-Gatsheni, S.J. (2015) Decoloniality as the future of Africa. *History Compass* 13 (10), 485–496.
Ochs, E. (1979) Transcription as theory. In E. Ochs and B. Schieffelin (eds) *Developmental Pragmatics* (pp. 43–73). New York: Academic Press.
Otheguy, R., García, O. and Reid, W. (2015) Clarifying translanguaging and deconstructing named languages: A perspective from linguistics. *Applied Linguistics Review* 6 (3), 281–307.
Probyn, M. (2009) 'Smuggling the vernacular into the classroom': Conflicts and tensions in classroom codeswitching in township/rural schools in South Africa. *International Journal of Bilingual Education and Bilingualism* 12 (2), 123–136.
Rampton, B., Tusting, K., Maybin, J., Barwell, R., Creese, A. and Lytra, V. (2004) UK linguistic ethnography: A discussion paper. See http://www.lancaster.ac.uk/fss/organisations/lingethn/documents/discussion_paper_jan_05.pdf (accessed 24 October 2020).
Tyler, R. (2018) Semiotic repertoires in bilingual science learning: A study of learners' meaning-making practices in two sites in a Cape Town high school. Doctoral dissertation, University of Cape Town.
Tyler, R. (2021) Transcribing whole-body sense-making by non-dominant students in multilingual classrooms. *Classroom Discourse*. doi:10.1080/19463014.2021.1896563
Weedon, C. (1987) *Feminist Practice and Poststructuralist Theory*. Oxford: Basil Blackwell.
Western Cape Education Department (2014) Curriculum FET minute: DCF 0003/2014. Teaching the language of assessment across the curriculum. See https://wcedonline.westerncape.gov.za/circulars/minutes14/CMminutes/edcf3_14.html (accessed 24 October 2020).
Williams, C. (1996) Secondary education: Teaching in the bilingual situation. In C. Williams, G. Lewis and C. Baker (eds) *The Language Policy: Taking Stock* (pp. 39–78). Llangefni: CAI.

Part 2

Delinking from Coloniality in Teacher Education

Part 2

Delinking from Coloniality in Teacher Education

5 Visual Essay: Teaching and Learning beyond the Classroom: What Can We Learn from Participating in Struggle with our Students?

Kate Angier, Carolyn McKinney and Catherine Kell

Currently caught in the grip of the COVID-19 global pandemic, our campus is again closed for face-to-face teaching and learning, with fences, bollards and security guards denying access, and its teaching venues, avenues and plazas deserted. All staff and students have been physically displaced. Although the cause of closure is different, we are again teaching in a time of crisis, and our experience over the past five years has forced the realisation that we need to prepare students and ourselves, as educators, for teaching and learning in turbulent times. During the course of this year there can be few who have not experienced some form of loss as a direct result of the COVID pandemic – millions of people have lost their livelihoods, hundreds of thousands their lives, the reported figures of gender-based violence have increased dramatically – but in all cases the experience of this pandemic has been shaped profoundly by our positionality. The photographs in this essay, taken in previous periods of rupture or crisis that also led to closures of the campus, have been curated from 'our' perspective – teacher educators on a PGCE programme working at an elite, historically white public university in South Africa.

In her discussion of colonial era travel writing, *Imperial Eyes*, Mary Louise Pratt uses the concept of 'contact zones'. She describes them as:

> social spaces where disparate cultures meet, clash, and grapple with each other, often in highly asymmetrical relations of domination and subordination – such as colonialism and slavery, or their aftermaths as they are lived out across the globe today. (Pratt, 2008: 7)

The avenues and plazas, the programmes and lecture halls, and, above all, 'our' classrooms, are contact zones and we, staff and students, work

Figure 5.1 Typical lecture theatre space for PGCE students
Source: CC Discott, https://en.wikipedia.org/wiki/File:UCT_Leslie_Social_Science_lecture_theatre_class.JPG.

within their borders. They are assemblages of age, race, gender, sexuality, religion, nationality, languages, and are alive with asymmetrical relations of power. Nowhere is this more visible than in the core Education lectures, compulsory for all Post Graduate Certificate in Education (PGCE) students, held in one of the oldest lecture theatres on the university campus (see Figure 5.1). This is an airless space complete with steeply raked, wooden benches and desks (Thesen, 2007), where even the most creative attempts to disrupt the normative hierarchy through engaging in a critical pedagogy struggle to overcome the experience of being positioned as a 'sage' on the 'stage' (McWilliam, 2009).

The national protests to decolonise education which were initiated by students on UCT campus in 2015 (#RMF), and against gender-based violence (GBV) which were triggered by the brutal rape and murder of a first-year student in a local post office in 2019, closed down these 'normal' teaching spaces and took us, literally and intellectually, into the in-between spaces, the contact zones. The photographs that follow illustrate 'moments' where, as educators, we taught and learned, with and from our students in the atrium of 'our' education building, the plaza of 'our' campus, the forecourt of 'our' parliament – liminal spaces of learning.

Series 1: #RhodesMustFall and #FeesMustFall in 2015

The first protests began in March 2015, becoming the #Rhodesmustfall (#RMF) movement. What began as student struggle/protest/activism to remove a statue of 19th century mining magnate and master capitalist of colonialism, Cecil John Rhodes, from the university campus, evolved into

Figure 5.2 The removal of the statue of Cecil John Rhodes from the plinth on UCT upper campus a month after the beginning of #RhodesMustFall protest movement
Photo credit: Michael Hammond/CMD UCT, 9 April 2015.

a broader critique of the culture of coloniality that pervades the university and a call for its decolonisation. In April 2015, after a month of protest, campus authorities arranged to remove the statue (see Figure 5.2).

Later in the year, the #RMF movement joined a larger national student movement calling for 'free decolonised' education, and the in-sourcing of maintenance and cleaning workers on campuses, #FeesMustFall (#FMF). Fallist students shut down campuses across the country, and at UCT classes were suspended (see Figure 5.3).

In 2015 the university had to close for 'official' teaching from 19 to 30 October, due to the protest action. By this time we on the PGCE had completed our academic course work. Initially, staff and students participated in the protests as individuals, not foregrounding our position as Education colleagues. As the days went by we started to engage with questions about what this meant for us as educators in a teacher education programme.

Figure 5.4 shows a mass meeting on UCT campus (estimated 3000 people) on the main plaza, following a march to parliament. These were moments of unity, as UCT faced its past. But as the struggles developed nationally into the call for free education and for the closure of universities until this demand was met, tensions started to emerge. These often fell along the same fault lines of race, gender and class that have characterised South Africa's history.

As the protests intensified, conflict increased. Figures 5.5 and 5.6 show security deployed in front of buildings, including the library. While access

Figure 5.3 Teaching suspended

Figure 5.4 UCT protest gathering
Photo credit: Roger Sedres/CMD, UCT, 22 October 2015.

Teaching and Learning beyond the Classroom 85

Figure 5.5 Here students are facing private security, controversially brought in by university senior management, who are preventing their entry to a university building
Photo credit CMD, UCT.

Figure 5.6 Blocking the Doors to Learning. Private security officers preventing access to the main university library, named after mining magnate and contemporary of Cecil John Rhodes, Ernest Oppenheimer
Photo source: Pam Christie.

to official knowledge was barred in order to 'protect' the books from students, learning continued to take place in alternate, in-between spaces across the campus.

Teaching Moment 1

During the 2016 university shutdown, students in the PGCE teacher education programme and staff were faced with the dilemmas presented by the demands of the protesting group and the fractures across the student and staff body. In this time of intense tension, we met to discuss what our response should be, how we could respond as educators and whether we could use this as a teaching moment, a moment to 'be in that contact zone'. Protesting students were trying to prevent teaching from happening, but other cohorts of students wanted it to continue. We agreed on a series of activities that could enable engagement across these fault lines, and bring our different cohorts of students together. One activity was that in place of the lecture series which was due to begin, staff and students would jointly plan and host a voluntary 'teach-in' to be held in the open courtyard of the building on the following day in place of the usual lectures. Students organised the first two activities, which included negotiating a contract for rules of engagement followed by a silent conversation and gallery walk (Facing History and Ourselves, 2020) generated by seven different prompts on newsprint.

While acknowledging that there can be no 'safe spaces' because of the power relations between and within the staff and student bodies as well as the broader university context of coloniality, we wanted to draw all participants' attention to their own voice and the voice of others. To listen and be heard. Students who had already participated in 'Contracting' in their teaching methods classes using a Facing History methodology drew up an initial set of guidelines for engagement which were then workshopped with the larger class. From here a set of criteria was established for conducting respectful, productive dialogue in the contact zone where the intellectual and emotional are entangled.

Silent conversation

A second methodology drawn from the students' teaching methods classes was a silent conversation, which provided a space in which students could dialogue without individual voices dominating the space. This strategy had been used to discuss source material relating to historical events that evoked powerful emotions. During our workshop the staff and students annotated, wrote, highlighted and responded to textual and visual prompts selected by the student facilitators, and to each other. It is a methodology that gives participants time to process what they are seeing and reading, allows for multiple voices from different positions to co-exist

Figure 5.7 Poster from the Silent Conversation
Photo credit: Carolyn McKinney.

and, rather than forcing a resolution to complex issues, surfaces additional difficult questions – an unresolved dialectical dialogue.

The conversations on newsprint were later put up on the walls of the department for wider reading and ongoing conversation (see Figures 5.7–5.11).

Privilege paperclips

The next activity was designed to raise consciousness about race and social class privilege. One of the student organisers offered an adaption of a privilege walk, with each participant making a chain of paperclips that represented their privileged position relative to others (see Figure 5.12). We realised after completing the activity that those who had lost (or had never acquired?) all their paperclips (and thus were most marginalised) became invisible as they had no paperclips left to hang on the line. In future we agreed to adapt the activity such that participants should hold on to their last paperclip. As one of the student facilitators, Uzair Ben-Ebrahim, commented, this activity enabled a space for 'grappling with the other's narratives and experiences' and becoming 'aware of (not knowing) the various lived experiences of their own students'.

Figure 5.8 Engaging in the moment with heart and head
Photo credit: Carolyn McKinney.

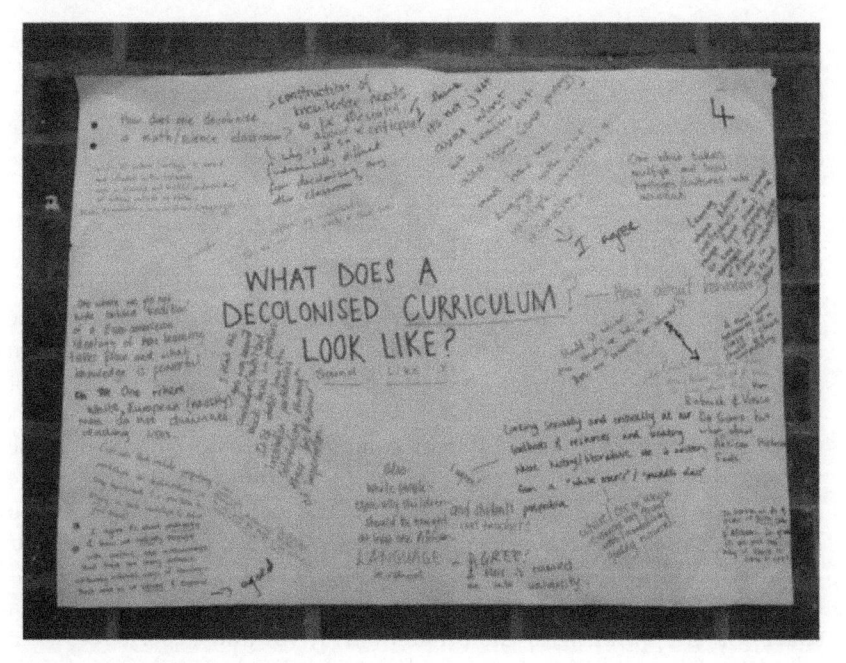

Figure 5.9 Imagining alternatives
Photo credit: Carolyn McKinney.

Teaching and Learning beyond the Classroom 89

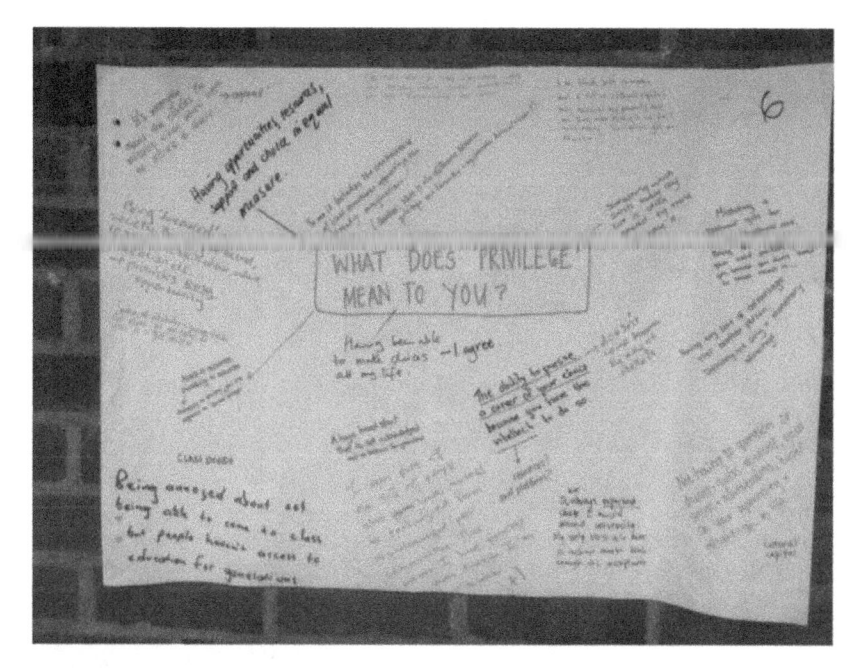

Figure 5.10 Probing privilege
Photo credit: Carolyn McKinney.

Figure 5.11 Thinking further
Photo credit: Carolyn McKinney.

Figure 5.12 Privilege paperclip chains hanging across the courtyard. As one of the student facilitators, Uzair Ben-Ebrahim, commented, this activity enabled a space for 'grappling with the other's narratives and experiences' and for education staff to become 'aware of (not knowing) the various lived experiences of their own students'
Photo credit: Carolyn McKinney.

The session ended with a 'Learning to Listen' pair activity. Our aim was to enable students and staff to pair with people from different courses, or who 'looked different' from them and with whom they had not previously engaged. For three minutes they were required to focus on hearing one another's perspectives and accurately reflect these back without evaluation or judgement. The silent conversation prompts had acted as a 'thinking space' before this pairing, and this listening activity flowed into a plenary 'sharing' session. Through this sequence of activities we wanted to demonstrate how a 'think-pair-share' teaching strategy, to which students had been introduced in our methodology classes and which was used to encourage participation in the large Education lecture course, could be repurposed in this different learning context.

Series 2: Student Protests against Gender-based Violence (GBV) in Response to the Rape and Murder of UCT Undergraduate Student Uyinene Mrwetyana

In 2019, the rape and murder of UCT undergraduate student Uyinene Mrwetyana sparked nationwide protests against gender-based violence and caused the shutdown of the UCT campus for two days. Again, staff and students were faced with dilemmas about how to respond. The series of images in Figures 5.13–5.15 document student teachers and lecturers making protest posters together in the early morning before their participation in the mass march to Parliament in Cape Town where President

Figure 5.13 PGCE students and staff making placards together using art materials requisitioned from the Creative Arts Methodology course, 4 September 2019. Director of the School of Education, Catherine Kell, is circled. In the background the formal student teaching spaces and computer labs are closed
Photo credit: Dick Ng'ambi.

Cyril Ramaphosa received a petition and addressed the crowd of thousands (Figures 5.16 and 5.17). Staff members and students travelled together to the city on buses and shared experiences, with some staff members exploring their memories of taking part in marches during the anti-apartheid struggle with young students, for whom this was their first experience of taking part in a public protest. The march was followed by a memorial service on campus, led by UCT Chancellor Graça Machel (Figure 5.18).

Teaching Moment 2

Following the march to parliament, it became essential to find ways of bringing staff and students in the School of Education together to 'process' the murder and students' and staff members' own experiences of GBV. This needed to be done with great care since the events had acted as 'triggers' for many people's own experiences which had often been repressed. Together, we created a series of open spaces which were carefully constructed as 'horizontal', where any staff members and any students could come together with no hierarchy in place, but simply to grieve or share. Thus, cleaning staff, professional and support staff, as well as academic staff members, attended, along with undergraduate and postgraduate students. Simply being together, with no regard for the usual roles or positions, or for the usual clamour of debate with its reliance on language, was important. Silence played a large part in this 'togetherness', enabling

Figure 5.14 Making placards in the in-between spaces of our building, 4 September 2019
Photo credit: Dick Ng'ambi.

witnessing and the sharing of emotions. Further spaces were then created within the university, which were curated together with psychologists who could assist in a process of communal grieving and sharing, and students and staff members were encouraged to attend these as well as to seek out counselling, if needed. These moments led to some students and staff members disclosing, for the first time, their own experiences of gender-based abuse and harassment.

These experiences fed into a further set of such 'horizontal' moments within the PGCE class specifically. The students had returned from their teaching practice placements in schools where they had encountered or come to know of numerous incidents of harassment and abuse, even among young children. Students were expressing a sense of trauma, which was heightened by the events on campus. Given that there had been a call for the ongoing suspension of classes, together we opted to take up some of our lecture periods in the lecture hall with these open, horizontal moments, in which students could share and grieve. These were powerful

Figure 5.15 March to parliament
Photo credit: Je'nine May/CMD, UCT.

periods in which students shared their rage and their sorrow, as well as their frustration, at the general state of education as well as their apprehension about their future roles as teachers in schools racked by the inequality and violence that are the predominant characteristics of South African society. As staff members, we had to 'hold' these spaces as well as undertake whatever actions we could to address students' concerns.

These were powerful moments in which the usual pedagogies were disrupted and spaces where affect was dominant. For some of us, they

Figure 5.16 March to parliament. School of Education staff and students join (tens of) thousands of other protestors outside parliament
Photo credit: Je'nine May/CMD, UCT.

Figure 5.17 Aerial view of march to parliament
Photo credit: Je'nine May/CMD, UCT.

were reminiscent of earlier experiences (during the 1980s) of anti-apartheid struggles for what was seen as a 'People's Education'. These memories, however, were also tinged with sadness, as we confronted the fact that 25 years after the end of apartheid, we continue to face a deeply divided and traumatised society (Figures 5.19 and 5.20).

Figure 5.18 UCT Chancellor Graça Machel addressing the Memorial Service for Uyinene Mrwetyana on campus
Photo credit: Je'nine May/CMD, UCT.

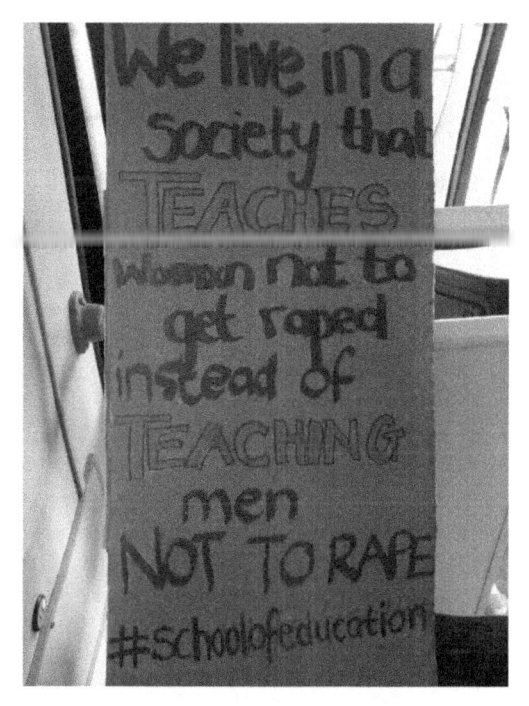

Figure 5.19 Student GBV placard displayed in the building after the march to parliament
Photo credit: Carolyn McKinney.

Figure 5.20 Poster created by a PGCE student and carried first to the demonstration outside parliament and then returned to be displayed within the School of Education

Conclusion

Over the course of several periods of student-initiated activism, we, as teacher educators, shifted our position from individual participation as allies, to a more collaborative and intentional transformation of 'disruption' into teaching moments. These are lessons we continue to learn in the context of COVID, where we have been disconnected physically from our students and forced into the virtual 'contact zone' of Emergency Remote Teaching.

We continue to experiment with ways to teach and learn, in and through turbulent times. In the context of coloniality in which we live and work there is no 'objective' vantage point from which to observe, but we are still faced with the far older question of what role we should as academics, as teacher educators, play in these moments. Should we abandon teaching and take to the barricades? Should we abandon the barricades to our students whose traditional role it is to take the struggle forward? As many of the chapters in this book attest, we continue to grapple with how to be agentic teachers within the contact zone, how to create space for intergenerational alliances and learning and how to model teaching for social justice across our courses.

Postscript

The events of the past few years have demanded the discomfort of self-reflection. As we turn our sights to the coloniality of our context, we are conscious of the situated nature of our gaze, our own place within the matrix of power. For all our good intentions to demonstrate solidarity with 'our' students, and our desire to use these crises as 'portal' moments, as opportunities for transgressive teaching and learning, we remain conscious of the ambiguity of our position. The privilege of our race, wealth and security leaves us wondering if we were/are/can ever really participate (with), or if we are simply part of the audience – as witness, or voyeur? And yet, to watch the students grow in confidence and capacity, learning through the experience of struggle, has been an opportunity to (re)learn the possibility and power that stems from collective action, lessons unlearned with age and comfort. The students' actions have changed the conversation on campus and in the Education courses. They have been a reminder that this work of teacher education in which we are involved is a 'journey of hope' (to borrow from Raymond Williams, 1983), and a public statement of our commitment to the 'long revolution'.

Acknowledgement

Thank you to Pam Christie for her input, and for sharing her images, and to Lerato Mduna from the Central Marketing Department (CMD) at UCT who helped source the CMD images.

References

Facing History and Ourselves (2020) *Building a Silent Conversation*. Resource Library/Teaching Strategies. See https://www.facinghistory.org/resource-library/teaching-strategies/big-paper-silent-conversation (accessed 27 September 2020).

McWilliam, E. (2009) Teaching for creativity: From sage to guide to meddler. *Asia Pacific Journal of Education* 29 (3), 281–293.

Pratt, M.L. (2008) *Imperial Eyes: Travel Writing and Transculturation*. New York: Routledge.

Thesen, L. (2007) Breaking the frame: Lectures, rituals and academic literacies. *Journal of Applied Linguistics* 4 (1), 33–53.

Williams, R. (1983) *Towards 2000*. London: Chatto & Windus.

6 Learning Science from umaGogo: The Value of Teaching Practice in Semi-rural School Contexts

Annemarie Hattingh

A Case of Learning to Teach Science in Under-resourced School Contexts

Teacher education programmes need to prepare prospective teachers to work with student populations in diverse economic and sociocultural contexts. They also need to cultivate students' understanding of the complex dynamics that impact on schooling, including their different contexts and resource levels, their organisational capacities and the quality of teaching and learning in classrooms. In South Africa, the historical legacy of apartheid schooling brings additional complexities, in that prospective teachers need to work in the existing system with its multiple intersecting inequalities, while also engaging in accountable ways to work against these inequalities. While knowledge of context diversity and social positioning may be programmed into teacher education curricula alongside content knowledge and pedagogical competence development, prospective teachers also need to deepen their understanding of social justice issues. As Maulucci (2013) points out, social justice perspectives are important for the ongoing task of achieving more caring, equitable and agentic schooling.

One approach to creating space for prospective teachers to engage with aspects of social justice in education beyond the theoretical constructs of course work is through teaching practice. Internationally, there is consensus that teaching practice, also referred to as work integrated learning, is fundamental to the preparation of teachers for both personal and professional development (Fafunwa, 2001). A common finding in research on pre-service teacher education is that student teachers perceive practical teaching during field placements to be the most influential part of their preparation (Guyton & McIntyre, 1990; Hollins & Guzman, 2005). With teaching practice playing a significant role in pre-service teachers' professional learning, a topic that is seriously debated among teacher educators is which types of schools should be used for pre-service teacher placements (Ronfeldt, 2012). One argument favours placement in high functioning, well-resourced schools which have high learner achievement outcomes, where it is assumed that effective schooling practices and exemplary pedagogy may be observed and passed on to aspiring teachers (Ronfeldt, 2012). It is, however, important to challenge the logic put forward by Ronfeldt (2012), as schools with more resources and better infrastructure do not necessarily have better results due to the quality of teaching practices, but rather due to structural advantages or privileges, or student segregation or selection. Therefore another conversation about what 'counts' as valuable to learn during teaching practice is also important, including how social justice issues might be addressed.

For example, soon after the 2015–2017 university protests calling for the decolonisation of higher education institutions in South Africa, schools also attracted media attention for various racial incidents affecting staff as well as students. One such incident was the dismissal of a Black teacher appointed at an all-girls high performing school in Cape Town, while at another school nearby, a Grade 9 Black girl had to apologise for writing a poem on the continued mispronunciation of her name. Both of these schools were used as preferred sites for teaching practice placements due to their high performing status, assumed effective leadership and pedagogical practices. Yet the limited inclusivity in these schools raises questions about how student teachers might learn about social justice and schooling for all from schools such as these. This in turn raises questions about the types of schools where prospective teachers might learn significantly about teaching practices as well as explore issues of social justice and the purpose of schooling for all.

In this chapter, I argue that educational experiences in challenging under-resourced schools in semi-rural environments may offer opportunities for teachers to deepen their understanding of social justice while also developing pedagogical competence. In addressing social justice issues, the South African teacher education landscape needs to go beyond boundaries of formal teaching practice school placements to include non-traditional spaces, even though this may be difficult, emotionally demanding and perhaps traumatic. In proposing this, I draw on the ideas of Paulo Freire (2007 [1974]), who promoted the necessity to deepen students' consciousness of a situation where they will work to understand it as a historical reality that may require transformation. The challenge for teacher educators is to explore how placements for doing practical teaching – in this case in physical science – might be imagined and enacted in such schools.

The aim of this chapter is to provide a critical reflection on an intervention preparing pre-service teachers for teaching practice in under-resourced semi-rural schools for a six-week period. In these schools, the most basic physical resources associated with teaching science (e.g. basic laboratory with basins, running water and equipment) were absent (Hattingh *et al.*, 2007). In addition, language diversity was a consideration, since the medium of instruction in secondary schools in South Africa is English or Afrikaans, and these are not the home languages of most students in rural schools. The chapter shows how student teachers were prepared for their placements in schools such as these, and it presents three vignettes to provide examples of how students engaged with issues of social justice while also developing their pedagogical competence in their teaching practice placements.

The chapter proceeds as follows. The next section sets out the theoretical framework underpinning the intervention, its context and design principles and the pedagogy for supporting teaching practice in under-resourced schools. Following this, the chapter presents the vignettes of student learning, and it concludes with my reflections as a teacher educator, on social justice and science teacher preparation.

Science Education and Social Justice: A Theoretical Framework

As mentioned earlier, socially just teaching is an evolving mission for more caring, equitable and agentic schooling (Maulucci, 2013). In science education, teaching for social justice recognises the position of science in society and the potential role it may play in determining positions of power, privilege or marginalisation. A social justice approach invites traditionally marginalised groups of participants such as girls, especially Black girls, into the field of science. Social justice through science teaching responds to the need to foster youth's sustained interest in and ownership of science (Basu & Calabrese Barton, 2007). Youth as stakeholders of collective scientific literacy (Roth & Calabrese Barton, 2004) have a vested interest in a nurturing and sustainable natural environment and ecojustice (Mueller & Tippins, 2007). In addition, a more pluralistic view of science represents multiple cultures and different traditional ways of knowing (Mushayikwa & Ogunniyi, 2011; Odora-Hoppers, 2002).

Giroux (1992) has used the metaphor of 'border crossing' in proposing a border pedagogy to challenge the existing knowledge boundaries and to create new ones. In this framework, science education is viewed as the acquisition of a culture that requires developing proficiency in the discourse and semiotics of science (Gee, 2004; Lemke, 1990). Where science learning is viewed from a cultural perspective, students incorporate science knowledge into their cultural schemata in a process of border crossing (Aikenhead, 2001). Students may experience difficulty in navigating their 'ways of being' within school culture and therefore may have difficulty in achieving the success associated with schooling (Piliouras & Evangelou, 2012). Furthermore, the semiotics and language of instruction is the second, if not the third language of the majority of students and this inevitably impacts upon academic performance. How conflictual a cultural border is depends to a great extent on the learning process and the science teacher who mediates the process. Although all students have to cross a border into the culture of science, school science has connotations of power and social status that may put students at a disadvantage either due to non-alignment with their home cultures (Gilbert & Yerrick, 2001) or linguistic differences (Zuniga *et al.*, 2005).

Ladson-Billings' (1995) work on culturally relevant pedagogy recognises that discontinuity between home and school cultures may have negative effects on students' science achievement and proposes a framework for teaching strategies that intersect home, Indigenous and science cultures in order to create potentials for learning, empowerment and systemic educational change. Ladson-Billings (1995) explains that a dynamic relationship exists between: (a) students' academic success; (b) students' cultural competence; and (c) students' critical social consciousness. Students' academic performance improves when teaching provides access to content knowledge in a way that is congruent with values and competencies that are characteristic of a particular cultural group. Similarly, Moll *et al.* (1992) argue that within students' cultural competence may be found 'funds of knowledge', which these authors define as historically accumulated cultural knowledge, skills and resources that students bring from their home environments. Teaching strategies that are congruent with students' funds of knowledge are more likely to be relevant to their interests and habits of mind. Culturally responsive and sustaining pedagogy requires teachers to: (a) value students' cultural and language backgrounds; (b) have knowledge of the nature of science; and (c) be able to make the connections between science and home experiences (Lee, 2004; Lipka, 2002; Paris & Alim, 2014). In what they term a 'loving critique', Paris and Alim (2014) warn against possible problems with approaches based on culturally responsive pedagogy. In particular, they caution against the tendency to foreground 'heritage' cultural practices without recognising that youth identity and culture are dynamic and evolving. They also stress the need to maintain 'a clear-eyed critique of the ways in which youth culture can also reproduce systemic inequalities' (Paris & Alim, 2014: 85).

Learning to Teach Science in Under-resourced School Contexts

Design considerations

The intervention to foreground socially just science education was situated in a physical science methodology course which was part of a one-year full-time postgraduate professional teacher education qualification. The prerequisite for enrolling in the professional qualification was a

Bachelor's of Science degree with majors in Physics and Chemistry which are required to teach Physical Science from Grades 10 to 12. In the physical science methodology course, student teachers had three hours of contact sessions per week for 30 weeks and two practical teaching placements of six weeks each in schools. For one of the practical teaching placements, student teachers could volunteer to do their teaching practice in under-resourced schools which were in a semi-rural environment in an area of low socioeconomic status five hours' drive away from the university. None of these schools had school laboratories with equipment for demonstrating or doing hands-on practical work. If practical work was to be conducted, a teacher had to be creative, knowledgeable and resourceful to work with whatever was available in a kitchen or bathroom, waste materials or any other resources they could activate, or make equipment and models themselves.

The underpinning theoretical framework of the intervention was informed by culturally relevant and culturally responsive pedagogy. In preparation for the practicum, student teachers were required to design learning tasks and teaching strategies that enabled students (a) to make the connections between science and home experiences, and (b) to value and incorporate students' cultural and language backgrounds. For the aim stated in (b), the notion of 'incorporate' meant going beyond the inclusion of a few Indigenous examples to study science curriculum material. 'Incorporate' signalled hierarchical levels of complexity of practices of which illustrative productive pedagogy cases were researched in South African schools and portrayed by Hattingh (2015), based on the Bank's Typology, which ranged from simple example integration to curriculum and systemic reform.

Nature and necessity of support

A study by Heeralal and Bayaga (2011) confirmed that teaching practice efficacy in semi-rural schools in South Africa was minimised by isolation and low levels of school-based mentor teacher expertise, and that student teachers reported high levels of stress due to severely inadequate support by schools. Most schools in these environments do not offer science beyond the compulsory Grade 9 general science curriculum due to a persisting shortage of Grade 10–12 teachers. Where physical science is offered, teachers have not necessarily majored in chemistry and/or physics (Prince *et al.*, 2010), which are the requirements for teaching physical science. Grisham *et al.* (2000) lament the distressing situations that arise when pre-service teachers are placed in classrooms without thoughtful orientation and continuous support. However, accountable teacher education cannot shy away from a difficult and stressful task. Therefore, it was decided that for the entire six-week placement, the university science methodology lecturer would accompany the student teachers. Staying at the same venue afforded opportunities for maximum interaction and support which took many forms such as the mentoring of student teachers on academic, emotional and professional dimensions.

Reflective learning

According to Cohen-Sayag and Fischl (2012), doing reflection tasks in teacher education promotes professional learning by mediating the dissonance between existing and new knowledge. It is also about 'breaking habitual ways of thinking, enhancing the development of meta-cognition, increasing awareness of tacit knowledge, facilitating self-exploration, and working out solutions to problems' (Kerka, 2002: 1). Pre-service teachers recorded their daily classroom observations, activities, contextual issues or any information about school leadership, and collegial interactions in their reflective journals. Their reflections were guided by a set of reflective questions, namely: What happened? What did you experience? Why did things happen like that? What does this mean? What could have been done differently? How do education theories explain praxis and vice versa? Jindal-Snape and Holmes (2009) identify conversation as a beneficial method of reflective practice, especially when conversations occur with a mentor. Conversations not only offered guidance and covered strategies, but also enabled knowledge exchanges and offered a supportive professional learning community. At the end of each school day a reflection session opened spaces for sharing concerns, including the emotional and pedagogical challenges of the school day. Weekends were used as consultation sessions where student teachers brainstormed and presented their ideas on science lesson designs to the lecturer and peers for feedback.

Methodological Pathways

Drawing on their reflective journals and exploratory interviews after the six-week teaching practice, students were asked to draw storyline graphs of significant episodes of professional learning enriched by field experiences. Storyline methodology aims to help convey the complexity of human actions and relationships by uniting cognitive, affective and imaginative dimensions (Jonasson, 2016) over a time period. In the storylines, significant episodes were those moments that had a transformative effect, either positive or negative, on participants' content knowledge, knowledge of self, beliefs about students, pedagogy and curriculum. Graphing storylines as an *ex post facto* activity (see Figure 6.1) afforded student teachers opportunities to go beyond daily journal reflections, to retrospective meta-reflection on their most significant moments of learning. For this chapter, only those episodes that relate to a social justice theme are addressed. In Figure 6.1, Peak 5, labelled 'Just get it', is an example of an

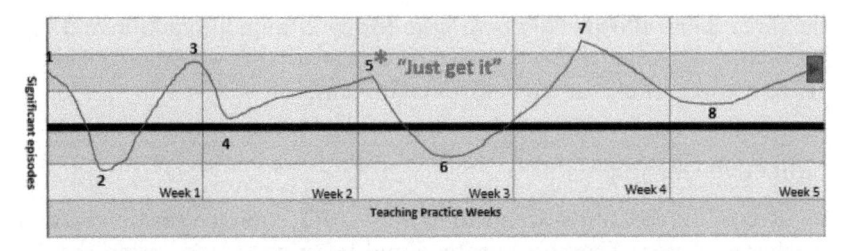

Figure 6.1 Example of storyline of significant episodes of professional learning
Note: *Significant episode related to 'social justice'.

episode that provided evidence for a social justice theme that will be discussed in the data section to follow.

The data units that provided *evidence* of social justice episodes are engaged with through vignettes in the next section. Constructing vignettes is a technique used within social science research to capture how meanings, beliefs and actions are situationally positioned (Barter & Reynold, 2000).

Data Vignettes and Discussion

Two themes emerged that related to teaching physical science from a social justice perspective: (a) translanguaging as a linguistic resource that enabled epistemic access to physical science content knowledge; and (b) accessing science-related cultural Indigenous knowledge and community resources for teaching. The vignettes were constructed by the researcher, originating from the data presented by student teachers from the various sources.

Vignette 1

Meshing languages while grappling with science concepts: Teaching Ohm's Law

A significant episode was reported by Thembelihle and Janet. The school where two student teachers, Thembelihle and Janet, were placed had only one Grade 11 physical science class, which necessitated that both student teachers be placed with the only science teacher in the same class. The home languages of both student teachers were not the language of learning and teaching (LoLT), which was English. Thembelihle was bilingual in seSotho/English and Janet in Afrikaans/English. The majority of students in the physical science class were seSotho home language speakers. The two student teachers decided to jointly prepare and teach science lessons, except for the critique lessons which were individually evaluated. The science curriculum content dealt with Ohm's Law (Ohm's law equation: $V = I \times R$ (V = voltage, electric potential difference, ΔV, or

E = electromotive force (emf = voltage) and I = current (direct current, Ampere)). The following excerpts are drawn from interviews with Thembelihle and Janet, explaining their rationale for choosing this particular episode as significant to them.

Thembelihle explained the following:

> The purpose of science teaching is that students should really 'just get it'. That should be the aim of teaching after all, but from my own experiences of learning physics at school and even during my BSc years, there were so much that I didn't understand or were confused by. Yes, I know learning is a process and you don't always get it the first time, but I do think, now that I do a methods course myself, that my teachers could have been more thoughtful in their teaching – they could have made life easier ... understanding the material is tricky and trying to learn it if not taught in one's mother tongue is really not easy. That is why Janet and I decided we will do whatever is necessary to help kids understand the work. We also noticed the teacher code-switching all the time though it was discouraged by the Department of Education. (Thembelihle)

In the interview, Janet mentioned that Thembelihle and the students conversed mostly in seSotho and that Thembelihle responded with detailed explanations which had the effect that 'a rather passive class started asking more questions and perhaps felt more connected to the subject'.

Janet reported a significant episode where she felt that a group task actually worked as intended:

> As you know we brought prac work electric board circuit kits to use for teaching the section on electricity and power. We divided the class into five groups where they had to plan an experiment to confirm Ohms Law. Now remember, these kids have never planned a 'real' experiment themselves. Usually they are given the law and formula and have to do calculations based on the equation $V = I \times R$. So while groups were working, they were talking in their mother tongue, but using subject-related English words in between such as 'dependent', 'independent variable', 'constants', 'data table' which made me wonder about the seSotho terminology for these science words. As their teacher I was a bit worried that I could not follow their planning ideas and I was concerned about the accuracy of their planning. When asking Thembelihle, she ensured me that students were actually on task, debating 'dependent and independent variables' and attempting to correct peers in the group. They were also arguing about which variable should go where when recording readings in the data table and plotting on a graph's 'x' and 'y' axis. That for me was indication that some meaningful groupwork was taking place. (Janet)

Discussion: The vignette confirms that a gap exists between the official language policy, where English is the LoLT, and the enacted language practices in the classroom. In practice, the learning took place via translanguaging and practices like code-switching and translation which is the seSotho/English mesh. Both pre-service teachers strove for their students to '*just get it*', which implied learning for understanding. '*Doing what is necessary*' highlights the joint decision they made to encourage students to use their home language to grapple with science concepts. As Msimanga and Lelliot (2014) have argued, conceptualisation may take place in any language. In rural communities, exposure to spoken and written English is limited outside the school context. The use of seSotho as home language interwoven with English became a linguistic resource that enabled epistemic access to science concepts. The point for social justice is that mixing languages in the classroom (and thereby transgressing the official LoLT policies) enabled students 'to just get it' and learn for understanding.

Also highlighted by the vignette is that a case can be made for co-teaching in multi/bilingual teaching environments. In the seSotho-dominant classrooms it was the English speaker who needed help with understanding the students' home language discussions which was mediated by the seSotho speaking student teacher.

Vignette 2

Amandla ngawethu (Zulu: Power to the people); matla ke a rona (Victory is certain): Teaching 'power; energy, work, resistance'

A significant episode was reported by Ross. Ross selected a significant episode where he observed the science teacher introducing a Grade 11 physics theme on 'power, energy, work and resistance' by asking students to explain their understandings of the terminology. In explaining these concepts, the teacher used words like 'Amandla ngawethu' and 'matla ke a rona'. For students and teachers in South African schools, classroom discussions on liberation, power, resistance and democracy are common occurrences. In Ross's words:

> It struck me that the science teacher had anticipated the everyday interpretations of these words by the kids. He then continued to explain the difference between the everyday use of these words, especially the term 'power' in a political sense and how students would learn about 'power, energy, work, resistance' in physics. (Ross)

Discussion: What the student teacher had observed in this significant episode highlights the different layers of language required when teaching and learning science concepts. Layer 1 is home language, Layer 2 is English as everyday language, Layer 3 is English as technical subject language (nomenclature), Layer 4 is ratio representation by a formula, Layer 5 is the scientific symbols, and Layer 6 is mathematical language used to develop conceptual understanding or solving of physics problems.

First, in students' home languages terminology has particular meanings (e.g. Matla, Amandla) and, second, the terminology in home languages does not necessarily have the same meanings as in English. For

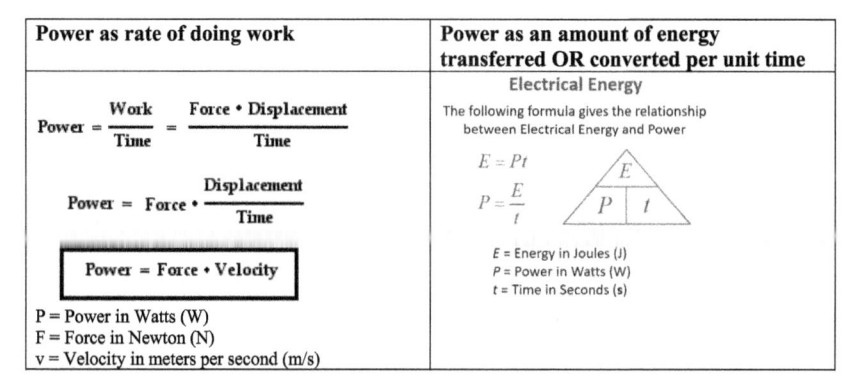

Power as rate of doing work	Power as an amount of energy transferred OR converted per unit time
$\text{Power} = \dfrac{\text{Work}}{\text{Time}} = \dfrac{\text{Force} \cdot \text{Displacement}}{\text{Time}}$ $\text{Power} = \text{Force} \cdot \dfrac{\text{Displacement}}{\text{Time}}$ $\boxed{\text{Power} = \text{Force} \cdot \text{Velocity}}$ P = Power in Watts (W) F = Force in Newton (N) v = Velocity in meters per second (m/s)	Electrical Energy The following formula gives the relationship between Electrical Energy and Power $E = Pt$ $P = \dfrac{E}{t}$ *E* = Energy in Joules (J) *P* = Power in Watts (W) *t* = Time in Seconds (s)

Figure 6.2 Two physics definitions of the concept of 'power', with ratios, scientific symbols and representations for each.

example, Amandla, Matla translated to everyday English as 'power' has an array of meanings such as control, influence, authority, supremacy or rule. Adding to these two language layers is a third, where everyday English words take on a different meaning in a science context – whether students are home language speakers of English or not. In a subject context, an everyday English word becomes a technical subject word, foregrounding the link between meaning and context (Probyn, 2015).

Furthermore, and herein lies compounded complexity for physics teachers (or any subject teacher), is the case that both conceptual and language proficiency need to operate *simultaneously* and *interactively* when teaching. For example, in physics 'power' is defined in two *different* ways. One meaning of 'power' in physics is the rate of doing work, and another meaning is the rate of transferring heat, i.e. the amount of energy transferred or converted per unit time. The two meanings of 'power' can then be communicated and represented as ratios and relationships in a format referred to as formulas (see Figure 6.2). In the formulas, the subject-specific technical words can be represented by scientific symbols, followed by mathematical language which incorporates variables (denoted typically by 'x' or 'y') as well as numbers.

Conversations in the Borders with Two Language Experts, Robyn and Soraya

In preparation of prospective science teachers, how could a teacher educator make sense of the multiple layers of language required for teaching for understanding?

Robyn:
I think the notion of register is important here. Register – as clustering or co-occurrence of lexical and grammatical items – shapes the

meanings we make. Given only the word 'power', a variety of meanings can be made. We might imagine we are present at a political rally, or that we are listening to a news report about Eskom (national electricity service provider), or that we are reading an explanation of a scientific equation. Each situation shapes the meaning we make of the word 'power'. We can only be certain of the meaning if we understand the register of the broader text.

This has implications for meanings and definitions in different languages. My intuition is that scientific English borrowed the word 'power' from an older English register for speaking about interpersonal human force and influence. A different, but related meaning layer was ascribed to the word when scientists needed a term for the rate of doing work. If a language, such as isiXhosa, is to be employed for meaning-making purposes in science, then a similar borrowing and meaning layering process needs to take place. Or, a new term needs to be coined and space made for it in the existing lexicon. For example, as scientific isiXhosa develops, the term 'amandla' might be borrowed from another register of isiXhosa to refer to scientific meaning. Or perhaps a new term 'i-power' will be coined in a similar way to how 'photosynthesis' was coined in scientific English. As a language develops for different purposes, it borrows and moulds items from other languages and registers.

Of course given, as your data shows, that science registers are also realised in mathematical equations and the English terms have become sedimented into these equations (e.g. P = power), it may make most sense for isiXhosa to develop the term 'i-power' which still retains the letter 'p' prominently which is a link for students and scientists to the 'P' in the equations.

Pedagogically speaking, there are many routes in and out of the scientific meaning of 'power'. I always suggest that when teachers begin with a new concept, they withhold the technical term until the students have had a chance to grapple with the meaning – in whichever language, i.e. as students engage in activities around the rate of doing work, they will see the need for a term to describe this, then the teacher can be ready with the term 'power', and its meaning in the scientific register will have already been established.

Soraya:
Taking Robyn's comments and your diagram into account, from a literacy lens, the registers are crossing from every-day to scientific language to another mode or register, namely ratio and scientific symbols or 'formula'. So you are demonstrating how the teacher is trying to support learning across different registers (every-day and scientific) as well as mathematical and scientific symbols. It problematizes the

idea that you can 'just get it'. When to understand 'power' you have to understand 4 levels of meaning or 6 levels of meaning as you stated previously. Perhaps the point is, the more levels or connections the teacher can reveal to the students, the deeper the understanding of the concept and how it shifts across domains. The social justice is in demystifying the languages of science and making visible the shifts and variance to lead the students out of a confusion that power is about one thing only. Then another grade emphasizes a different aspect of power, leaving learning unconnected and fragmented for students and entrenching the belief that science is only for a select few who have special affinity for it based on gender for example.

Vignette 3

Learning science from umaGogo: Teaching 'saponification' in organic chemistry by activating local Indigenous knowledge

A significant episode was reported by Mpho.

[Note: The process of making soap is called saponification and is one of the earliest examples of using organic chemistry to produce a human-made product that involves the chemical reaction of triglycerides – natural fats and oils – with sodium or potassium hydroxide (Plummer, 1987).]

Mpho explained that one of her significant learning episodes was her observation of the science teacher's integration of local Indigenous knowledge to introduce a topic on organic chemistry. Mpho said that:

> The introduction to the topic on 'dehydrohalogenation' captured my imagination for several reasons. For the past two years, the teacher invited one of the *umaGogos* (grandmothers) to demonstrate her lye soapmaking technique during science periods despite a dense curriculum that have to be covered. Initially I was perplexed because *UmaGogo* did not know any chemistry and nor could she speak a word of English. This, however, did not seem to be a hinderance to learning. In fact, this was bringing an everyday life practice into the science classroom ... I am not quite sure whether kids understood the theoretical chemistry of 'dehydrohalogenation' better, but it definitely made the topic more fascinating. What I found interesting was that while the grandmother was talking about her actions, the students and their teacher felt that they had to translate her explanations into English as there was a visiting student teacher from the States that joined us on teaching practice. In my journal I have also reflected on what should be examined in the final exam: the typical chemical reactions have to be examined of course as much of the chemical industry is built on this process, but should we also include the Indigenous aspects of 'dehydrohalogenation' and how? Perhaps the Indigenous techniques can be assessed in a practical exam? (Mpho)

Discussion: The student teacher explained that this significant pedagogical episode she observed contained multiple principles of culturally relevant pedagogy. A local practice and knowledge possessed by an elderly woman from the community was *valued* as a resource for learning about the application of chemistry. The fact that the elderly woman could not speak English was not positioned as a deficit – on the contrary, her talk as she demonstrated her practice was translated by home language seSotho students for the visiting monolingual English speaking student teacher to follow. This positioned the student teachers as the students and the uma-Gogo and the seSotho speaking translators as the owners and disseminators of valuable knowledge. Not only was the demonstration a good pedagogical decision, but cultural knowledge from the community not documented in a textbook was valued and utilised.

The student teacher's reflective thoughts documented in her journal opened a space to re-explore curriculum content to be assessed. While the canon of knowledge in science is fundamental to access careers in science, technology, engineering and mathematics fields, a reformatory science curriculum could include local knowledges that co-exist, extend or critique 'the' canon with the aim of designing local sustainable science-society-technology-environmental solutions to pressing problems.

Reflective Considerations on Learning to Become Socially Just Science Teachers

I am left with thoughts on science teacher education to ponder. First, did the practice teaching experience of student teachers in 'constraining' under-resourced learning environments cultivate a social justice disposition, while also developing professional identities and competence as high school science teachers? From the significant episodes the student teachers reported, it is possible to trace the pedagogical designs that they had implemented and observed in teaching science curriculum material in ways that provided conceptual access.

Placements in 'constraining' under-resourced contexts

On the basis of this intervention, I would propose that it is possible to design and support teaching practice placements in under-resourced semi-rural school contexts that are affirming and liberating for the developmental trajectory of prospective science teachers who have to teach in diverse schools settings. In these so-called constraining learning environments, the student teachers were not constrained in their professional learning. On the contrary, they reported rich learning experiences for socially just science teaching. These student teachers extracted resources related to translanguaging and Indigenous local cultural knowledge and practices for teaching and learning science meaningfully.

Abundant resources in the science class: Language repertoires

In the schools that were under-resourced in terms of equipment for doing hands-on science practical work, student teachers themselves mobilised another powerful resource – languaging for learning (Guzula *et al.*, 2016). As Msimanga and Lelliot (2014: 1180) point out, 'Language can afford or constrain epistemic access'. By utilising the full language repertoires that students and teachers possess in a flexible and interwoven manner, the students in these schools were not as 'passive and uninterested' as one teacher had expected them to be. By articulating questions and ideas in ways that made language sense to students, potential misconceptions and shortcomings in prior knowledge could be identified and pedagogically mediated. It seemed that once students could construct science knowledge that made sense to them conceptually, the specialised technical terminology and evidence-based argumentation that are central for learning science, especially in Grades 10–12, followed in a naturalistic manner. More recently, the terms 'translanguaging' and 'trans-semiotising' are being used in South African pedagogical contexts (a) as a normative communicative practice among bi- and multilinguals which incorporates semiotic modes beyond language and (b) as an ideological position which resists the notion of languages as bounded and autonomous objects (McKinney & Tyler, 2019; Probyn, 2015; Setati *et al.*, 2002).

What knowledge is valued by whom? Canonical knowledge – dwelling in the borders of STEM fields

Doing teaching practice in these schools enabled the repositioning of such schools as having useful and relevant resources that resonate with students' prior knowledge, particularly their sociocultural knowledge. This is documented in the South African science curriculum from Grades 4–12 as follows:

> Physical Sciences investigate physical and chemical phenomena. This is done through scientific inquiry, application of scientific models, theories and laws in order to explain and predict events in the physical environment. This subject also deals with society's need to understand how the physical environment works in order to benefit from it and responsibly care for it. All scientific and technological knowledge, including Indigenous Knowledge Systems (IKS), is used to address challenges facing society. Indigenous knowledge is knowledge that communities have held, used or are still using; this knowledge has been passed on through generations and has been a source of many innovations and developments including scientific developments. Some concepts found in Indigenous Knowledge Systems lend themselves to explanation using the scientific method while other concepts do not; this is still knowledge however. (DoE, 2011: 8)

The science curriculum that was implemented since 1994 is progressive in that it enables teachers to work pedagogically with culture as a vehicle not only to advance students' understanding of robust, equitable science education, but for acting in a systemic way to create it as well. Previous studies (e.g. Mushayikwa & Ogunniyi, 2011; Seehawer, 2018) have reported how teachers have creatively engaged with sociocultural and Indigenous knowledge when teaching science. Based on the Banks Typology (Banks, 2001), my own research (Hattingh, 2015) foregrounds science pedagogic practices that manifest on various levels of complexity, ranging from integration and critique to generative levels.

Having done teaching practice in schools pushed the thoughts of one student teacher to imagine another type of high-stakes exit exam where teaching is not done through culturally relevant lenses only, but where Indigenous scientific knowledge is evaluated in examinations, signalling the value of sociocultural knowledge as scientifically laden and useful for situated problem solving. These thoughts raised by the student teacher touched on the following concerns mentioned in a study conducted by Maulucci (2013), quoting Nieto (2002) in *Language, Culture and Teaching*:

> Nieto stresses the importance of listening to students' concerns and general input ... I find it slightly hypocritical to suggest to students that their culture and beliefs are important and then teach them the 'canon' or the rest of the curriculum that does not prioritize multiculturalism. (Maulucci, 2013: 469)

While the established canon of knowledge in science is fundamental for access to careers in the fields of science, technology, engineering and mathematics, a reformatory science curriculum pushes beyond the boundaries of the canon. Recent protests in higher education demand a type of 'cognitive justice' that requires education based on affordances across various knowledge and science systems. Fataar (2018: vii) argues for 'inclusion of all knowledge forms bequeathed to humanity including African, Indigenous, Aran-Islamic, Chinese, Hindo, Indo-American, Asiatic and Western knowledge forms' to create a more inclusive canon which may also address the curiosities and problems that the present canon is grappling to find solutions for. A conversation between STEM fields and Humanities would be timely on how to extend the canon to include multiple ontologies, epistemologies and methodologies that may contribute to resolving the challenges of a natural environment in need of healing and caring, while creating work opportunities amid high levels of unemployment in South Africa and critically engaging in the Fourth Industrial Revolution.

In conclusion, I argue that doing teaching practice in different types of schools cultivates professional dispositions for socially just education that dissolve the boundaries between perceived 'functional well-resourced' and 'less-functional under-resourced' schools. The prospective teachers faced the challenges of classroom teaching and creatively activated internal and external resources for students to learn science productively and enthusiastically.

Making Connections/Entanglements

Editors' note: We encourage readers to use Google Translate to access the Afrikaans and SeSotho (Southern Sotho on Google Translate) meanings.

The author/researcher's linguistic repertoire: 'Dumela, Good Day and Goeiedag'
Hometown for me was Pretoria, the capital city of South Africa where I attended an Afrikaans primary school in the early 1970s with an arts and culture orientation – Pierneef primary school was situated next to the residence of the fine arts painter Pierneef. Tweetaligheid (bilingualism) was 'n doelwit vir alle kinders van graad 1 tot graad 12 in die apartheidskurrikulum en gevolglik was Engels as tweede taal aangebied. I had ample opportunity to speak English through the many friends I met at ice-skating and Children's Theatre which were extra mural activities I was involved in. In die Kinderteater produksie genaamd 'Peter Pan' moes ek die rol van die hond (dog) Nana vertolk en net woef-woef blaf omdat ek nie die Engelse woorde wat die karakter Wendy moes praat 'behoorlik' in Engels kon uitspreek nie. At the time my Afrikaans pronunciation of English words in the play was not good enough to be staged ... so as Nana the pet dog, I barked. In my last years of primary school seSotho was introduced as a conversational language and till this day I remember the wonderful songs that were used as instructional method to learn vocabulary. In this song the tsjipi (bell) is calling all children to come to school: Banna ba sekolo, Banna ba sekolo; tlang sekolong, tlang sekolong, Tsjipi ya la bitsa, Tsjipi ya la bitsa, Tling-Tlong-Tlang; Tling-Tlong-Tlang.

During my childhood years I was also exposed to the isiZulu language when visiting my sister and her family who were farmers in rural KwaZulu Natal. The entire family – two boys and youngest daughter – were rather fluent speakers of isiZulu and I admired them for being able to speak the language while playing with their friends. In Afrikaans is daar 'n gesegde wat lui 'hulle het hulself gate uit geniet en hul dae omgespeel' in die naby geleë Shongweni dam. My exposure to isiZulu and my good friend Nthombi Ngobela inspired me to select an Indigenous language, Northern seSotho, as one of my Grade 12 subjects along with mathematics and physical science. Other elective languages on offer at the school were Latin, French and German. By

> the time I matriculated in 1983 I was very well aware that Afrikaans was seen as the language of the enemy. I was deeply saddened and angry about the death of Hector Peterson during the Soweto uprising, 1976. At the time youth protested against Afrikaans as the medium of instruction in their local schools.
>
> In my career, which started as a high school teacher and since as a teacher educator, I would intentionally arrange work integrated learning opportunities, also called teaching practice, with groups of student teachers who spoke English, Afrikaans and Northern Sotho in schools in semi-rural areas to teach mathematics, physics and chemistry. The maths and science teachers of the future and I live and work in a multicultural, multilingual society and translanguaging makes perfect sense as enabler of learning for understanding, enjoyment of these subjects and for exploring the usefulness of these subjects in daily lived experiences.

References

Aikenhead, G.S. (2001) Students' ease in crossing cultural borders into school science. *Science Education* 27, 1–52.

Banks, J.A. (2001) *Cultural Diversity and Education: Foundations, Curriculum and Teaching* (5th edn). Boston, MA: Allyn & Bacon.

Barter, C. and Reynold, E. (2000) 'I want to tell you a story': Exploring the application of vignettes in qualitative research with children and young people. *International Journal of Social Research Methodology* 3 (4), 307–323.

Basu, S.J. and Calabrese Barton, A. (2007) Developing a sustained interest in science among urban minority youth. *Journal of Research in Science Teaching* 44, 466–489.

Cohen-Sayag, E. and Fischl, E.C. (2012) Reflective writing in pre-service teachers' teaching: What does it promote? *Australian Journal of Teacher Education* 37 (10).

DoE (Department of Education) (2011) *National Curriculum Statement. Physical Science. Curriculum and Assessment Policy Statement*. Pretoria: Department of Basic Education.

Fafunwa, A.B. (2001) Crises and challenges in higher education: An overview. In A.U. Akubue and D. Enyi (eds) *Crises and Challenges in Higher Education in Developing Countries: A Book of Readings*. Ibadan: Wisdom Publishers.

Fataar, A. (2018) Decolonising education in South Africa: Perspectives and debates. *Educational Research for Social Change (ERSC)* 7 (June), vi–ix.

Freire, P. (2007 [1974]) *Pedagogy of the Oppressed*. New York: Bloomsbury.

Gee, J. (2004) *Situated Language and Learning: A Critique of Traditional Schooling*. New York: Routledge.

Gilbert, A. and Yerrick, R. (2001) Same school, separate worlds: A sociocultural study of identity, resistance, and negotiation in a rural, lower track science classroom. *Journal of Research in Science Teaching* 38 (5), 574–598.

Giroux, H.A. (1992) *Border Crossings: Cultural Workers and the Politics of Education*. New York: Routledge.

Grisham, D.L., Laguardia, A. and Brink, B. (2000) Partners in professionalism: Creating a quality field experience for preservice teachers. *Action in Teacher Education* 21 (4), 27–40.

Guyton, E. and McIntyre, D.J. (1990) Student teaching and school experiences. In W.R. Houston (ed.) *Handbook of Research on Teacher Education* (pp. 514–534). New York: Macmillan.

Guzula, X., McKinney, C. and Tyler, R. (2016) Languaging-for-learning: Legitimising translanguaging and enabling multimodal practices in third spaces. *Southern African Linguistics and Applied Language Studies* 34 (3), 211–226.

Hattingh, A. (2015) Relevante onderrig van fisiese wetenskappe: Benutting van kulturele en inheemse kennisbronne in semilandelike skoolkontekste. *Suid-Afrikaanse Tydskrif vir Natuurwetenskap en Tegnologie* 31 (1), 1–13.

Hattingh, A., Aldous, C. and Rogan, J. (2007) Some factors influencing the quality of practical work in science classrooms. *African Journal of Research in Mathematics, Science and Technology Education* 11 (1), 75–90.

Heeralal, P.J. and Bayaga, A. (2011) Pre-service teachers' experiences of teaching practice: Case of a South African university. *Journal of Social Sciences* 28 (2), 99–105.

Hollins, E. and Guzman, M.T. (2005) Research on preparing teachers for diverse populations. In M. Cochran-Smith and K.M. Zeichner (eds) *Studying Teacher Education: The Report of the AERA Panel on Research and Teacher Education* (pp. 477–548). Mahwah, NJ: Lawrence Erlbaum.

Jindal-Snape, D. and Holmes, E.A. (2009) A longitudinal study exploring perspectives of participants regarding reflective practice during their transition from higher education to professional practice. *Reflective Practice* 10 (2), 219–232.

Jonasson, J.T. (2016) Connecting the past, present and the future: A story about the travel of education through time. In P.J. Mitchell and M.J. McNaughton (eds) *Storyline: A Creative Approach to Learning and Teaching*. Cambridge: Cambridge Scholars Publishing.

Kerka, S. (2002) Journal writing as an adult learning tool. *Practice Application Brief* 22, 3–4.

Ladson-Billings, G. (1995) Towards a theory of culturally relevant pedagogy. *American Educational Research Journal* 32, 465–491.

Lee, O. (2004) Teacher change in beliefs and practices in science and literacy instruction with English language learners. *Journal of Research in Science Teaching* 41, 65–93.

Lemke, J. (1990) *Talking Science: Language, Learning and Values*. Norwood, NJ: Ablex.

Lipka, J. (2002) *Schooling for Self-determination: Research on the Effects of Including Native Language and Culture in the Schools*. Charleston, SC: ERIC Clearinghouse on Rural and Small Schools.

Maulucci, M.S.R. (2013) Emotions and positional identity in becoming a social justice science teacher: Nicole's story. *Journal of Research in Science Teaching* 50 (4), 453–478.

McKinney, C. and Tyler, R. (2019) Disinventing and reconstructing language for learning in school science. *Language and Education* 33 (2), 141–158.

Moll, L.C., Amanti, C., Neff, D. and Gonzalez, N. (1992) Funds of knowledge for teaching. *Theory into Practice* 31, 132–141.

Msimanga, A. and Lelliott, A. (2014) Talking science in multilingual contexts in South Africa: Possibilities and challenges for engagement in learners' home languages in high schools. *International Journal of Science Education* 36 (7), 1159–1183.

Mueller, M.P. and Tippins, D.J. (2007) Citizen science, ecojustice and science education: Rethinking an education from nowhere. In B.J. Fraser, K. Tobin and C.J. McRobbie (eds) *Second International Handbook of Science Education*. London: Springer.

Mushayikwa, E. and Ogunniyi, M. (2011) Modelling the integration of IKS into the teaching and learning of science. In *19th SAARMSTE Conference Proceedings* (pp. 409–425). Mafikeng: SAARMSTE.

Odora-Hoppers, C.A. (2002) *Indigenous Knowledge and the Integration of Knowledge Systems*. Claremont: New Africa Books.

Paris, D. and Alim, H.S. (2014) What are we seeking to sustain through culturally sustaining pedagogy? A loving critique forward. *Harvard Educational Review* 84 (1), 85–100.
Piliouras, P. and Evangelou, O. (2012) Teachers' inclusive strategies to accommodate 5th grade pupils' crossing of cultural borders in two Greek multicultural science classrooms. *Research in Science Education* 42 (2), 329–351.
Plummer, T. (1987) *An Introduction to Practical Biochemistry*. London: McGraw-Hill Book Company.
Prince, T., Snowden, E. and Matthews, B. (2010) Utilising peer coaching as a tool to improve student-teacher confidence and support the development of classroom practice. *Literacy Information and Computer Education Journal (LICEJ)* 1 (1), 49–51.
Probyn, M. (2015) Pedagogical translanguaging: Bridging discourses in South African science classrooms. *Language and Education* 29 (3), 218–234.
Ronfeldt, M. (2012) Where should student teachers learn to teach? *Educational Evaluation and Policy Analysis* 34 (1), 3–26.
Roth, W.M. and Calabrese Barton, A. (2004) *Rethinking Scientific Literacy*. New York: RoutledgeFalmer.
Seehawer, M. (2018) South African teachers' strategies for integrating indigenous and Western knowledges in their classrooms: Practical lessons in decolonisation. *Educational Research for Social Change* 7 (June), 91–100.
Setati, M., Adler, J., Reed, Y. and Bapoo, A. (2002) Incomplete journeys: Code-switching and other language practices in mathematics, science and English language classrooms in South Africa. *Language and Education* 16 (2), 128–149.
Zuniga, K., Olson, J.K. and Winter, M. (2005) Science education for rural Latino/a students: Course placement and success in science. *Journal of Research in Science Teaching* 42 (4), 376–402.

7 Engaging Deficit: Pre-service Teachers' Reflections on Negotiation of Working-class Schools

Rochelle Kapp

Introduction

This chapter uses data from a case study on the reflective practices of pre-service teachers to describe and analyse the ways in which three postgraduate, pre-service teachers grappled with challenges in low-fee, under-resourced high schools during their teaching practicum. Drawing on research on learning, literacy, identity and reflection in teacher education, my research is focused on how pre-service teachers make meaning from their experiences and on understanding reflective writing as a literacy practice. In contrast to many of their peers, the three participants used reflective writing productively to position themselves in agentic ways in order to engage critically with the deficit constructions of learners that characterised the black working-class school environments in which they taught. I argue that the participants' conceptualisation of reflection, as well as their reflective writing practices, offer important insights for teacher education about pre-service teachers' positioning and about mediating and scaffolding reflective writing.

Teacher Education legislation in South Africa makes it compulsory for pre-service teachers to experience teaching practice in diverse schooling contexts (DHET, 2015). As a consequence of the still remaining structural legacy of an unequal apartheid system of education, pre-service South African teachers encounter school practice teaching contexts that are extremely different in terms of levels of resources, racial demography, linguistic profile, school location, class size, school culture and teaching and learning discourse practices (Christie, 2018; Christie & McKinney, 2017; Soudien, 2007). The vast majority of learners are educated in under-resourced schools and are taught through the medium of their second language, English. In addition, in the last 25 years, the South African educational context has been characterised by rapid curriculum and educational policy shifts and strong contestation around issues of resources, race, social positioning and social justice in both school and higher education contexts. In public discourse, education is described as a panacea and is constructed as key to enabling economic advancement. There is a constant public outcry about the severe underperformance of learners, particularly in black working-class contexts. These issues contribute to challenging teaching practice contexts that are often fraught with tension, stress and disquiet.

In my experience as a teacher educator, the process of negotiating the borders of markedly different and difficult schooling contexts is often life changing for pre-service teachers as they are forced to step outside the boundaries of race, class and language and their own experiences of schooling. While their experiences may result in discomfort and unease, the disruption of taken-for-granted assumptions about learners and learning also provides an opportunity for pre-service teachers to reflect on their social positioning and the effects of structural inequalities, and to imagine possibilities for agency and change (Carrington & Selva, 2010; Ryan, 2011).

However, a significant body of research has described the ways in which teachers mimic the pedagogy that characterised their own schooling, and the difficulties experienced by teacher education programmes in disrupting the investment in strongly held beliefs about classroom norms, appropriate pedagogy and literacy practices that are the consequence of student teachers' own experiences of school discourses (see, for example, Christie, 2018; Ryan, 2011). While crossing borders and dwelling in what Anzaldúa (2012 [1987]) calls 'borderland' spaces can be transformative, it can also serve to confirm existing stereotypes, deficit constructions of learners and problematic notions about what constitutes appropriate teaching and learning (Asher, 2009; Gelfuso & Dennis, 2014; Mendelowitz, 2017; Mendelowitz & Dixon, 2016). In Christie's (2018: xxiii) words, 'experience is always partial and often incoherent; and it requires critical reflection to sift and refine'. An understanding of *how* pre-service teachers reflect and position themselves within this divided terrain carries potential benefits for teacher education to rethink how to support pre-service teachers' development and engagement with the complexities of a social context.

In some ways, the three participants who are the subject of this chapter were very well prepared for the task in that all three were students with strong undergraduate and postgraduate degrees in their subject areas, as well as prior, informal teaching experiences and experiences of activism in working-class contexts. They have varying degrees of proficiency in isiXhosa and Afrikaans, the predominant home languages of the learners in their teaching practice schools. They had benefited from being educated in high-performing, well-resourced schools and expressed a strong commitment to making a difference in the lives of children from working-class backgrounds through teaching.

Notwithstanding their high levels of motivation and resources, the participants' verbal and written reflections provide insight into the considerable intellectual and emotional difficulties they experienced in coping with the material challenges of, inter alia, large classes, language and literacy issues, classroom management, violence, teacher and learner absenteeism and late-coming, and temporal and spatial arrangements that characterised the working-class, commuter schools in which they taught. Most significantly, they experienced dissonance with the (often consequent) constructions of learners as deficit, and the instrumental, test-driven pedagogy that characterises many South African schools.

The chapter shows how the three teachers reflected critically by drawing on prior discourses and multiple sources – strategising and positioning themselves in order to understand the classroom and social context, to situate their experiences and to negotiate tensions between their theoretical conceptions of teaching, learning and schooling and the material conditions and discourse practices within the schools. Drawing on academic literacy theorists, I conceptualise reflection as a literacy practice to describe the ways in which the pre-service teachers used writing as a tool to construct their teaching practice as inquiry as they negotiated boundaries. The chapter ends with a consideration of how the participants' insights can be harnessed to enable pedagogy that facilitates critical reflection.

Reflection and Teacher Education

Within the discipline of teacher education, reflection has long been positioned as central to learning to teach (Gelfuso & Dennis, 2014; Loughran, 2002; Nkambule & Mukeredzi, 2017; Schön, 1987). Ussher and Chalmers (2011: 95) usefully define it as 'the process of assessing and comparing existing practice and knowledge in order to predict, speculate and answer questions'. This definition foregrounds the notion of the teacher as an inquirer who draws on theory to describe and interpret practice with a view to transforming practice. In the literature on teacher education, reflection is viewed as: a crucial resource for learning from experience; a tool for making meaningful connections between theory and practice; a means to integrate content, pedagogical knowledge and practice; and a tool for informed decision-making and the development of pedagogical reasoning and professional judgement.

With increasing disciplinary recognition of the centrality of identity to becoming a teacher, reflection has also been recognised as key to the process of constructing one's unfolding identity as a teaching professional (Cheung *et al.*, 2015; Kŏrkkŏ *et al.*, 2016).

Hoadley-Maidment (2000: 160) points out that it is often assumed that, through reflection, students will 'gradually learn to reframe problems and solutions within the discourse of the profession'. And yet, as Loughran (2002: 33) argues, in many teacher education programmes reflection is ill defined and simplistically conceptualised as 'thinking about a problem' and, as Scott (2000) demonstrates, while the term 'reflective practitioner' is positioned as central to teacher education, its pedagogical and writing implications are relatively ill defined (see also Vassilaki, 2017).

My research is focused on how pre-service teachers read, interpret and make meaning from their teaching practice experiences and the role of literacy in that process. Following New Literacy theorists' conceptions of literacy as multiple and socially situated, I locate literacy practices in discourses (Bangeni & Kapp, 2017; Gee, 1990; Lea & Street, 1998; Thesen & van Pletzen, 2006; Vassilaki, 2017). In this sense, the ways of knowing and valuing that are considered appropriate within academic disciplines are ideological, and inextricably bound to specialised ways of using language and literacy and constraints about what constitutes appropriate positioning of self within the discourse (Gee, 1990). In Gee's terms:

> [t]here is no such thing as 'reading' or 'writing', only reading or writing something (a text of a certain type) in a certain way with certain values, while at least appearing to think and feel in certain ways. (Gee, 1990: xviii)

Reflective writing is thus a literacy practice located within the discourse of teacher education (see also Scott, 2000; Vassilaki, 2017). It is not a decontextualised activity and, as Donohoe (2015: 802) argues, 'depends on the development of meta-cognitive skills together with a grasp of and an acceptance of the perception that actions and events are located in, and influenced by, multiple historical and socio-political contexts'. In the context of teacher education, reflecting critically entails learning to recast a personal (often emotional) experience into a moment of learning about teaching practice. This activity requires proficiency in a meta-language, a language in which to question, describe and analyse practice with a view to developing teaching strategies that are pedagogically and contextually appropriate. It entails engagement with one's own assumptions and prior discourses as well as multiple (and often conflicting) theoretical perspectives. The knowledge that needs to be grasped is often tacit (Ussher & Chalmers, 2011). As such, the act of engagement in reflective thinking and writing is intellectually and emotionally challenging (Crowe & Berry, 2007; Rodgers, 2002). It represents a shift away from conventional academic literacy practices which tend to foreground conceptual thinking and reasoning, mastery over secondary reading and the development of a relatively constrained, distanced authorial stance (Clark & Ivanič, 1997; Hyland, 2005; Kapp & Bangeni, 2009; Vassilaki, 2017).

While a social view of literacies implies an understanding of how disciplinary discourses work to construct 'normative, literate' varieties that position individuals (Blommaert, 2010: 85), it also implies an understanding of agency: the choices and decisions made by individuals; what individuals 'do' with literacy (Barton et al., 2000: 6); how they interpret the very different social spaces that they inhabit; and how they make meaning from the constructions of literacy and subject positions they are offered by discourses (Kapp, 2012). Drawing on a range of theorists who view identity as central to learning, I am interested in how pre-service teachers process their experiences, invest in certain positions and construct subject positions within the constraints, affordances and contradictions of the literacy practice of reflective writing (Cheung et al., 2015; Herrington & Curtis, 2000; Norton, 2000; Thomson, 2009; Walker, 2010).

Research Design and Methodology

This chapter is drawn from a larger qualitative case study of the reflections of 52 pre-service teachers over the course of one year. The participants were all registered for the Post Graduate Certificate in Education (PGCE), a one-year programme located in the School of Education at the University of Cape Town. They volunteered to participate in the project in January 2019 and signed ethical permission. Although I usually teach on the programme, I was on sabbatical during the period of research, which provided a unique opportunity to engage in discussion with the participants and to analyse their writing without the usual degree of investment and power relations.

Safia, Beverley and Anna (all pseudonyms) were purposefully selected, both because they experienced their first teaching practice in a context very different from their own schooling and because, while many of the participants' reflections produced fairly conventional analyses of their classroom contexts and their possibilities for improvement, these three participants engaged critically, using writing as a tool to explore and engage contextually and conceptually.

The data comprise: (1) a background questionnaire, designed to elicit biographical information and to gain a preliminary sense of participants' motivation to become teachers; (2) participants' reflective writing over the course of the year, consisting of one observation journal and two teaching practice journals (the journals provided insight into participants' understanding of the concept of reflection, their reflective writing practices and their positioning as teachers); (3) an assignment comprising transcripts of a single lesson and participants' analysis and reflection on their classroom talk in relation to learning which provided valuable evidence of their ability to reflect on their actual (rather than reported) practice; and (4) two semi-structured, audio-recorded interviews of 26 of the participants, selected with the purpose of obtaining a diverse spread of race, gender, age and subject area profiles. The interviews were conducted immediately after each teaching practice period and sought to probe participants' understandings of the concept of reflection and its relationship to learning, their attitudes to writing and their positioning as teachers. They also enabled me to ask specific questions about participants' written reflections and I used critical incidents in participants' journals and/or raised by them in the interviews as prompts to stimulate discussion on how they made meaning and learnt from their teaching practice experiences.

In addition, Safia, Beverley and Anna agreed to participate in an unstructured focus group discussion with me after they had read a draft of this chapter. The 90-minute focus group discussion yielded rich insights in terms of the participants' experiences of reflective writing as a literacy practice and its potential for fostering critical engagement. This data source is reflected through comments in the margins of this chapter. The use of the participants' comments in dialogue with my analysis highlights the crucial role that students can play as co-contributors to meaningful curriculum development, knowledge production and change (Thesen, 1997). As academics, we so often talk about students' experiences without inviting them to be participants in the academic conversation.

Tracing patterns, exceptions, silences and contradictions within and across data sources was essential to the data analysis of both the interviews and the participants' writing. Critical discourse analysis (Fairclough, 1995; Janks, 2010) was used to analyse participants' writing and positioning. Rather than merely describing instances of discursive practice, critical discourse analysis 'aims to systematically explore often opaque relationships of causality and determination between (a) discursive practices, events and texts and (b) wider social and cultural structures, relations and processes ...' (Fairclough, 1995: 132). I focused on the topics foregrounded within their reflective writing, the way in which the writing was structured, the level of description and analysis and the register. I also found Hyland's (2005, 2011) work on positioning and stance highly generative in identifying how participants positioned themselves in relation to their writing.

My research process concentrated on participants' perceptions, attitudes and meaning-making processes and positioning. I am interested in the ways in which they constructed their subject positions in writing and in speech. What is significant is the 'activity of identifying [within participants' narratives] rather than its end product' (Sfard & Prusak, 2005: 17). As Leander and Boldt (2012) point out, texts do not constitute practice. While the pre-service teachers' experiences are important, my focus is on how they *process* their experiences, how they conceptualise reflection and engage with it as a literacy practice.

Conceptions of Reflection and Writing

The PGCE teacher education programme requires students to keep a reflective journal during their period of observation in schools and during their two periods of teaching practice. They are asked to produce daily entries as well as a reflective summary at the end. Students are scaffolded into the practice of reflection during tutorials and lectures and are provided with models of journal entries and extensive written guidelines which include prompt questions, diagrams and suggested topics. They also engage in joint analysis of video-recorded lessons. The purpose and audience of the journal are outlined in the school experience handbook as follows:

> During teaching practice you will keep a personal journal, which is made available only to your supervisors and, should they request to see it, your Methods lecturers. The purposes of the journal are to track your professional growth during the two teaching practice sessions and to encourage you to reflect on school experience. The TP journal also provides a record of evidence that can be used in the final School Experience ePortfolio. For supervisors, the journal offers a valuable perspective on your progress, and a record of your time spent in schools.

This extract highlights the hybrid nature of the journal. It is both 'personal' and available to multiple figures in authority. It is constructed as a development tool and as a tool used to monitor progress and development (Vassilaki, 2017).

> Anna, Beverley and Safia were all critical of how the journal is framed and the degree to which reflective writing was taught and scaffolded within the programme. Beverley commented that while reflective writing is 'somewhere between free-writing and essay writing', many pre-service teachers with limited experience of writing have the impression that it is free writing, rather than a complex sense-making process.

The participants' journals were of variable quality, with many confined to narratives that identified and described practical problems in fairly discrete, decontextualised terms, with generic, surface-level solutions, such as improving the quality of the PowerPoint or the quality of the instructions given to learners. Participants often foregrounded their own performance and the immediate, micro-context of their own classrooms (for similar remarks and findings, see Ryan, 2011; Ussher & Chalmers, 2011). Particularly in under-resourced schools with large classes, the problems identified were overwhelmingly focused on concrete, visible challenges, such as classroom management in large classes or issues related to time on task and use and/or lack of resources, with very little analysis of learners and learning and of the significance for teaching and learning in the context. When participants were critical of pedagogy or aspects of schooling, they tended to foreground the power relations of the teaching practice context and the need to be deferential, to 'know my place'.

The participants' interview commentaries on their conceptions of the role of these reflections and on their processes of writing shed light on the nature of their reflections. During the first interviews, participants foregrounded their strong awareness that the journal was a course requirement which would be handed in regularly during teaching practice and which would form part of their assessment. Many spoke of how they tended to delay writing until it became necessary to hand in the journal to their supervisors, by which point they had often forgotten the details of their week. They prioritised lesson planning and viewed journal reflections as arduous, time consuming and, in some ways, a diversion from teaching. They also expressed difficulty with the genre of the journal. For example, some participants assumed that the journal needed to be stripped of emotion, as in the following comment:

> … there were examples of what reflections look like, so I tried to base my reflections off of what I saw and because I tried doing that it was hard for me to express what I wanted to say …. I am a very emotional kind of person. I like using expressive language and I felt constricted as well. Because they said that you can't be emotional and stuff …. (Farida)

As a consequence of her effort to make distinctions between her 'personal' diary and the journal, and her perception that 'you can't be emotional', Farida suppressed analysis of a classroom incident which challenged her authority and positioned her as subordinate because it was 'too painful'. Her journal thus provided only a glimpse of the difficulties she experienced and yet she expressed gratitude for the opportunity to reflect and share within the interview. While participants could articulate the purpose of the journal in terms of their own development and 'improvement' as teachers, it seemed that many only came to appreciate the value of reflective writing for their learning quite late in teaching practice, often in response to a supervisor's prompt questions and comments or when they were re-reading the journal at the end of teaching practice in order to write the final summary.

In contrast, participants like Safia, Beverley and Anna, who had had prior academic experience of producing the genre of reflective writing, could see the personal benefit of reflection and, in particular, of reflective writing. All three conceptualised writing as a tool for learning, but described quite specific functions of the reflective writing during their teaching practice and quite distinct writing processes. Safia distinguished 'in class', mental reflection from the physical act of writing as follows:

> Anna commented on how students who are not used to reflective writing and who are feeling the pressure of assessment in teaching practice may also suppress information about disastrous lessons rather than viewing it as a tool for growth and development. Beverley commented that as an older student with work experience, she also felt more confident in describing mistakes and seeking help. Significantly, the discussion also focused on the extent to which assessment often presupposes growth and development, whereas the paths to learning and the development of teachers' professional identities are often non-linear.

> … In writing the thought can carry on all the way to its completion and it is a way of thinking through a process, so even though I know that I have to rearrange the desks, I don't know why. The reflective practice helps me to complete the thought as to why, in terms of hierarchical space and now I can link it very easily to curriculum theory about learning space and I am able to assess the learners more easily, so the writing process takes me to that end point … (Safia)

In this statement, Safia conceptualised reflection as a journey and assigned agency to the writing process which 'takes' her 'to that end point'. She articulated a very clear understanding of how writing can help thinking ('complete the thought') and how it can lead from the particular event (and her intuitive action of rearranging the desks) to making theoretical connections, to contextualisation and to externalised explanation of the significance for teaching practice. At the same time, Safia was aware that she was always negotiating multiple discourses, that the task of reflective journal documentation was Janus-faced in that it entailed personal processing, within the constraints of the academy and high-stakes assessment, and also that it required her to straddle discourses, that she was being 'watched' and assessed by multiple audiences with different lenses:

> … there is that performativity within this course and within this framework, where I am being watched, not only by students, but by someone else and being assessed … (Safia)

This high level of meta-awareness of the complexity and affordances of reflection as a literacy practice was also evident in Beverley's interview. She described how the process of reflective writing created a space which 'actually forced me to debrief after a day'. She said that the writing enabled her to 'vent' her frustrations and served as the basis for planning the next day's lessons. The act of writing enabled expression of emotion, but also enabled critical detachment as she situated the everyday in a broader context of structural inequality:

> … you just sit there and you just see like all these faults coming up, but I think, for me, in that regard, I think the journal is useful because then I can go back and realise like, you know, this is not an isolated thing, it is a more societal thing and where people start realising that, I feel then they sometimes become even more isolated or they feel more isolated because they can't do anything but I'm a Marxist so I [laugh], so I can actually see the solution as well and not get caught up in that situation … (Beverley)

Here, Beverley drew on a subject position from a prior discourse, Marxism, to place her experiences and feelings in context and to position herself as an agent, able to 'see the solution'.

Like Beverley, Anna viewed the journal as a vehicle for working through her personal positioning and everyday classroom events in order to focus on the social context, her place within it and the consequences for teaching and learning. She described the journal as a physical 'place' where she could 'orienteer' herself and deal with 'difficult' issues. She developed a process-orientated approach where she would 'jot down' issues during the week. Over the weekend, she would read her notes and engage in internet research in an attempt to provide 'context and some point of reference' for her struggles – to try to understand the difference between her own schooling and her teaching practice experiences and to find practical classroom strategies. She would then write a better developed reflection that explored the limits and possibilities of the research for her practice. She commented that the journal became 'a very helpful thing to read' and 'I feel like the journal became a little bit more and more about practice and less and less about what was happening in the day ... I guess it became a bit more reflective'.

Anna's comments show her awareness of writing as a process of exploration, but she also expressed a clear idea of the complexity of the genre of reflective writing. She believed that her background in ethnographic research had led her to this approach where she constantly thought about 'what has happened, what has led you to be here and what are the implications going forward'.

All three participants thus conceptualised the act of reflective writing as a process that enabled them to narrate issues, to contextualise their experiences and to connect and consolidate ideas. They also viewed it as a vehicle for figuring out their possibilities for agency within the constraints of the contexts. Their prior experiences with reflective writing within academia enabled them to conceptualise a discursive positioning that took into account the complexity of negotiating the audience and purpose of the genre within academia.

Participants' Journal Reflections

The three pre-service teachers constructed writing as both an emotional and an intellectual resource and viewed it as central to their meaning-making processes, and to their understanding of the considerable challenges experienced by teachers and learners in under-resourced schools. This meta-awareness of the affordances of writing is evident in their reflective journal writing. The participants described problems within their classrooms and then set about revisiting the issues over the course of the six weeks of teaching practice. They recruited the views of teachers, supervisors, readings and their own prior and current experiences of schooling; in Loughran's (2002: 42) terms, they sought to 'frame and reframe' the problems from multiple perspectives. For example, Anna grappled with the issue of teaching time in large, junior high school classes in a township school. In her first week of observation, she remarked:

> Today I was thinking a lot about the amount of time there is to actually teach learners. Schools which are lower resourced often have more for the teachers to do over and above teaching (finance, lunch systems, sick bay etc.) which affects teaching time. There are also more learner related interventions that exist to try and get learners better equipped; lots of time being spent on different control tests, school awards, school wide tests etc. Both of the above factors lead to less time for teaching content.

On top of this you have bigger classes and often more confusion because of a lack of individual attention. The above was making me think through how one optimises one's time with a lot of learners, in a small amount of time to give learners the best opportunities. I don't have the answer but it has been interesting to see how my 2 different mentor teachers approach it; Mr T gives few difficult examples which covers all content while Mrs M has morning classes to try to give learners as many examples as possible. It becomes a game of choosing what and whoever have to sacrifice certain things for others. I feel like I am leaning towards structure to be a saving grace but will have to see if this works when I begin teaching next week. I hope that by being well prepared, having a structure and potentially by having lots of examples available to learners if they want them on top of homework, that I will provide learners with the most productive use of our time together. (Anna)

In this extract, Anna positions herself as an ethnographer 'observing', contextualising and analysing the constraints of the environment – as a student teacher, learning from experienced professionals, and also as an agent, taking responsibility for her learning and figuring out how best to strategise to maximise time for individual learning in her class of 65 learners. As is evident in the repetition of the first person, she positions herself firmly within the text, but she does so with the low-modality caution that carries authority within academic discourse. Her writing reflects a delicate balance between low-inference observation, 'objective information' and 'subjective evaluation' (Hyland, 2005: 180). Anna articulates a clear, but cautious, low-modality stance, which is visible in 'I feel like I am leaning towards', 'but will have to see', 'I hope'. The 'our' in the last line signals her belief in learner-centred pedagogy which is sustained throughout the journal. It also signals her ethical stance, her strongly expressed moral commitment and her sense of responsibility within the context (Christie, 2005). Over the course of the next few weeks, her journal entries reflect high levels of stress as she battled with trying to develop an environment conducive to learning mathematics for all students:

We got through all of the content of the lesson which is great (despite only getting through 3 examples) but I am struggling to know if learners understand the content or not. I need to find a balance in coming lessons between understanding the example on the board and moving on to another example where they may find more or different meaning …. I am trying to make sense of whether one can move on despite having learners in the class who clearly don't understand.

… I realised that he [mentor teacher] really does just let go of the learners who are struggling. I asked [him] about his strategy and he said that it is up to the learners to make good of their time. If they do not, then it is their fault. It is very difficult for me to leave learners behind but what [he] said is true to a certain extent and with that class size, not focusing on the weaker learners is the main way you are able to push the stronger learners.

> With my Gr9s I feel like I am flailing. My tutor ... said 'go with the learners who are going' which is true to a certain extent but as I said before it is difficult to put into practice ....

> ... I may need to understand that I won't catch all learners and then develop a strategy which moves on despite some learners not understanding. This however is a very difficult thing for me to do as I feel leaving a learner confused means I haven't done my job. (Anna)

As reflected in these examples, Anna continued to engage openly about her difficulties in discussion with experienced professionals. She attempted to view the problem from multiple perspectives and constantly questioned herself about her perspective as a 'privileged, white' woman. While she drew from her experience of ethnography to position herself as a 'small fish because small fishes learn a lot', she did not accept the well-worn refrain in township schools of 'going with the learners who are going' (Kapp, 2004), and persisted with researching and developing appropriate strategies to engage all the learners and to develop a 'safe classroom' environment which 'involves all learners'. Over the weeks, Anna's journal documents how she worked on building learner confidence and participation through positive affirmation, inducting learners into non-verbal hand signals to facilitate quick informal assessment and by drawing on her verbal fluency in isiXhosa, the learners' home language to build rapport (a 'relating point'). She introduced stronger classroom management systems by engaging privately with disruptive learners, reorganising the classroom space, developing groupwork strategies to facilitate peer learning, and creating points systems to keep learners accountable for keeping noise levels down. She celebrated the moments in which these worked, but also engaged openly with the moments when she was 'flailing'.

Beverley was similarly disappointed by the way in which the school's streaming practices and some teachers' classroom practices labelled learners who did not excel in mathematics and science in deficit terms. She reflected on how a teacher prepared in exactly the same way for two classes which were at different levels and on the lack of attention to individual learners in large classes. She critiqued the instrumental examination-focused imperative to 'rush through content' and tasks 'as a box ticking exercise' which resulted in the provision of model answers rather than a focus on 'scientific' inquiry and experimentation. She described how teachers 'resorted to fabricating perfect results for learners to discuss' rather than engaging in 'a more constructivist model of learning from mistakes or imperfect results in experimentation'. Over the course of teaching practice, her journal reflects her deepening understanding of how structural issues such as the 'prescriptive, content-heavy curriculum', 'the pressure from the Education Department to conduct control tests', the streaming and poor organisation within the school, and teacher stress all play a role in reinforcing rote-learning and 'reproducing further academic inequalities'.

While the journal documents her empathy for the teachers and the stresses they face and for the learners who travel long distances to school, Beverley actively resisted teachers' deficit constructions of learners and worked hard at building learners' confidence levels by: 'relating to them as mature young adults capable of critical thinking'; drawing on prior learning; engaging in experiments to induct them into the 'scientific method' which foregrounded inquiry; setting up 'a competitive environment where everybody wins'; rearranging the classroom space to enable group work; and engaging in formative assessment. Her journal described how she 'took every opportunity to ensure that teaching scientific content was not devoid of critical content' and to show learners 'how societal influences shape their learning'.

> Beverley commented in the focus group that she came to the view that teachers constructed learners in deficit terms over time. In the beginning, she believed that teachers were merely 'justifying' why learners performed badly.

When she became frustrated with learners' lack of knowledge of notation in a physics class, Beverley researched the issue by engaging with teachers about the learners' prior knowledge in both mathematics and physics. She consequently reframed the lesson:

> I told the learners that I acknowledge that what I was doing yesterday was challenging for them, but we are not going to leave it without understanding as I believe they can do it. ... It was clear they did not understand WHY we use that method, so I went through the 'long way' of rearranging the equations with learners to make sure they understood. I even got a learner who was not a 'star pupil' to demonstrate on the white board how to do it. (Beverley)

Safia's journal was also directly critical of the school management, the pedagogy and the deficit construction of learners in her school: 'I got warned by several teachers that the learners are below average and that it doesn't matter how much effort I put into lessons, most of the learners aren't capable of succeeding'. She reflected that:

> All of the teachers that I've observed use the same approach to teaching. They present the lesson and then give the class an activity. I haven't seen any group discussions, pair work or other forms of interaction that don't involve the teacher leading the discussion. (Safia)

Drawing on theory from the PGCE programme, Safia was critical of the 'presentational' style of teaching, the fact that there was very little exploratory work with learners and that learners were seldom asked questions.

Safia organised her journal reflection using the evaluation questions in the teaching practice marking rubric and critically analysed her own teaching using these criteria. Over the weeks, she drew on her prior teaching and work experience, her supervisor's feedback and her PGCE theory, and grappled with how to enable student 'voice' and facilitate active student engagement. Her strategising to increase learner participation is visible and incremental in her journal as she reorganised the desks, slowed pace, modelled her expectations, worked on giving learners individual attention, encouraged use of their home language, isiXhosa, and paused to give learners time to think. Her classroom talk assignment provides evidence of her conscious reflection on how to improve her classroom talk for learning to develop her feedback turns and to ask higher order questions.

> Safia commented on the constant tension between trying to connect to the learners' present level, while not lowering expectations.

Because her mentor teacher was absent for long periods, Safia had to take responsibility for her learning and, unlike most of the participants, she had to think carefully about how to structure, sequence and select content beyond single classes. While this placed inordinate pressure on her, she used the opportunity to develop theme-based work and resources to contextualise and scaffold learning as well as to circumvent the siloed repetition within the curriculum.

At the same time, Safia reflected on her ongoing battle to create and retain appropriate boundaries:

> ... I found myself raising my voice and shouting to stay above the general noise in the classroom. ... I don't mind noise, but I could hear that students were not engaging with the work. I would like to find a way to stop the class when this happens and know what to do in order to get back on track and not feel helpless. (Safia)

Safia witnessed incidents of sexual harassment, verbal abuse and physical violence in her classroom and in the school; she was deeply critical of her own inaction and her tendency to raise her voice. After a critical incident of verbal sexual harassment, she stopped her class:

> When I returned to my class, I told them that I don't tolerate violence and that we have to try and resolve our differences without violence. I then said that I found the kissing sound [made by male students] to be violent against the female students. All of the boys strongly disagreed with me and the girls sat there silently. The boys told me that girls like it and we spent time arguing back and forth. None of the girls felt comfortable to speak but they applauded me after everything I said. The argument ended with me shouting, 'I am more than just an object for a man to use for sex'. The boys were quiet and the girls clapped loudly. I went back to teaching and everyone was quiet, but engaged. The learners were raising hands to answer questions and I thought, 'Wow, maybe I got through to them'. At the end of the lesson, as the bell went, some of the boys started making the kissing sound again. I'd like to relate this action to Resistance Theory, because I think it is an act of resistance, but I'm not sure what they are resisting. I want to address this subject again as well as violence in the practical work. (Safia)

While Safia did not manage to resolve the issues of violence and sexism, what is striking is the manner in which she persisted in developing strategies to address the issues, drawing on the concept of 'peace discipline' learnt within the PGCE to adjust boundaries and 'to model the behaviour that I wanted from learners and consistently explaining my expectations and reasons for my decisions'. She did not blame learners or construct them in deficit terms, but worked to help them to understand their behaviour and to establish boundaries. She also drew on critical pedagogy, using prescribed texts to help learners engage with how power works and to teach values. Her journal reflects enormous empathy for teachers in working-class schools, but she was also critical of their apathy, comparing them to her own teachers:

> For me, my teachers were emotionally, within my emotional life, teachers were support and my constant, and was a way for me to get out of where I was at, so if there is no constant for them either, I don't see how successful learning can happen. (Safia)

By the middle of Safia's teaching practice, students were participating actively in her classes and learners who were not registered for her subject were clamouring to attend her classes.

Conclusion

The data illuminate the challenging path that pre-service teachers navigate as they straddle multiple discourses and concomitant subject positions. I highlight the ways in which Safia, Anna and Beverley located themselves within the borders, simultaneously placing themselves in learning positions and enacting considerable agency in order to counter deficit constructions of black working-class learners. While many pre-service teachers struggled to reflect critically, these three students used reflective writing productively as a tool to construct their teaching practice as inquiry in order to understand how structural inequality worked within the school context, to negotiate contradictory discourses about teaching and learning, and to work through challenges to their values and notions of pedagogy in critical moments. They also strategised to develop pedagogy appropriate to the teaching and learning context.

The participants' processes illustrate the complexity of reflection as a literacy practice. The genre is so complex precisely because, while its starting point is the narration of (often painful) personal experience, it also requires detached evaluation and analysis which connects practice to subject disciplinary knowledge, to pedagogy and to context. In effect, it operates across domains of everyday and disciplinary ways of knowing and using language. While the everyday notion of reflection values speculation and exploration, within the discipline the personal subject position is circumscribed. In the discipline of teacher education, reflection fulfils a number of purposes and addresses multiple audiences. As Vassilaki (2017: 43) argues, it is both an academic genre and a professional development practice. While the notion of reflective writing generally implies a safe space for private contemplation, within the discipline it entails high-stakes assessment, an issue which was foregrounded by participants and which influenced how they approached the task. The hybrid nature of the genre reflects the multifaceted subject positions, the border crossing required by teaching practice. Pre-service teachers are required to assume identities as knowledgeable authority figures within their classrooms, and at the same time to place themselves in deferential positions in relation to the profession and the academy.

There is much for teacher education to learn from the way in which Safia, Anna and Beverley conceptualised reflection and reflective writing as a meaning-making process, as a tool in their process of crossing boundaries. They used the writing process to express their frustrations and emotions, to question assumptions and to situate their experiences in their classrooms and in the school and social context. Aware of their own social privilege and difference, they solicited multiple sources to make sense of their context. They observed and engaged with their peers, mentor teachers, learners and supervisors in discussions; they drew on their prior discourses and they actively sought to connect teacher education theory to practice in order to learn from the context over time. Importantly, they also reframed problems.

Rather than constructing learners as victims and lowering their expectations, they strove to develop ethical approaches to resist deficit constructions of learners, the exam-driven pedagogy and gender violence in the classroom. While they all had to deal with challenges from learners, they sought to treat their learners with respect and to understand the difficulties they faced, while maintaining the structures that would enable them to deal with large classes. Rather than confining themselves to finding neat solutions to discrete classroom problems, they took risks, positioned themselves as agents and explored possibilities for change. They actively developed appropriate ways to build learners' confidence and engagement, to develop resources, to scaffold learning, to draw on learners' linguistic resources, to build positive teaching and learning environments, to engage in critical pedagogy and to challenge their learners within the limitations of teaching practice.

> The discussion endorsed this view, with participants commenting that many students emerged from teaching practice with their stereotypes confirmed. We discussed ways to turn the journal 'from a monologue into a dialogue' through active discussion with mentors, supervisors and peers, which helps students to extract the value from their writing and challenges students' analyses and positions

The research confirms the potential for reflection to result in thin description, rationalisation/justification and instrumental, surface-level solutions rather than developing meta-awareness and questioning assumptions in order to facilitate change in practice (Loughran, 2002; Ussher & Chalmers, 2011). It is significant that Safia, Anna and Beverley all had prior academic experience of reflective writing in academic contexts. Both the interviews and the reflective writing journals demonstrate the need for engagement with reflective writing as a literacy practice which requires explicit mediation as well as practice. We need to provide sustained *in situ* support and feedback to help pre-service teachers to see the intrinsic benefit of reflection and the need for critical engagement with their positionality within school contexts. It is clear from the data that we also need to make explicit the complex, hybrid nature of the genre within the discourse of teacher education. These two goals are inextricably linked. Experience of diverse contexts has the power to enable new ways of thinking and engaging, but careful scaffolding and guidance is required to disrupt taken-for-granted norms and values and to enable meaningful, critical reflection and agency.

> The students agreed that the journal should be used in class. Beverley commented that the journal constitutes 'data' which could enrich classroom discussion and facilitate joint understanding of teaching and learning in working-class schools.

References

Anzaldúa, G. (2012 [1987]) *Borderlands/La Frontera: The New Mestiza*. San Francisco, CA: Aunt Lute Books.
Asher, N. (2009) Decolonization and education: Locating pedagogy and self at the interstices in global times. In R.S. Coloma (ed.) *Postcolonial Challenges in Education* (pp. 67–77). New York: Peter Lang.
Bangeni, B. and Kapp, R. (eds) (2017) *Negotiating Learning and Identity in Higher Education: Access, Persistence and Retention*. London: Bloomsbury.
Barton, D., Hamilton, M. and Ivanič, R. (2000) *Situated Literacies: Reading and Writing in Context*. London and New York: Routledge.
Blommaert, J. (2010) *The Sociolinguistics of Globalization*. Cambridge: Cambridge University Press.
Carrington, S. and Selva, G. (2010) Critical reflection and transformative learning: Evidence in pre-service teachers' service-learning logs. *Higher Education Research and Development* 29 (1), 45–57.
Cheung, Y., Said, S. and Park, K. (eds) (2015) *Advances and Current Trends in Language Teacher Identity Research*. London: Routledge.
Christie, P. (2005) Education for an ethical imagination. *Social Alternatives* 4 (4), 39–44.
Christie, P. (2018) Foreword. In Y. Sayed, N. Carrim, A. Badroodien, Z. McDonald and M. Singh (eds) *Learning to Teach in Post-apartheid South Africa: Student Teachers' Encounters with Initial Teacher Education* (pp. xxiii–xxvi). Stellenbosch: Sun Press.
Christie, P. and McKinney, C. (2017) Decoloniality and 'Model C' schools: Ethos, language and the protests of 2016. *Education as Change* 21 (3), 1–21.
Clark, R. and Ivanič, R. (1997) *The Politics of Writing*. London: Routledge.
Crowe, A. and Berry, A. (2007) Teaching prospective teachers about learning to think like a teacher: Articulating our principles of practice. In T. Russell and J. Loughran (eds) *Enacting a Pedagogy of Teacher Education* (pp. 31–44). London and New York: Routledge.
DHET (2015) *Revised Policy on the Minimum Requirements for Teacher Education Qualifications*. Government Gazette 596, No. 38487. Pretoria: Department of Higher Education and Training.
Donohoe, A. (2015) Reflective writing: Articulating an alternative pedagogy. *Procedia – Social and Behavioral Sciences* 186, 800–804.
Fairclough, N. (1995) *Discourse Analysis*. London and New York: Longman.

Gee, J. (1990) *Social Linguistics and Literacies: Ideology in Discourses*. London: Falmer Press.
Gelfuso, A. and Dennis, D. (2014) Getting reflection off the page: The challenges of developing support structures for pre-service teacher reflection. *Teaching and Teacher Education* 38, 1–11.
Herrington, A. and Curtis, M. (2000) *Persons in Process: Four Stories of Writing and Personal Development in College*. Urbana, IL: National Council of Teachers of English.
Hoadley-Maidment, E. (2000) From personal experience to reflective practitioner: Academic literacies and professional education. In M. Lea and B. Stierer (eds) *Student Writing in Higher Education* (pp. 165–178). Milton Keynes and Philadelphia, PA: Open University Press and Society for Research into Higher Education.
Hyland, K. (2005) Stance and engagement: A model of interaction in academic discourse. *Discourse Studies* 7, 173–192.
Hyland, K. (2011) Projecting an academic identity in some reflective genres. *Iberica* 21, 9–30.
Janks, H. (2010) *Literacy and Power*. New York and London: Routledge.
Kapp, R. (2004) 'Reading on the line': An analysis of literacy practices in ESL classes in a South African township school. *Language and Education* 8, 246–263.
Kapp, R. (2012) Students' negotiations of English and literacy in a time of social change. *JAC* 32 (3–4), 591–614.
Kapp, R. and Bangeni, B. (2009) Positioning (in) the discipline: Undergraduate students' negotiations of disciplinary disciplines. *Teaching in Higher Education* 14 (6), 587–596.
Kõrkkö, M., Kyrö-Ämmälä, O. and Turunen, T. (2016) Professional development through reflection in teacher education. *Teaching and Teacher Education* 55, 198–206.
Lea, M. and Street, B. (1998) Student writing in higher education: An academic literacies approach. *Studies in Higher Education* 23 (2), 157–172.
Leander, K. and Boldt, G. (2012) Rereading 'A Pedagogy of Multiliteracies': Bodies, texts, and emergence. *Journal of Literacy Research* 45 (1), 22–46.
Loughran, J. (2002) Effective reflective practice: In search of meaning in learning and teaching. *Journal of Teacher Education* 53 (33), 33–43.
Mendelowitz, B. (2017) Conceptualising and enacting the critical imagination through a critical writing pedagogy. *English Teaching: Practice and Critique (ETPC)* 2 (16), 178–193.
Mendelowitz, B. and Dixon, K. (2016) Risky writing: Working with a heteroglossic pedagogy to deepen pre-service teachers' learning. *Perspectives in Education* 34 (1), 120–134.
Nkambule, T. and Mukeredzi, T. (2017) Pre-service teachers' professional learning experiences during rural teaching practice in Acornhoek, Mpumalanga Province. *South African Journal of Education* 37 (3), 1–9.
Norton, B. (2000) *Identity and Language Learning: Gender, Ethnicity and Educational Change* (1st edn). London: Longman.
Rodgers, C. (2002) Defining reflection: Another look at John Dewey and reflective thinking. *Teachers College Record* 104 (4), 842–866.
Ryan, M. (2011) Improving reflective writing in higher education: A social semiotic perspective. *Teaching in Higher Education* 16 (1), 88–111.
Schön, D. (1987) *Educating the Reflective Practitioner*. San Francisco, CA: Josey-Bass.
Scott, M. (2000) Writing in postgraduate teacher training: A question of identity. In M. Lea and B. Stierer (eds) *Student Writing in Higher Education* (pp. 112–124). Milton Keynes and Philadelphia, PA: Open University Press and Society for Research into Higher Education.
Sfard, A. and Prusak, A. (2005) Telling identities: In search of an analytic tool for investigating learning as a culturally shaped activity. *Educational Researcher* 34, 14–22.

Soudien, C. (2007) The 'A' factor: Coming to terms with the question of legacy in South African education. *International Journal of Educational Development* 27, 182–193.
Thesen, L. (1997) Voices, discourse and transition: In search of new categories in EAP. *TESOL Quarterly* 31 (3), 487–511.
Thesen, L. and van Pletzen, E. (eds) (2006) *Languages of Change*. London and New York: Continuum.
Thomson, R. (2009) *Unfolding Lives: Youth, Gender and Change*. Bristol: Policy Press.
Ussher, B. and Chalmers, J. (2011) Now what? First year teachers' reflective journal writing. *Waikato Journal of Education* 16 (3), 99–110.
Vassilaki, E. (2017) Reflective writing, reflecting on identities: The construction of writer identity in student teachers' reflections. *Linguistics and Education* 42, 43–52.
Walker, M. (2010) Critical capability pedagogies and university education. *Educational Philosophy and Theory* 42 (8), 898–917.

8 Thirdspace Thinking: Expanding the Paradigm of Academic Literacies to Reposition Multilingual Pre-service Science Teachers

Soraya Abdulatief

In South African schools, the official language of instruction or language of learning and teaching (LoLT) is English or Afrikaans from Grade 4 onwards, and thus all the textbooks, written materials and assessments are only available in these two languages (see Chapter 2 on the language of instruction in South Africa). However, in poorly resourced schools (see Chapter 6 for a more detailed discussion) where African languages are spoken by teachers and learners and are the languages in daily use, science is primarily taught in an African language/English mix using a chalkboard, textbook and/or worksheet. In these schools, many without laboratories and equipment, where even a textbook is a scarce resource, science is primarily learned through memorisation and rote, with almost no experiential learning. This chapter takes a disciplinary approach to academic literacies and focuses on supporting students with their lesson plans, an academic writing genre that is specific to teacher education. Although not considered a typical academic literacies text like the essay, the writing in the lesson plan is crucial as it can directly influence classroom interaction and what the learners have access to.

Using theories of academic literacies (Lea & Street, 1998; Lillis, 2001), thirdspace (Gutiérrez, 2008; Soja, 1996) and decoloniality (Mignolo, 2007), I show the importance of multimodality and experiential learning, along with academic writing practices, in the development of science students' repertoires and identities as pre-service teachers. Further, I argue for the importance of including multiple spaces as sites of learning to support pre-service teachers' creation of interactive lesson plans, focusing in particular on the role these spaces play in developing awareness across multiple modes to create an expanded academic and science literacies repertoire. In doing so, I draw on Neely and Samura's (2011) argument that the spaces a person has access to can affect the texts she/he produces. Creating more interactive lesson plans can signal a point of development for student teachers who learned science primarily through a textbook, and how students can be encouraged towards more multimodal science teaching is discussed below.

The chapter presents a segment of the research findings of a larger project on academic literacies for multilingual postgraduate science students in a pre-service teacher education programme at the University of Cape Town. Drawing on the experiences of four pre-service science teachers (Lera, Xara, Zinzi and Kagiso) and their visits to the Cape Town Science Centre, I show how the alternative learning space provided opportunities for deeper understanding of the multimodality of science in developing students' repertoire of literacies and teaching practice. The chapter begins by arguing for the importance of multimodal and experiential learning in science education, particularly in the academic literacies initiatives offered by universities to support science students. Then, drawing on research examples, it illustrates how spaces outside of the university may offer extended learning opportunities for student teachers to engage with science.

Thirdspace, Academic Literacies and Multiple Modes

A number of South African universities provide academic literacies support for students and often institutions describe students that need support as 'underprepared' for university study because of their schooling backgrounds. This notion of students being 'underprepared' is challenged by various scholars (Fataar, 2018; O'Shea, 2016; Smit, 2012). O'Shea (2016: 61), for example, writes that 'it is important not to simply position students as problematic and instead recognise the overarching constraints that this cohort may operate within', while Fataar (2018) states that it is not that students are underprepared for university but that universities are underprepared for these students. Often the academic literacies support on offer to students may follow the dominant approach and emphasise study skills or academic socialisation which may be exclusively text based, and may also involve students learning to write outside of their academic courses (Lea & Street, 1998). Learning to write essays unrelated to subject and disciplinary areas can create more confusion and hardship for multilingual science students, who may already be facing challenges such as reading academic English or understanding practices and processes in their course. Archer (2006: 451) states that 'the overemphasis on logocentrism [in academic literacies] has led to the neglect of other modes and their interconnectedness'. She argues 'for an approach [to academic literacies] which recognises the different semiotic dimensions of representation, in other words, a multimodal approach to teaching and researching academic practices' (Archer, 2006: 449). It is not only the constraint of logocentrism and writing in English that students face when learning academic writing; they also face additional constraints on identity. Archer (2006: 451), for example, notes that 'expressions of affect in the written mode may be more suppressed and implicit than in the visual [or experiential] mode'.

While Archer (2006) and Kress (2010) call for the field of academic literacy to include modes other than the written text, the conception of science learning as multimodal and interactive has been argued by several scholars (Jewitt & Oyama, 2001; Kress *et al.*, 2001), including Jay Lemke's research and work on science education. Lemke (1998), a physicist and science educationist, argues that multimodality is important to learning and doing science, despite the scientific discipline's attempts to distance and erase the human physical body from scientific processes. In certain scientific processes, bodily sensation and experiencing the physical effects of processes form part of writing the results and reporting on the experiment. For example, one of the students in my study, Xara, during the experiment on light, commented on the fact that she could feel the battery heating.

Lemke argues that intertextuality is a feature of science and that we make sense of each item we read or hear or see partly by comparing it with other things we have read, heard or seen somewhere else (Lemke, 1998: 12). He says further that while disciplines like science and mathematics may strive for clarity and completion, these states are never really reached, as all texts continually refer to other texts during meaning-making (Lemke, 1998: 12). One example of why science has to be multimodal, says Lemke, is that:

> Natural language gives us no clue as to which is larger: seven elevenths or eight twelfths? But a geometric representation would be quite clear on this point. In general, the resources of visual representation were better able to handle matters of proportion and ratio, and complex shape, pathway, or direction of motion, than natural language. (Lemke, 1998: 16)

In order to de-link (Mignolo, 2007) from logocentrism and develop students' academic literacies, multimodality and use of multilingualism as a resource, I designed an academic literacies intervention for the pre-service science teachers in my study, working in support of and parallel to but outside of the official PGCE course. The intervention consisted of: one-to-one academic literacies sessions focused on improving students' academic writing using their coursework essays and writing assessments; introducing basic science experiments; and visiting various sites and spaces outside of the university. The site visit to the Science Centre as well as the science experiments the students conducted were designed to connect multimodal practices with the academic literacies required in the lesson plans that the students had to prepare for teaching methodology courses and for practice teaching in schools. The design of my intervention drew on thirdspace theory and thinking, viewing literacies – both academic writing and reading and scientific literacies – as interconnected and spanning several modes. It also allowed for learning outside of formal curriculum spaces.

Space and Learning

Edwards and Clark (2002: 153) explore how space influences the provision of learning opportunities and knowledge production. In answer to the question of how space influences learning and knowledge production, Soja (1996) refers to the spatial theorist, Lefebvre (1991), who states: 'To underestimate, ignore and diminish space amounts to the overestimation of texts, written matter, and writing systems, along with the readable and the visible, to the point of assigning to these a monopoly on intelligibility' (Soja, 1996: 48). Soja describes Thirdspace as 'a creative recombination and extension, one that builds on a Firstspace perspective that is focused on the "real" material world and a Secondspace perspective that interprets this reality through "imagined" representations of spatiality' (Soja, 1996: 6). This means building on and going beyond a Firstspace perspective that focuses on the 'real' material world, and a Secondspace perspective that interprets 'reality' through representations, to reach a Thirdspace of multiple 'real-and-imagined places' (Soja, 1996: 6). Thirdspace theory provides a theoretical place of 'openness' where multiple theories – in this case, academic literacies, decolonial theory, science education and the spatial – are layered and combined in an intervention that can create different and enriched conceptual and experiential iterations of learning and literacy for isiXhosa/English multilingual students. I return to this point later in the chapter.

Expanding on thirdspace theory, Scherff comments as follows:

> Moje *et al.* (2004) and Barton, Tan and Rivet (2008) summarize three perspectives on hybrid/Third space. First, such spaces can be viewed as a scaffold between academic and out-of-school (for example marginalized) knowledge. Second, third spaces can be seen in terms of how people can cross between different discourse communities. Third, third spaces can be described as places where differing beliefs, cultures, knowledge, and ways of talking come together to create both new and out-of-school knowledge. (Scherff, 2015: 82)

This approach means that academic literacies practices for pre-service science teachers need to cross between different discourses of science, education and academic literacies, and to allow for multimodal and experiential learning.

Why Do Pre-service Teachers Need Support?

Supporting the learning and development of pre-service teachers is important because, as Darling-Hammond (1996: 5) states, 'Students' right to learn is directly tied to their teachers' opportunities to learn what they need to know to teach'. Darling-Hammond observes that teachers without sufficient preparation focus on 'rote methods of learning, [are] more autocratic in the ways they manage their classrooms, less skilled at managing complex forms of instruction aimed at deeper levels of understanding, [and are] less capable of identifying children's learning styles and needs' (Darling-Hammond, 1996: 5). My intervention was designed to support pre-service science teachers from resource-poor historically black schools who had not necessarily been taught in the variety of modes that are necessary for teaching and learning science. Thus, it was important to consider how these student teachers could be supported so that they could teach a more enriched and engaging version of science education than they themselves had experienced. Part of this support was to ensure that they did not replicate the impoverished, text-based science they were taught while they were in school. But in order to teach interactively, science students first had both to learn to do science as a social activity and to learn to create lesson plans that actively engaged learners in the necessary curriculum content and the interactive and multimodal activities that learning through an enriched version of science education entailed. Teaching interactively requires planning and implementing active learning pedagogy involving multiple modes where learners interact with each other and apparatus in order to understand and enjoy science.

Guidelines on what pre-service teachers needed to know and what they needed to do during their school-based teaching practice (hereafter TP) were shared in carefully prepared department handbooks such as the Teaching Practice Handbook that the School of Education provided for students. The Teaching Practice Handbook contained samples of writing such as an example of a lesson feedback sheet given to students after a lesson was assessed during TP. The Handbook also contained an example of a supervisor's report, and an example of a journal entry written by a student. These examples allowed students to gain some understanding of the type of writing that was required for TP. The Handbook also contained the outcomes pre-service teachers should achieve and what aspects of TP students would be assessed on. In the Teaching Practice Handbook, the Outcome 1 heading states 'Plan and organize systematically and imaginatively', and this heading is followed by sub-points: 'Plan lessons and tasks which reflect knowledge and understanding by the student; show imagination, insight, and an ability to plan beyond the expected' (Teaching Practice Handbook, 2016: 9). The implicit assumption of Outcome 1 was that students understood how to create lessons and lesson plans that 'show imagination, insight, and an ability to plan beyond the expected', when what is considered imaginative, creative and unexpected is often culturally learned. This implicit cultural knowledge can differ between universities, schools and content knowledge subjects. Constructions or conceptualisations of what 'insightful' or 'imaginative' mean in education, and in science education in particular, vary widely.

The way a student interprets or misinterprets Outcome 1 – 'show imagination, insight, and an ability to plan beyond the expected' – is illustrated in the case of Xara. In an interview about her first TP experience, Xara revealed the initial disparity between her understanding of what was required in a lesson plan and what was expected by her science method lecturers. She said:

> In my lesson plans, I would be like, 'this content I understand'. 'I will do this, this way and then it will come back so well'. But 'hayi' then the marks come and it is 40% … But I worked so hard. (Xara, Interview)

Xara's words reveal her confidence in her content knowledge ('this content I understand'), but her decisions around pedagogy or learning activities ('I will do this, this way and then it will come back so well') are given a low mark of 40%, and her dismay at the result is revealed in the words, 'But I worked so hard'. Thus Xara becomes aware that there is a difference between 'knowing the content' as emphasised in her mostly textual experience of science at school, and the expectation of the lecturer marking the lesson plan who anticipates a lesson plan that employs interactive pedagogy and learning activities.

The lack of interactivity or lack of planning for active learning and interaction with learners in Xara's lesson plans resurfaced in her TP at a highly resourced elite English-medium school. In her first TP journal, on 13 April 2016, Day 6 of her TP, she reflected on teaching a Grade 9 biology lesson on the human respiratory system and its related diseases and wrote:

> The PowerPoint was full of words and there were no pictures to show the different diseases of the respiratory system. (Xara, TP1 Journal entry)

As the academic literacies facilitator, Xara's words reveal two important realisations about literacies and multimodal teaching. The first was that creating and writing out a lesson plan is one type of literacy activity, while learning to use and compose a lesson in PowerPoint is a different type of literacy activity, with its own demands and challenges. The literacy composition was thus occurring across two genres of connected texts (lesson plan and PowerPoint presentation), both of which were new to the student. Also, the literacy activity and multimodality of the lesson plan and PowerPoint were different. The lesson plan was descriptive and featured the different parts a lesson was divided into, with each section providing brief descriptions of content as well as learner activities, time allocations, materials needed, procedures and processes and lesson sequencing. The PowerPoint contained the actual subject content and instructions for activities that the learners had to perform or engage with. Each content subject had specific ways in which learners had to engage. Second, after observing the mentor teacher, Xara grew aware of the multiple modes of teaching biology and the lack thereof in her lesson is revealed in her words, 'there were no pictures to show the different diseases'. The link between teacher content and learner output was made even clearer when the students were unable to label a diagram of the respiratory system during the class exercise. Xara noted in her journal that, after the learners 'were asked to close their books and try labelling the diagram, they were unable to. For this I blame the way I insufficiently used the PowerPoint' because it lacked images and diagrams (Xara, Day 6, 13 April 2016). She realised the significance of the visual mode to biology learning and assessments and the connection between the content of the lesson plan and PowerPoint presentation and learner experience. Two days later, Xara made another realisation and on 15 April wrote in her TP1 journal, bullet point three, 'Areas of Improvement: Use of different apparatus to enhance learning', showing an awareness that she had to make the lessons more interactive and interesting.

Xara learned that she needed to add two important aspects of multimodality to her lesson plan, namely images and apparatus. This growing awareness of the multimodality of science learning was possible because Xara was at a resource-rich school and she was agentic by applying to her own lessons what she observed the mentor teachers doing.

However, Lera, another pre-service teacher who was part of the study, had a different experience during TP, since she was placed at a resource-poor school where the mentor teacher skipped the science experiments because the school had no laboratory. Lera, who was observing and following the mentor teacher's example, was not learning to teach science interactively. Lera reports:

> In Physics ne, where he [the mentor teacher] would come across that part, where they needed to perform a critical exercise, he'd be like, 'ha, just jump that part, cause we don't have um, the labs'. (Lera, Interview)

As a result Lera only came to the realisation that she needed to make learning interactive at the very end of her TP1, when her supervisor failed her and wrote 'at this level (Gr 9) you need to be practical' (Lera's TP1 lesson evaluation report). Xara came to the realisation of the multiple modes in science teaching much earlier as she observed science being taught in a resource-rich environment and thus passed TP1 successfully. As the variation in Lera's and Xara's experience showed, and as their previous failed lesson plans demonstrated, there remained a need to develop their understanding of interactive and experiential pedagogy so that they could draw on these learning experiences when they created lesson plans. There was thus a need to scaffold and develop the understanding of multilingual pre-service teachers so that they could move away from mainly text-based Initiation Response Evaluation (IRE) or Initiation Response Feedback (IRF) classroom discourse to a more experiential pedagogy (Gibbons, 2009). The students needed to learn and engage in pedagogical practices and processes that were diverse so that they could enact multimodal science in any context, regardless of whether the other teachers were able to model the behaviour for them.

Access to Material Resources: Kagiso and the Economics of Interactivity

Teaching science interactively is also a matter of economics and access to material resources that enable the teacher not only to envision but also to buy or acquire the apparatus needed. In the extract below, Kagiso and I were discussing the draft of an essay comparing his TP1 and TP2 experiences. We were discussing a TP1 lesson plan identifying problems that he solved in TP2 in order to show how he improved and developed in TP2. In the TP1 lesson on gravitational potential energy and kinetic energy, Kagiso was meant to drop a ball, showing how potential energy changes to kinetic energy, but his experiment did not work properly because he used an apple instead:

Kagiso:	It was not actually a ball. It was an apple. I had an apple on that day
Facilitator:	Oh sorry
Kagiso:	But ja, I said initially a ball but it was an apple
Facilitator:	Ok
Kagiso:	And even my Supervisor complained ... 'why did you use a ball instead of an apple?' [repeating the supervisor's question]. Just because she wanted me to let the ball fall but she couldn't do that just because I had an apple. I didn't have a ball.
Facilitator:	Ok ... oh she asked you, why you didn't use a ball because you used an apple?
Kagiso:	Ja

(Kagiso and Facilitator, TP Essay draft discussion)

Kagiso substitutes an apple for a ball, making do with what he had because he did not have the money to spend on a ball that he would only use once in his TP2. His apple does allow the learners to see the movement from potential energy to kinetic energy, in a single small demonstration; once the apple drops, it stops on the ground or may roll a little and stop. However, dropping a rubber ball to demonstrate the change in energy from potential to kinetic energy means that a longer continuous process from potential to kinetic energy is visible to the learners. Also, a ball bounces back to a lower height than it was thrown from, showing that its potential energy has decreased. Kagiso's demonstration using an apple is thus less effective than if he had used a ball. Scherff cites Barton *et al.* (2008), who note that 'What one is able to do in a setting, is dialectically related to what one can access and activate in that setting' (Scherff, 2015: 89). Although Kagiso knows that he has to participate in interactive experiential science through demonstration, he is hampered by his earlier school experiences based on text-based science as well as a lack of funds to purchase the rubber ball that he needs. His substitution of an apple makes the demonstration less effective as he cannot expand upon the demonstration by asking the learners questions about the height of the bounce nor could he allow them to feel the rubber getting warm as would have happened had he repeatedly dropped the ball. Kagiso's experience shows how 'underpreparedness' is constructed historically and economically.

Thirdspace and Remediating Pre-service Teacher Experience

In the intervention I designed, the two visits to a Science Centre played a role in providing missing information on the multiple modes of science including the many ways of enacting science, using materials and ways of demonstrating science that were new to the students. The Science Centre allowed the students to observe and develop a store of knowledge that was not completely dependent on the people (like mentor teachers) they had access to or the school placements that they were in. Jean Anyon, in one of the classic studies of inequality and stratification of schooling along social class lines, notes that public schools 'make available different types of educational experience and curriculum knowledge to students in different social classes' (Anyon, 1980: 67). Anyon also found in her study that 'the variety and amounts of teaching materials in the classrooms increased as the social class of the school population increased' (Anyon, 1980: 73). This variation in the amount of school resources is a phenomenon that was specifically racialised and engineered by apartheid and remains a reason why the majority of black schools in South Africa are severely under-resourced even two decades after apartheid. Gutiérrez argues that in the thirdspace the constraints on learning and

> the historically generated practices around schooling can be re-mediated through the reorganization of learning and pedagogy, their relationships, and cultural resources for thinking. Specifically, our focus has been on developing new tools, ... that promote new roles and activities and, thus new opportunities to extend social and cognitive development. (Gutiérrez, 2008: 156)

Using Gutiérrez's theory of thirdspace, and the idea of re-mediating school experiences, the intervention sought to change students' science learning experiences by introducing them to spaces where the diverse modes of a space/site like the Science Centre was intended to provide what Gutiérrez (2008: 156) refers to as 'cultural resources for thinking'. As mentioned earlier, thirdspace refers to 'in between spaces', 'beyond' both the physical and conceptual where different kinds of knowledge, conceptualisations and discourses meet, often transforming and transitioning to something new (Bhabha, 1994; Gutiérrez, 2008; Gutiérrez *et al.*, 1999). As facilitator, I wanted to recast the students as science practitioners able to perform practical experiments and provide deeper levels of understanding for their learners through enacting the multiple modes of science. This re-mediation and broadening of understanding science as multimodal was regarded as important for developing the academic literacies of the pre-service teachers whose lesson plans would only improve if their conceptions of both the science content and the pedagogy were developed and expanded. I thus treated the multimodal science practices and academic writing as connected. The students' improved lesson plans would be intersections of the modes of content knowledge and the textual demands of the lesson plan genre. Moreover, I sought to provide students with an understanding of science content and its multimodality that went beyond a writing consultation focused on correcting or meeting the genre requirements of a single lesson plan. From an academic literacies perspective that includes thirdspace theory, textual production involves movement to new places, spaces and kinaesthetic experiences and reading new texts.

The Science Centre (Figure 8.1) is a valuable and scarce resource for children and science learning in that it is the only one of its kind in Cape Town and one of a few in South Africa. In relation to other similar centres in the United States, for example, it would be considered miniscule, but here it plays a crucial role. The Science Centre is an open warehouse type space with white walls and exposed metal beams and 'more than 250' installations, to quote their website. It is mainly a space designed for school children, and from the children's free movement between games and installations it was clear that there were very few conventions or 'rules' that participants had to adhere to. These were explicit and visible at the entrance to the Science Centre and at a few installations that guided interaction with the apparatus. Being well located and accessible via bus and minibus taxi, the Science Centre also engaged in community outreach where schools and preschools could attend the centre for free on specific days. It also provided jobs for science students from a historically black university in the region who worked as assistants and demonstrators. The small number of African language speaking people participating in this space consisted of some students in white lab coats, the service staff who

Figure 8.1 Site visit to the Science Centre

Figure 8.2 Xara and Lera view the Marvels exhibit at the Science Centre

worked as cleaning staff, security persons, assistants at the café and the pre-service student teachers. To facilitate the students' visit I sponsored their entrance fee and we drove together to the centre. I also wanted to direct students' learning in this space so I provided students with a worksheet where they had to choose an activity or experiment that linked to a school curriculum content area in science and describe how they would emulate or implement the observed science for learners in a classroom setting. I asked the students to use the worksheet to guide them towards material for an imagined lesson plan. The worksheet was a way of opening up the space for the students and was meant to shift them to thinking like a teacher/researcher about how the environment could be used as a resource for teaching science. Students were able to walk around and explore the Science Centre, playing games and using apparatus.

The students (Xara and Lera) in Figure 8.2 are looking at an exhibit called 'Marvels' which featured examples of applied science that influenced and shaped modern-day living. Xara and Lera are 'marvelling' at the turning mechanism of the lipstick which allows a product to rise in a tube through rotation. By viewing the Marvels exhibit, Lera and Xara were able to read about and gain deeper knowledge of many small objects in use today such as digital watches and spark plugs that can be seen in the forefront of the photograph.

The Science Centre Visit and Personal Knowing

Xara speaks about the significance of going to the Science Centre and how that experience affected the way she experienced teaching:

The visit to the Science Center, it really helped 'cause in the last few days [of TP2], I taught the learners, it was light, visible light, and the whole experiment that they did [at the Science Centre], in terms of what you can see on a pin hole and things like that, ja it really helped, because I was able to relate to that when teaching the learners and I knew then even way before asking them to do the pin hole [clapping her hands], I knew, I knew what they were expecting to see and why and then I was able to explain it to them in more scientific terms. (Xara, Interview)

Xara's excitement at knowing on an experiential level what the outcome of the science experiment would be is expressed in the words, 'it really helped, because I was able to relate to that when teaching learners', and in her enthusiastic gestures when she clapped her hands and repeated the words 'I knew … I knew, I knew', positioning herself as confident and knowledgeable. Her experience of contrast between dark and light as well as what she observed of the demonstration created the opportunity to enact Outcome 3: 'Conduct lessons confidently on the basis of knowledge' (Teaching Practice Handbook, 2016: 9–10). Her words reveal that she now felt able to use apparatus in science experiments and that her experience allowed her to position herself as a competent knower. Xara's sense of knowing was shaped by her experience of the visible light experiment at the Science Centre. She, like the other visitors, was taken to a dark room where a few of the people standing at the back were asked to move away from the window, allowing a tiny sliver of daylight to shine through the blacked-out windows. The Science Centre assistant then directed our attention to the properties of light, that it travels in a straight line, that it can be reflected, refracted, diffused and diffracted. The assistant also explained how colour is seen. Following this experiment on light, we went into another dark room where the camera obscura was demonstrated and shown. We were also free to ask the assistants questions about the camera obscura and how it worked. Xara's textbook knowledge about light was thus enhanced through the visible light experiment and deepened with her witnessing and experiencing how light was used by the camera obscura in a darkened room to reflect the street, moving cars and buildings in real time many metres away.

By watching the assistants doing science practically, the students were able to observe and experience many examples of applied science. The following aspects were modelled: how to demonstrate scientific concepts and how to respond to learner questions in a positive way, as well as providing a practical example of how light is used by the camera obscura, an example of applied science. Visiting the Science Centre, a space she had not been in previously, allowed Xara to gain the experience she needed to teach a particular concept (visible light) successfully during her second TP. Specifically, it connected to the Outcome 1 on planning and organising imaginative lesson plans.

A Repertoire is Built by Different Experiences

Traditional ideas of development, argues Gutiérrez, are often tracked vertically through time or a curriculum; however, the notion of 'repertoires of practice' is a more expansive conceptualisation of development and includes 'forms of expertise that develop within and across an individual's practice ... this includes not only what students learn in formal learning environments such as schools, but also what they learn by participating in a range of practices outside of school' (Gutiérrez, 2008: 149). Next, I show how Xara's repertoire of scientific practice developed over time, space and modes. During a week-long workshop, 11–15 July 2016, which was part of the intervention, I had encouraged the students to take the science resource book, *Super Science Experiments* by Miles Kelly (2014), which they had used for experiments in the workshop, home for a few days to examine and link to school science content and the curriculum. The idea was to help the students think about and select content in preparation for TP2, which was going to happen a few weeks after the workshop. Xara had taken the book home for a few days to have a look at the content. During the week of workshops the students did two experiments, creating an electromagnet and lighting a lightbulb. Figure 8.3 shows the conclusion to an experiment on creating an electrical circuit. Xara and Zinzi use two A4 batteries connected to aluminium foil paper to conduct current to a tiny lightbulb, causing it to light up.

The experiments were conducted in the morning and were followed up with a visit to the Science Centre in the afternoon. On the second visit to the Science Centre, Xara and the other students experienced the visible light demonstration in the dark room. Weeks later, in her lesson plan shown in the top half of the image in Figure 8.4, Xara draws on both the science book and her experience at the Science Centre. The demonstration was part of her lesson plan for a Grade 8 science class on visible light in TP2. The image shows a photo from the book and a screenshot of Xara's lesson plan.

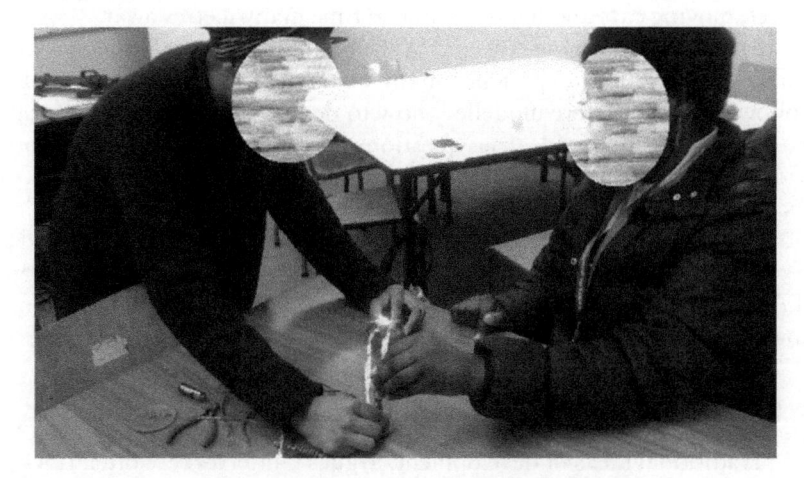

Figure 8.3 Xara and Zinzi perform the electric circuit experiment

Arguably, then, it was a combination of the practical experiments the students did in the workshops with me as facilitator, viewing and reading experiments about light in Miles Kelly's book *Super Science Experiments* (Component 1), as well as the experience of participating in the visible light experiment at the Science Centre (Component 2) that provided Xara with the experiences needed to move her from text-based science to demonstrating science to her learners. This shift is revealed in Component 3 of Figure 8.4, which shows the image of the lesson plan that Xara created,

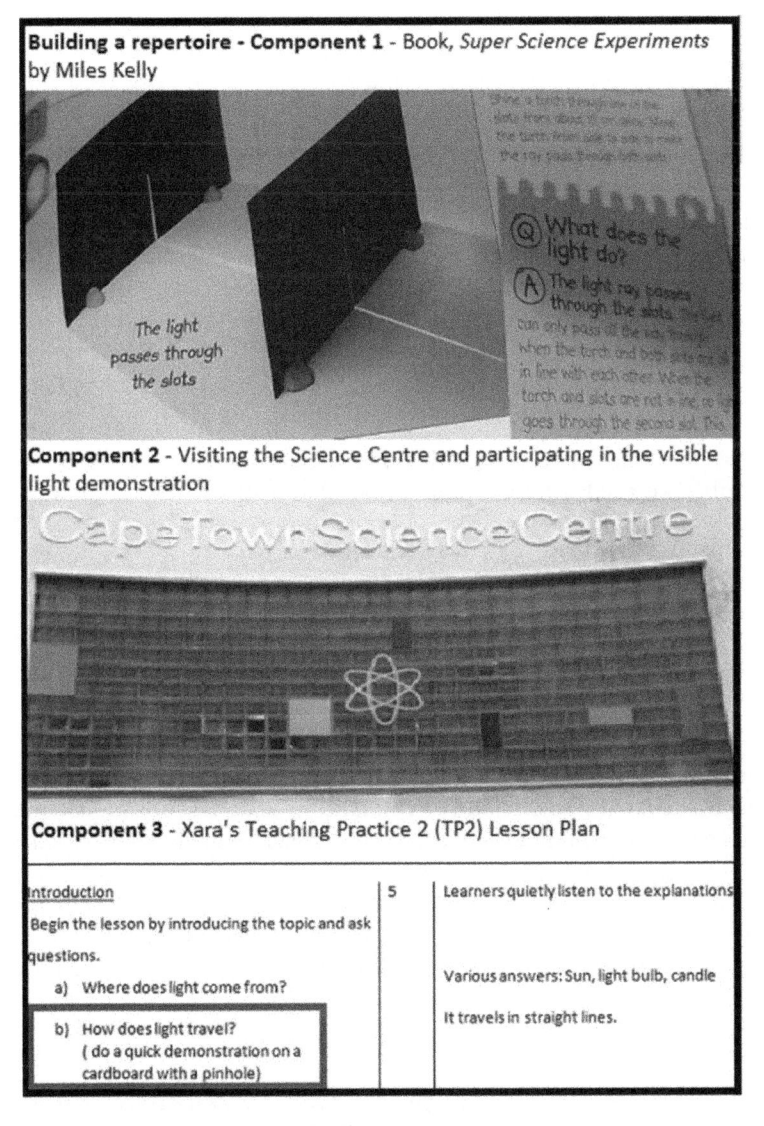

Figure 8.4 A repertoire consists of different experiences

showing how she used the light travelling through a pinhole, originally demonstrated at the Science Centre using a dark room with the windows blacked out in which a small hole was made that allowed a ray of sunlight into the dark. She replicated the experiment in the classroom by making a pinhole in cardboard and used a torch to demonstrate a property of light, namely that it travels in a straight line. Thus, Xara used the materials of the book but, instead of using slots, she used a pinhole seen in the lesson plan text above, where she wrote 'do a quick demonstration with a cardboard and a pinhole' which was similar to the experiment on visible light that she had experienced at the Science Centre.

New Spaces and their Influence on Teacher Roles

By using Gee's (1996) 'social semiotic toolkit' to bring together multiple modes, I facilitated extending students' repertoires of practice in ways that enabled them to become 'designers of their own [and their learners] social futures' (Gutiérrez, 2008: 156). Gutiérrez (2008: 150) asks the question, 'How can these experiences [in spaces students had not been in before] provoke and support new capacities [and identities] that support students' repertoires of practice?'. Zinzi's words provide some sense of how ideas about learning can shift when students are introduced to new practices and modes. When asked about the Science Centre visits, Zinzi said:

> I enjoyed the site visits because I'll be a science teacher and so obviously I will take my learners for site visits. And for me, um ... for you [the Facilitator Soraya] to take us for those site visits, they helped because you kind of showed me what I need to do when I'm teaching because we didn't go there just to walk around and go around, you also gave us worksheets isn't it so that we can sort of link our visit to what the worksheet is saying. So that was useful. Even though when the lecturer gave us an exam, something like that I couldn't answer. I don't know why, I just went blank. (Zinzi, Interview)

Even though this was Zinzi's first visit to the Science Centre, she was able to envision herself taking learners to learning sites when she said, 'I'll be a science teacher and so obviously I will take my learners for site visits'. Zinzi stated a future intent to be a teacher who values taking learners to learning spaces outside of the school classroom. Also, her five-year-old son was with her at the Science Centre and she could see his enjoyment and engagement with the artefacts and educational toys which added a personal motivation to her experience. Another learning experience that Zinzi reflected on was the use of the worksheet I had provided when she said:

> You kind of showed me what I need to do when I'm teaching because we didn't go there just to walk around and go around, you also gave us worksheets isn't it so that we can sort of link our visit to what the worksheet is saying. So that was useful. (Zinzi, Interview)

Zinzi clearly recognised the aim of the worksheets, which was to turn the Science Centre visit into a guided learning experience for the students. My intention was to link the practical applied scientific examples at the Science Centre to creating practical and creative lesson plans, using the worksheet to make this connection.

What I Learned as a Facilitator: Student Feedback on the Worksheet

Although the students seemed to enjoy the Science Centre visit, their encounter at the Centre was not homogeneous. This variation in experience was revealed in the discussion or feedback session on the Science Centre visit the following day. Although Zinzi had commented positively on the worksheet, other students had abandoned the worksheet as they went from installation to installation, trying out experiments, observing others or playing games. They needed to experience the Science Centre space for themselves first. I had seen the worksheets folded in their back pockets and realised that it was only the second time that the students had visited the Science Centre and there was much that they had not yet explored and experienced. Xara said that she had abandoned the worksheet, saying that she found it difficult to link to a specific curriculum topic since there were so many examples to choose from. Zinzi, who had been to a well-resourced school and was more familiar with experiential learning, had filled in the worksheet although she found it hard. She said 'I struggled with this' and did not complete it fully. The contradiction between wanting the students to learn (using the worksheet) and to play only became apparent to me after I saw the worksheets folded and tucked into the students' pockets. There were also words and terms on the worksheet that the students needed help with understanding that I should have explained and discussed with them.

Middle-class and wealthy learners would have started visiting the Science Centre during early childhood as evidenced by the many children under the age of 12 observed running around the Science Centre during our visit. Compared to the university students learning to be science teachers who were in their mid-20s and who had only attended the Science Centre for the second time, these children would have repeated the patterns of exploration, discovery and experience at the Science Centre many times, providing them with a store of modes and experiences that could serve as sources of knowledge.

Assessments and Outside-of-University Learning Experiences

Zinzi relates how reference to sites and site visits to spaces like the Science Centre was used during an assessment as part of a Physical Science method examination that took place when the university was reopened after the #FeesMustFall student protests. In this assessment, students had to write an explanation of how they would use a site visit to a Science Centre as a learning experience for their learners. Zinzi's reflection, 'when the lecturer gave us an exam, something like that I couldn't answer. I don't know why, I just went blank', revealed that linking learning from outside-of-university learning spaces to high-stakes assessments can be bewildering for students who have had limited or no similar experiences that they can draw upon.

A considerable amount of time had passed between Zinzi's visit to the Science Centre and when she and the other students had to answer a final examination. The visits to the Science Centre took place in July 2016, while the assessment was in November 2016 which was after TP2, the upheaval of the #FeesMustFall student protests and the university shutdown. After all these events and time, Zinzi states that 'I couldn't answer. I don't know why, I just went blank'. Zinzi's experience demonstrates how students from poorly resourced schools may be inadvertently disadvantaged by assumptions that are based on middle-class or elite values and practices established throughout childhood such as visiting spaces like a Science Centre, and how elite universities draw on specific types of cultural knowledge found in these spaces. When a visit to the Science Centre was used in the exam by the content lecturer, I learned the importance of scaffolding the worksheet and experience more carefully for the students and how students from low-resourced schools and communities are vulnerable in elite learning contexts.

Conclusion

I have tried to show through delinking (Mignolo, 2007) from logocentrism and by using 'creative recombination and extension' (Soja, 1996: 6), as well as the 're-mediation' (Gutiérrez, 2008) provided by thirdspace theory, that academic literacies support for student teachers of science demands movement into multimodal spaces outside of the university. The need for students to access different spaces is related to aligning the writing and content of the lesson plan with the disciplinary and subject requirements that science should be experiential and practical. Students visited a Science Centre to experience and observe multiple modes they could draw on when they created and wrote their lesson plans. Through a visit to a new space closely related to their field, students were positioned to learn new ways of participating in multimodal knowledge production that could improve their writing and expand their repertoires as science teachers.

The financial assistance of the National Institute for the Humanities and Social Sciences (NIHSS), in collaboration with the South African Humanities Deans Association (SAHUDA) towards this research is hereby acknowledged. Opinions expressed and conclusions arrived at are those of the author and are not necessarily to be attributed to the NIHSS and SAHUDA.

References

Anyon, J. (1980) Social class and the hidden curriculum of work. *Journal of Education* 162 (1), 67–92.

Archer, A. (2006) A multimodal approach to academic literacy practices. Problematising the visual/verbal divide. *Language and Education* 20 (6), 449–462.

Barton, A.C., Tan, E. and Rivet, A. (2008) Creating hybrid spaces for engaging school science among urban middle school girls. *American Educational Research Journal* 45 (1), 68–103.

Bhabha, H. (1994) *The Location of Culture*. London: Routledge.

Darling-Hammond, L. (1996) The quiet revolution: Rethinking teacher development. *Educational Leadership* 53 (6), 4–10.

Edwards, R. and Clark, J. (2002) Flexible learning, spatiality and identity. *Studies in Continuing Education* 24 (2), 153–165.

Fataar, A. (2018) Decolonising education in South Africa: Perspectives and debates. *Educational Research for Social Change* 7 (SPE), vi–ix.

Gee, J. (1996) *Social Linguistics and Literacies: Ideology in Discourse* (2nd edn). London: Taylor & Francis.

Gibbons, P. (2009) *English Learners Academic Literacy and Thinking: Learning in the Challenge Zone*. Portsmouth, NH: Heinemann.

Gutiérrez, K. (2008) Developing sociocritical literacy in the third space. *Reading Research Quarterly* 43 (2), 148–164.

Gutiérrez, K.D., Baquedano-Lopez, P., Tejeda, C. and Rivera, A. (1999) *Hybridity as a Tool for Understanding Literacy Learning: Building on a Syncretic Approach*. Quebec: American Educational Research Association.

Jewitt, C. and Oyama, R. (2001) Visual meaning: A social semiotic approach. In T. Van Leeuwen and C. Jewitt (eds) *The Handbook of Visual Analysis* (pp. 134–156). Thousand Oaks, CA: Sage.

Kelly, M. (2014) *Super Science Experiments*. Thaxted: Miles Kelly Publishing.

Kress, G.R. (2010) *Multimodality: A Social Semiotic Approach to Contemporary Communication*. London: Taylor & Francis.

Kress, G., Charalampos, T., Jewitt, C. and Ogborn, J. (2001) *Multimodal Teaching and Learning: The Rhetorics of the Science Classroom*. London: Bloomsbury.

Lea, M.R. and Street, B.V. (1998) Student writing in higher education: An academic literacies approach. *Studies in Higher Education* 23 (2), 157–172.

Lemke, J.L. (1998) Teaching all the languages of science: Words, symbols, images, and actions. Conference Keynote on Science Education in Barcelona.

Lillis, T.M. (2001) *Student Writing: Access, Regulation, Desire*. London: Routledge.

Mignolo, W.D. (2007) Delinking: The rhetoric of modernity, the logic of coloniality and the grammar of de-coloniality. *Cultural Studies* 21 (2–3), 449–514.

Moje, E.B., Ciechanowski, K.I., Kramer, K., Ellis, L., Carrillo, R. and Collazo, T. (2004) Working toward third space in content area literacy: An examination of everyday funds of knowledge and discourse. *Reading Research Quarterly* 39 (1), 38–70.

Neely, B. and Samura, M. (2011) Social geographies of race: Connecting race and space. *Ethnic and Racial Studies* 34 (11), 1933–1952.

O'Shea, S. (2016) Avoiding the manufacture of 'sameness': First-in-family students, cultural capital and the higher education environment. *Higher Education* 72 (1), 59–78.

Scherff, L. (2015) Service learning in third spaces: Transforming preservice English teachers. In E. Morrell and L. Scherff (eds) *New Directions in Teaching English: Reimagining Teaching Teacher Education, and Research*. New York: Rowman.

Smit, R. (2012) Towards a clearer understanding of student disadvantage in higher education: Problematising deficit thinking. *Higher Education Research & Development* 31 (3), 369–380.
Soja, E. (1996) *Thirdspace: Journeys to Los Angeles and Other Real-and-Imagined Places*. Malden, MA: Blackwell.
University of Cape Town. Graduate School of Education (2016) *Teaching Practice Handbook*. Rondebosch, South Africa.

9 Delinking from Coloniality and Increasing Participation in Early Literacy Teacher Education

Carolyn McKinney

In a conversation with interviewer Francis Wade, Kenyan scholar Ngũgĩ wa Thiongo explains that in Anglophone post-colonial spaces:

> The language of power is English and that becomes internalized, (…) You normalize the abnormal and the absurdities of colonialism, and turn them into a norm from which you operate. Then you don't even think about it. (Wade, 2018: n.p.)

One of the effects of the #RMF student protest movement at the University of Cape Town (UCT) was to force people to pay attention to how the abnormal had become and continued to be normalised in our university environment. Such normalisation processes continue to position black multilingual students as linguistically deficient while monolingual English speaking white students are positioned as linguistically adept. In my own and my collaborative teacher education work this normalising of the abnormal as a product of colonialism takes on particular significance because we are preparing teachers to teach in multilingual schooling contexts. Preparing teachers in this context thus needs to involve a repositioning of student teachers in relation to their language and schooling histories. In university classrooms where African language resources are usually invisible, we needed to convince African language speakers not just of the value, but of the necessity of their lived experience of multilingualism and of their language resources for teaching young children. On the other hand, in the case of privileged 'monolingual' English speakers, we needed them to acknowledge the gaps in their knowledge and experience, including lack of competence in African languages and lack of experience of typical schooling contexts in township and rural settings in South Africa.

Decolonial theory draws attention to the ways in which hierarchies of language and culture are crucial aspects of the colonial matrix of power (Ngũgĩ wa Thiongo, 1986). In Africa it is commonplace for colonial languages to dominate the education system and for proficiency in a European language and script to be seen as the *sole marker* of being educated. It is also the Western episteme that is largely responsible for monoglossic myths that construct monolingualism as normative in official university spaces. During protests at UCT, the deficit positioning of black students as educationally underprepared in their university classes was critiqued. This is a positioning that white students in South Africa seldom experience, with the assumption being that they have received high quality schooling and are adequately prepared for university study. However, especially given the slow pace of change in the ethos of previously white schools post-apartheid (Christie & McKinney, 2017; Soudien, 2007), there is an urgent need to also recognise the gaps in white, middle-class students' knowledge and resources that hinder them from engaging critically at university. Included in these gaps could be proficiency in African languages, consciousness of their own social positioning, including privilege, and lack of experience of typical schooling in South Africa. These potential gaps are especially significant for student teachers.

In this chapter I present a case study of one response to calls for decolonised education in a teacher education course on early literacy. One aim of the course was to foreground the multilingual resources and knowledge of our frequently marginalised African language speaking students and to enable our traditionally empowered English home language speakers to recognise the gaps in their knowledge and experience. Another aim was to prepare all students to work productively with multilingual learners in literacy learning. Activities were designed that required students to work collaboratively and multilingually across the three named languages of isiXhosa, Afrikaans and English that are dominant in our region, the Western Cape. I will present an overview of design elements of the course as well as a close analysis of the embodied responses of a smaller group of students who worked collaboratively in the course.

(De)coloniality (and Dwelling in the Borders)

The course was informed by theorising of coloniality, in particular the relationship between language and coloniality (Makalela, 2018, 2019; Ngũgĩ wa Thiongo, 1986) and the need for 'delinking' from coloniality (Mignolo, 2007), as well as for 'learning to unlearn' (Andreotti & de Souza, 2008; Tlostanova & Mignolo, 2012). In distinguishing between coloniality and colonialism, Maldonado-Torres (2007: 243) explains that coloniality describes what has survived colonialism: 'the long-standing patterns of power that emerged as a result of colonialism, but that define culture, labor, intersubjective relations, and knowledge production' in the present. Maldonado-Torres (2007: 243) reminds us that 'as modern subjects we breathe coloniality all the time and everyday'. The continuing marginalisation and invisibility of African language resources, alongside the hegemony of English, and the construction of monolingualism as the norm in a deeply multilingual society, is a powerful way in which we live and 'breathe coloniality all the time and everyday' in our education system. The exclusive valuing of English in a country where the majority of learners are African language speakers and multilingual has, as Ngũgĩ explains, become so normative as to be invisible.

It is the Western episteme that is largely responsible for monolingual myths that have underpinned research in applied linguistics and psycholinguistics (McKinney, 2017). While most children in the world grow up multilingually, theorising of language acquisition continues to assume that the typical, or normal, child is monolingual and acquires language sequentially in monolingual settings, as the ubiquitous terms 'first language acquisition' and 'second language acquisition' illustrate (Canagarajah, 2007; Ortega, 2014). Eurocentric language ideologies position monolingualism in a European language as normative and privilege monolingualism over multilingualism in 'other[ed]' languages. In South Africa, and other Anglophone contexts of coloniality, proficiency and literacy in particular forms of 'standard' English are the main markers of being educated. The dominant language ideology is *Anglonormativity*, 'the expectation that people will be and should be proficient in English and are deficient, even deviant, if they are not' (McKinney, 2017: 80). Yet, education in a foreign language or through a language in which a child is not proficient effectively removes the most valuable resource a child brings to formal schooling: their linguistic repertoire (Busch, 2017).

One of our challenges in teacher education is how to unlearn the dominant monoglossic and Anglonormative language ideologies while at the same time participating in a higher education and schooling system that reproduces and upholds these same ideologies. For Andreotti and de Souza (2008: 4), learning to unlearn is 'learning to perceive that what one considers as neutral and objective is a perspective and is related to where one is coming from socially, historically and culturally'. Unlearning involves developing recognition of language resources other than English, learning to hear/'see' African languages as resources, and learning to work multilingually. However, while we advocate bi/multilingualism in schooling and higher education, enabling children to develop their proficiencies in Indigenous African languages and English, we are aware that our students at most times have to perform as English monolinguals in the university space. It is in this sense that we position ourselves as dwelling in the borderlands (Anzaldúa, 2012 [1987]), dwelling in a space where we work multilingually to surface invisible language resources, while at the same time performing English monolingualism when required.

Coloniality, Race and Linguistic Repertoires

Working multilingually in the classroom requires students to become aware of their own and others' linguistic repertoires. Initially the concept of linguistic repertoire was coined by Gumperz to describe shared language resources among a speech community. More recently, Busch (2017) has expanded the notion of linguistic repertoire to take account of our embodied histories of language learning and use. Her notion of *spracherleben*, or the 'lived experience of language', is particularly helpful in the South African context, where the racialising effects of apartheid and its aftermath profoundly shape people's experiences of and with language use and learning. Rather than understanding repertoire as a 'set of competences' or a 'toolbox' from which we draw particular codes, Busch (2017: 355) describes linguistic repertoires as multidimensional. She sets out three distinct dimensions:

(1) interactional/anthropological, 'how we interact linguistically and socially with one another';
(2) post-structuralist or 'how we are constituted as speaking subjects by historical/political discourses'; and
(3) phenomenological or 'bodily/emotional prerequisites for speaking and experiencing language'.

This multidimensional approach thus 'interweaves social/interactive elements with historical/political and personal/biographical ones'. Significantly, language ideologies, or value-laden discourses about languages, language use and users, are active in all three dimensions. Busch (2017: 348) points out that language ideologies 'have a major influence on whether we feel that a language we speak brings respect, or whether we try to hide it from others or even to get rid of it'.

The experience of feelings of 'shame' linked to how we speak, as well as the resources in our linguistic repertoire, is one of the damaging effects of coloniality. Fanon (2017 [1952]) showed how the colonised are dehumanised through internalising myths of European superiority and exclusive use of European languages for 'legitimate' expression. Ngũgĩ wa Thiongo draws attention specifically to the ways in which the denigration of African people's language and cultural practices, their ways of knowing and being, had the effect of a 'cultural bomb':

> The biggest weapon wielded and actually daily unleashed by imperialism against that collective defiance is the cultural bomb. The effect of a cultural bomb is to annihilate a people's belief in their names, in their languages, in their environment, in their heritage of struggle, in their unity, in their capacities and ultimately in themselves. (Ngũgĩ wa Thiongo, 1986: 3)

My own research on girls' use of varieties of English in desegregated, elite schools, as well as Makoe's (2007) research on language practices and ideologies in primary schooling, have shown how children and youth express shame in relation to their language practices. For example, 16-year-old Cape Flats English speaker Sumaya positions herself deficiently in relation to her white English speaking peers:

> ok I feel like that like I hardly talk in class because of the way I normally speak like I'm scared to talk in class because of the way I speak. I speak differently from the way they do the way the rest of them do. (Sumaya)

Sumaya speaks English as her home language but feels silenced in school because she speaks a non-dominant variety of English with a non-prestigious accent. Makoe's research with children in Year 1 of schooling analyses how a learner refuses to answer her English speaking teacher's question in an African language when invited to do so because she has learned that only speaking English will garner praise and accolades (Makoe, 2007). We can also note that the children in Makoe's research in this volume declined to use languages other than English in their storytelling even though they were invited to do so (see Chapter 3, this volume). As in all of these examples, it is most often the language use of Black South Africans that is stigmatised in one way or another, either because the variety of the language used (of English or Afrikaans) does not conform to the ethnolinguistic repertoire of whiteness (Benor, 2010; McKinney, 2017) or because their Indigenous African languages are not used formally in the educational system beyond Year 3, and thus are not accorded status. As South Africans, becoming conscious of our linguistic repertoires means confronting how these are shaped by our colonial and apartheid/racialised histories, and how this is shot through with power relations. This confrontation, and understanding the way in which educational spaces are saturated with Anglonormativity, enable us to understand why a speaker's competence in a number of African languages, thus multilingualism, is less valued than monolingualism in English.

Research Methodology: Linguistic Ethnography

The teacher education course that is the site for this research focuses on how to enable students to teach early literacy and language multilingually. In a university and teacher education programme where lectures and assessments as well as prescribed reading materials are available in English only, this necessarily involves *modelling* a different kind of language and literacy practice in the classroom. The research aims both to describe and to understand/analyse what happened during the course as the lecturer worked to transform the normative interactional order from a monolingual to a multilingual one and from an order that privileged written discourse to valuing embodied and multimodal communication. Linguistic ethnography is especially well suited to addressing these aims as it enables us to look at the entanglement of macro social processes and structures and micro interactions (Copland & Creese, 2015; Lillis, 2008). A range of complementary data collection tools such as observation, audio-visual recording of naturally occurring interaction and collection of student work (artefacts) produce data that in combination make visible the interactions that unfold moment-by-moment. In describing a central insight of linguistic ethnography, Rampton and colleagues (2014: 2) write that 'language and the social world are mutually shaping, and that close analysis of situated language use can provide both fundamental and distinctive insights into the mechanisms and dynamics of social and cultural production in everyday activity'. I hope to show how the interactional order in the classroom was profoundly shaped by sociohistorical and political relations of the past, present and future.

My role was to observe and record the unfolding of the intervention. I did this through handwritten field notes, informal discussions with the lecturer, photographs of lecturer and students during the process of teaching and learning and of student-produced work, as well as audio-visual recording of some of the sessions. We did not video- or audio-record the first session, where observation was captured in field notes and a collection of documents. The lecturer, Xolisa Guzula, and I worked together on the analysis of some of the data as acknowledged below (see Abdulatief *et al.*, 2021). The course consisted of four three-hour sessions with 24 students, all of whom were completing a one-year postgraduate teacher education programme for Year 1–3 children (Grades 1–3; six to nine years of age). The main source of data in this chapter is field notes, accompanied by visual images and a transcribed student presentation.

Analysing participation

In showing how 'participation is intrinsically a situated, multi-party accomplishment' (Goodwin & Goodwin, 2001: 231), the Goodwins draw attention to its interactive nature, thus involving speakers and hearers in the joint accomplishment of participation. They also emphasise the need to pay attention to how 'speakers can adapt to the kind of engagement or disengagement their hearers display through constant adjustments of their bodies and talk'. Thus, participation must be analysed as fully embodied action. Given our aim of working multilingually and making visible marginalised language resources, a focus on student and lecturer language practices and discourses is central to the analysis. Equally important is attempting to account for participants' embodied communication through their facial expressions, gestures and stance, physical positioning in relation to each other and the materials they are presenting, as well as non-linguistic verbal cues such as laughter and hesitations. Participants' affect and their engagement is often more visible in these non-linguistic elements than it is in their words. The analysis is also inspired by Canagarajah's discussion of 'assemblage', in which he draws attention to how 'diverse semiotic resources' work in concert:

> The notion of assemblage helps us to consider how diverse semiotic resources play a collaborative role as a spatial repertoire (...) Assemblage corrects the orientation to non-verbal resources in scholars addressing 'multimodality'. From the perspective of assemblage, semiotic resources are not organised into separate modes [...] Rather [...] all modalities, including language, work together and shape each other in communication. (Canagarajah, 2018: 39)

Data Analysis: Constructing a Translingual Space

In describing and analysing one attempt to delink from the grammar of coloniality in a teacher education course, I have chosen to focus on four moments from the seminars.

Moment 1: Molweni

Seminar 1: Opening the class

> Xolisa begins by greeting the class in isiXhosa: *Molweni* [Greetings All] *Ninjani* [how are you all?] There are a few isiXhosa-English bilinguals in the room, and more in the class who have not yet arrived, but most of the students present are English dominant or English-Afrikaans bilinguals. Initially Xolisa's greeting is met with silence and then some students respond with *Ndiphilile* [I am well] and then a few self-correct with *Siphilile* [We are well]. A few students ask Xolisa '*Unjani?*' [how are you?].
>
> Xoli says '*I have to think because it's a long time ago*', then says '*Goed dankie*' [Good, thank you in Afrikaans] and students laugh at this. Xoli then asks '*are we all here?*'
>
> One student responds to Xoli in isiXhosa, explaining that some students coming from Khayelitsha are struggling with transport this morning. Xoli then introduces herself in isiXhosa, translanguaging to English, and asks the students to introduce themselves. I notice that some of the white students introduced themselves using isiXhosa. One isiXhosa/English bilingual student gave a much longer introduction in isiXhosa and telling about her family, clan name and where she comes from. (Field notes, 30 May 2017)

As an observer in the classroom, I saw a changing interactional order from the moment that the lecturer opened the class with her greeting in isiXhosa. This is likely the first time in the programme that the students would have been greeted in a language other than English in their methodology class. This may explain why there was a brief silence before students began responding to the lecturer's greeting. The lecturer then made another unexpected move by answering the students' question '*Unjani*' (how are you?) first with metacommentary in English (I have to think because it's a long time ago) and then with an appropriate reply in Afrikaans, *'goed dankie'*/good thank you. Answering in a language in which she was not confident, Xolisa positioned herself as a language learner, here of Afrikaans. She again disrupted the monolingual English norm and began to model a different kind of multilingual languaging where taking risks was to be encouraged. The students' laughter at Xolisa's answer in Afrikaans suggests that they do not associate her with this language. By way of contrast, they did not laugh at her opening greeting in isiXhosa. Racialised patterns of language use in South Africa make it unusual for fluency in Afrikaans to be included in the linguistic repertoires of African language speakers as they would have learned an African language as home language subject and English as additional language at school. The lengthy account for her peers' absence in isiXhosa that an isiXhosa speaking student gave in response to Xoli's question 'are we all here?' is also notable. This may be the student's attempt to create solidarity with the lecturer by speaking in a shared language. It also positions the lecturer as somebody who would understand the material living conditions of students who live a long distance away from campus and who struggle with public transport and taxi strikes. The longer self-introduction of another of the isiXhosa speaking students also shows how changing the language of introduction enables the student to draw on different 'ways with words', replacing the usually brief English introduction – My name is xx – with a way of locating oneself (using a family name, a clan name and giving your place of origin). This allows others to locate you within a wider community. In both cases, the isiXhosa speaking students' participation was enabled by the knowledge that their lecturer would understand both their language use and their message. Participation was thus interactively enabled and accomplished.

Moment 2: 'There are no monolinguals here'

Xolisa went on from the greetings to surfacing the language resources among the students in the room. Later on in the session, she put up a slide with the prompts:

Ndithetha...
I speak...
ek praat...
ke bua...
ngikhuluma ...

She asked the students to discuss in pairs their own language learning experiences and language resources before reporting back to the class.

> I notice that when Xolisa asks for feedback from the pairs, students seem hesitant to report back. A student from Zimbabwe explains that she can speak Shona but she cannot read it. Black students report back for

themselves or their partner's knowledge of Sesotho, isiXhosa, isiZulu, isiNdebele. White students sitting on the North side of room are quiet; one says I speak a bit of French, another says a bit of Portuguese; I can read Spanish. German and Korean are mentioned.

One student says 'Xhonglish'; Xoli writes up all the language names mentioned on newsprint including 'Xhonglish', and then adds 'Zunglish', 'Shonglish', 'Frenglish', 'Afriklish', 'Kombuistaal'. Xoli comments 'so we are very multilingual, very very multilingual here. There are no monolinguals here'. One girl responds with 'I am. I can only speak a little bit of Zulu'. And some of her colleagues comment 'and you can have a conversation in Afrikaans'. (Extract from field notes, 30 May 2017)

While Xolisa elicited from the students the named languages and varieties in their language repertoires, it was observable that not all students positioned themselves as bi/multilingual or as being able to claim proficiency in a language other than English. The student from Zimbabwe was hesitant to claim competence in Shona because she could not write the language; the spectre of shame hovered over her. Reporting of language resources was also racialised. Several white students in the class had studied Afrikaans at school for 12 years and had to pass it every year to complete their schooling, yet none of these students claimed competence in Afrikaans, never mind bilingualism. It seemed as if the students had a notion of multilingualism as linked exclusively to proficiency in African languages. We see this in the statement of one girl who responded to Xoli's affirmation that 'there are no multilinguals here' with 'I am. I can only speak a little bit of Zulu'. While her peers challenged her, saying 'and you can have a conversation in Afrikaans', she did not acknowledge her own competence in Afrikaans. This disavowal of language proficiency was not unfamiliar to me. It echoed years of experience where I have asked postgraduate students to share their language histories, and white English speakers consistently claim they are monolingual. Historical language ideologies around Afrikaans as either the language of oppression, linked as it was to Afrikaner nationalism and apartheid, or to the use of a less recognised and often stigmatised variety of Afrikaans, Kaaps, spoken on the Cape Flats in Cape Town (Antia & Dyers, 2019), play an important role in evoking feelings of shame, leading to disavowal. This confirms Busch's observation of the role language ideologies play in 'whether we feel that a language we speak brings respect, or whether we try to hide it from others or even to get rid of it' (Busch, 2017: 348).

Moment 3: Constructing definitions in three languages

Having surfaced the linguistic repertoires among the students in the room, Xoli gave the students an activity to do in groups of three or four in which they would revise one of the approaches to understanding early literacy or literacy pedagogy that they had been introduced to earlier in the year. Each group was tasked with writing a definition in the three languages, English, Afrikaans and isiXhosa, of one of the terms: emergent literacy; whole language; phonics approach; balanced approach. The activity required the students to work together across languages. The resources of isiXhosa and Afrikaans, usually invisible, became highly valued, as did speakers of these languages. Students constructed their definitions on newsprint to share with the rest of the class. In Figure 9.1, where students have produced definitions of emergent literacy, we can see evidence of a clear hierarchy among the three languages that reflects the valuing of these languages in education more broadly. English is dominant, written first and proclaiming the heading in large capital letters, while Afrikaans follows with a fairly large font size ('Oprysende Geletterdheid') and isiXhosa is squeezed in with smaller font sizes ('Iliterasi esaphuhlayo'). However, the students have made a concerted effort to explain the different aspects of their definition in the three languages and have been largely successful in doing this. The time that they

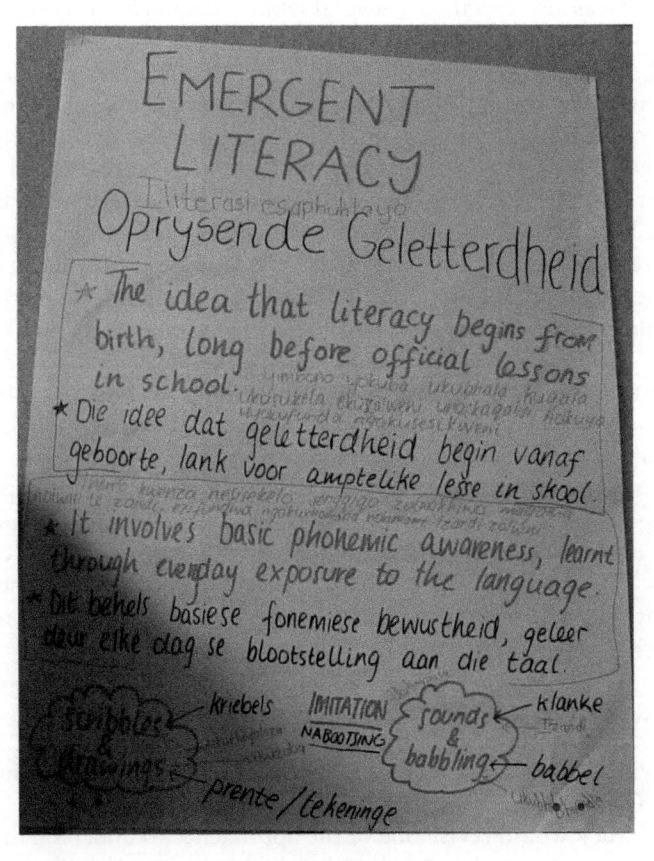

Figure 9.1 Defining 'emergent literacy' multilingually

spent grappling with meanings across three languages was significant in constructing the classroom as a multilingual space as well as constructing isiXhosa as an academic language. The way in which language resources have been represented on the newsprint simultaneously disrupts English monolingualism as normative and reproduces an ideology of language hierarchy: English, followed by Afrikaans and then isiXhosa.

Moment 4: *Mfondini awuzazi iintaka*/My friend (male) you don't know about birds.

The fourth moment I want to describe is taken from the third session in the course.

Xolisa designed the class around an oral performance that she gave of a story about a beautiful bird that brings rain. In order to decentre monolingualism, Xolisa first asked for equivalent terms for 'bird' in isiXhosa and Afrikaans and then elicited from the class their knowledge about different birds, recording the names in English, isiXhosa and Afrikaans on newsprint before eliciting relevant songs and rhymes. After her storytelling performance, Xolisa divided the class into four groups, each with a different task. Group 1 were to develop ideas for art activities related to the story and specific instructions for these. Groups 2 and 3 were tasked with developing action songs and rhymes to go with the story and drama/role play ideas and instructions, respectively. Group 4 were to develop ideas for book making and the accompanying instructions. The group work was followed by a plenary session where each group shared their ideas with the rest of the class. While Xolisa had herself been working multilingually and multimodally from the first class, she did not give specific instructions to the students that they were required to work multilingually in this activity (as had been the case with Moment 3, for example, when producing trilingual definitions, described above). It was thus interesting to see how the students continued to work multilingually to a greater or lesser extent in their groups.

One group of four female students who were to develop songs and rhymes set themselves the task of doing this multilingually and multimodally, thus taking up the pedagogy that had been modelled in the course. They began working as a group of three who were all home language English speakers with schooled knowledge of Afrikaans and very basic communicative proficiency in isiXhosa which they were currently learning during their teacher education programme. Shortly after they began, they were joined by Lisa, an isiXhosa/English bilingual student. As they were explaining the group task based on the story Xolisa had told, Lisa immediately began singing a well-known isiXhosa song about rain:

[Lisa singing] *Imvula, imvula,*
chapha chapha chapha, imanz' ilokhwe yam,

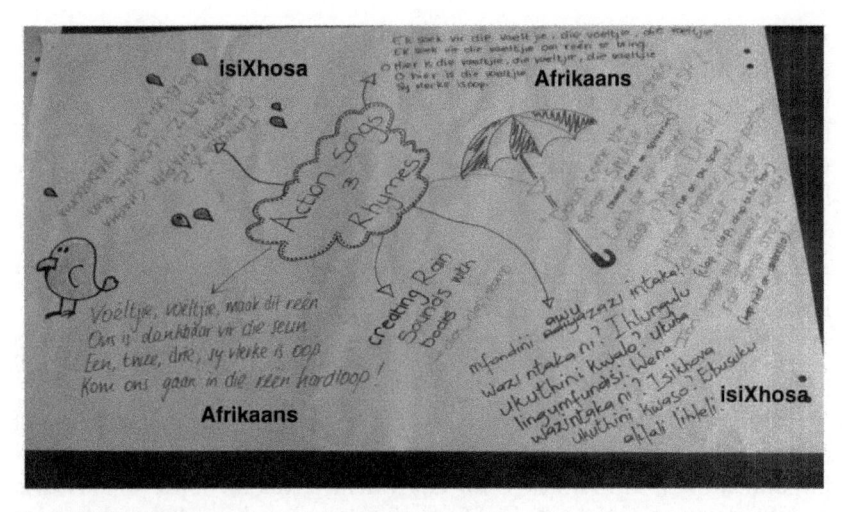

Figure 9.2 Multilingual and multimodal newsprint poster created by Group 2

chapha chapha chapha, imanz' ilokhwe yam,
gqum gqum kuyaduduma
gqum gqum kuyaduduma
imanz' ilokhwe yam, imanz' ilokhwe yam [end singing].

The group members were delighted by the song and asked Lisa to include it on the newsprint that they were preparing for their presentation to the class (see text in the top left-hand corner of Figure 9.2, 'Imvula x 2'). The group went on to create a multilingual and multimodal poster using the three distinct named languages, isiXhosa, Afrikaans and English, as can be seen in Figure 9.2. They chose not to include written translations of the songs/activities described. While the two isiXhosa songs/activities were well known to Lisa, the others were original compositions. In contrast to Figure 9.1, English, while still present, is less visibly dominant on this poster. It is used for the title in the centre and two of the six explanations.

In the group's presentation of their activities to the class, the first student performed an activity that used no verbal language but rather body percussion (stamping the feet; slapping hands on her thighs) to create the sound of rain. The students moved through presenting the isiXhosa, Afrikaans and English songs (in that order) and then concluded with the game that is described on the bottom right-hand side of the newsprint: *Mfondini awuzazi intaka* (Friend you don't know [about] birds). The extract is a transcript of Lisa's presentation of the game.
Mfondini awuzazi iintaka

1	Lisa:	And then the last is a game where they…
2	Xolisa:	You want to play it with me?
3	Lisa:	Andiva?

4	**Xolisa:**	You can play with me.
5	**Lisa:**	Ok. We can play together.
6	**Xolisa:**	Ok.
7	**Lisa:**	This one is where you are asking whether they know… what kind of the bird they know. 'Mfondini awuzazi iintaka.'
8	**Xolisa:**	'Ndiyazazi iintaka.'
9	**Lisa:**	'Wazi ntaka ni?'
10	**Xolisa:**	'Ndaz' ihlungulu.'
11	**Lisa:**	'Ukuthini kwalo?'
12	**Xolisa:**	'Uh… lifana nomfundisi, linxiba ikhola.' [X draws her hand from left hand side of her neck towards the right, gesturing a collar]
13	**Lisa:**	'Mfondini awuzazi intaka.'
14	**Xolisa:**	'Ndiyazazi iintaka.'
15	**Lisa:**	'Wazi ntaka ni?'
16	**Xolisa:**	'Uh… ndazi i… ndazi i… no… ndazi iskhova.'
17	**Lisa:**	'Ukuthini kwaso?'
18	**Xolisa:**	'Siyalala emini xa sivukile thina, siyavuka ebusuku.'
19	**Lisa:**	That's nice.

[Slight applause]

20	**Xolisa:**	So this one is a game… because the boys used to play it a lot when they go like chasing birds. And then they would test each other if they know birds. So you have to tell more about the bird. So they'll say; 'Hey you! You don't know birds.' And then the one says: 'I know a bird.'
21	**Lisa:**	'What kind of a bird is that?'
22	**Xolisa:**	'A raven.'
23	**Lisa:**	'What does it do?'
24	**Xolisa:**	'It looks like a priest. It's got a collar.' [X draws her right hand from left hand side of her neck towards the right, gesturing a collar]

[Some laughter]

26	**Lisa:**	'What else do you know about the bird? Which bird do you know?'
27	**Xolisa:**	'I know an owl.'
28	**Lisa:**	'What does it do?'
29	**Xolisa:**	'It sleeps in the day while we are awake and it wakes up in the night.' That's the game.
30	**Lisa:**	Oh!

[Applause from the class]

The activity that Lisa shared with the class was (as Xolisa explains in Turn 20) an isiXhosa game usually played by boys in rural areas and involving verbal competition; it begins with a challenge from one boy to

Figure 9.3 On the far left is Xolisa (lecturer) and facing her on far right is Lisa (student) (illustrated by Lana Manson)

another 'awuzazi iintaka/you don't know about birds'. As Lisa introduces the activity, Xolisa immediately offers her assistance, 'do you want to play it with me?', showing her recognition and knowledge of the game as well as her enthusiasm to participate with Lisa in demonstrating it for the class. Given her position as lecturer, Xolisa's joining in lends authority to Lisa's knowledge and positions her as a legitimate speaker. Xolisa sits on a chair facing Lisa while Lisa stands addressing her (see Figure 9.3). In Figure 9.3, we can see how Lisa is leaning in towards Xolisa, directly addressing her, and Xolisa's eyes are on Lisa as she waits to respond. The remaining three group members are onlookers, joining the rest of the class as audience. Xoli uses gesture alongside her verbal explanations, e.g. drawing her right hand across her neck from left to right when she says of the raven 'linxiba ikhola' [it wears a collar, Turns 12 and 20] as evidence for her claim that she knows the bird, raven (ihlungulu). Xolisa leans in towards Lisa as she speaks and Lisa walks towards and then away from Xolisa as she questions her. These bodily movements in the dialogue add to the competitive sense of the verbal game. As they end the game in isiXhosa (Turns 18–19), Xolisa goes on to give an explanation in English:

> So this one is a game… because the boys used to play it a lot when they go like chasing birds. And then they would test each other if they know birds. So you have to tell more about the bird. So they'll say; 'Hey you! You don't know birds.' And then the one says: 'I know a bird.' (Xolisa)

When Xolisa begins to describe how the dialogue would work in English, Lisa spontaneously joins in, mirroring Xoli's joining in earlier (Turns 7–8) and performing the game again with Xoli, but this time in English for the benefit of those students who don't understand the isiXhosa. The intense focus of the silent audience on Xoli and Lisa as well as their enthusiastic applause after the explanation and demonstration of the game in English is evidence of their engagement and pleasure. With the lecturer's support, Lisa was not only able to demonstrate an appropriate and engaging isiXhosa activity for the group, but was also able to extend the cultural repertoire of her peers who did not know of the game and who may well be teaching isiXhosa speaking children who do know this game. Lisa's participation using isiXhosa and her cultural repertoire enabled her to educate her peers, while Xolisa's support and joint participation with Lisa lent her knowledge authority and increased the volume of Lisa's voice, defined as the 'capacity to be heard' (Blommaert, 2005). This is a clear demonstration of the joint, interactive accomplishment of participation which highlights the significance of teachers'/lecturers' involvement in who speaks and for how long in seminars.

Conclusion

Returning to Gutiérrez' (2008: 152) definition of third space as 'a transformative space where the potential for an expanded form of learning and the development of new knowledge are heightened', I would argue that the course described in this chapter constituted such a third space. The transformative nature of the space was constituted in part by shifting from monolingual English to an explicit multilingual space where the use of a range of language resources was encouraged and where the use of the three named languages of isiXhosa, Afrikaans and English was required. Delinking from a colonial use of language, i.e. monolingual English interaction, was a necessary part of constituting third space, and a part of the first steps in an ongoing process of unlearning colonial myths about language (Makalela, 2018; see also Antia & Dyers, 2019; Hibbert & van der Walt, 2014, for innovative uses of multilingualism in South African higher education). In the different moments analysed, 'unlearning' can be seen as an active process through observation, participation and embodied communication. Learning that English monolingualism is insufficient involves unlearning the myths of the superiority and 'universal' utility of English and inferiority as well as the lack of utility of African languages. As students observed the skilful use of isiXhosa in classroom interaction, the rich cultural repertoires accompanying the language also became visible. Students who were proficient in an African language grew in their confidence to participate and to recognise the knowledge they had from their cultural repertoires which would be invaluable in teaching young children. Given the racialised nature of language proficiency in South Africa, working multilingually also meant disrupting racialised patterns of classroom participation where (mostly white) English home language speakers are more confident to contribute and hold the floor while (mostly black) African language speakers are less confident. The transformative role of the lecturer who herself modelled the affordances of working multilingually and who had knowledge to recognise cultural repertoires that are most often excluded in English monolingual spaces can also not be underestimated. The 'abnormal' of Anglonormativity can only be disrupted by working multilingually which enables othered ways of knowing, being and making meaning not only to become visible but to be recognised as essential for teaching and learning in multilingual contexts of [de]coloniality.

Making Connections/Entanglements

Editors' note: We encourage readers to use Google Translate to access the Afrikaans and isiXhosa meanings.

My own language history and linguistic repertoire is largely determined by apartheid language policy and education policy for white children, i.e. Christian National Education. Through my language use I 'live and breathe coloniality all the time and everyday' as Maldonado-Torres says and my apartheid upbringing breathes through my linguistic repertoire – English, 'suiwe' Afrikaans, and limited isiXhosa learned at university. Like the white students in this study, I learned Afrikaans as a second language at school and had to pass it every year in order to complete my 12 years of schooling. Unlike the students in this study, there was no possibility that I could learn any language other than Afrikaans, as bilingualism in Afrikaans and English was the compulsory goal for white South Africans schooled during apartheid. Partly because of anti-Afrikaans prejudice that lingered after the wars between competing colonists British and Dutch settlers in South Africa, and partly as I moved into high school and began to associate Afrikaans with apartheid and thus the language of the enemy, I strongly resisted learning the language, putting as little effort into it as possible. However, when television arrived in SA in the 1970s, the cultural boycott coupled with the state control of broadcasting meant that English and Afrikaans programming alternated daily. So if I wanted to watch popular children's programmes like 'die man van staal' en 'die man van Atlantis', ek moet dit in Afrikaans kyk. As ek by die klein winkel in ons Afrikaans gesprekende gebied van Blouwater Baai in Port Elisabet lekkers wil koop, moet ek die tannie en oom in Afrikaans groet. So ek was gedwing on Afrikaans te gebruik alhoewel ek wou nie en alhoewel ek het nie my self as tweetalig gesien nie. Soos die wit studente in die studente-onderwys klaskamer, ek vind dit nog steeds baie uncomfortable/ongemaklik om myself as tweetalig in Engels/ Afrikaans te beskruif. When I arrived at university, I was excited about the opportunity to learn an African language. It was 1991, the ANC had been unbanned and Mandela released – it was the dying days of apartheid. My isiXhosa course was more than 200 students strong and included Uncle Lionel Abrahams, respected Robben Islander who as a mature student said he wanted to learn the language of fellow islanders like Mandela. Despite the two years of isiXhosa, apartheid physical and social segregation which continues to this day prevented me from developing anything like the proficiency I have in Afrikaans. Ndidiniwe ukuthi ndithetha isiXhosa kancinci qua. Kufuneka ndiza kuzama harder kodwa ndine-excuses amanınzı, andınexesha, andinemali …. Teaching multilingualism in education has enabled me to accept my English/Afrikaans bilingualism and to appreciate that I can understand at least some of the local Afrikaans variety (Kaaps) that so many black people speak in Cape Town. It also gives me the opportunity to learn and use isiXhosa. The idea of the 'language of the enemy' resonates for me in two deeply uncomfortable ways – isiXhosa (along with other African languages) was framed as 'the language of the enemy' of the 'swart gevaar' (lit. black danger) while I grew up in white South Africa and Afrikaans was 'language of the enemy' (of apartheid regime) as I grew older. Language learning and language proficiency is deeply racialised in South Africa. In my experience of asking 100s of students about their language histories over more than 20 years, I've found white English speakers generally identify as monolingual and are largely enabled in this identification by the language ideologies in their schooling and South African society more broadly. Multilingualism it seems is only for African language speakers. My own entanglements with this positioning fuel my research, teaching and language activism.

References

Abdulatief, S., Guzula, X. and McKinney, C. (2021) Delinking from colonial language ideologies: Creating third spaces in teacher education. In Z. Bock and C. Stroud (eds) *Language and Decoloniality in Higher Education: Reclaiming Voices from the South.* London: Bloomsbury.

Andreotti, V. and de Souza, M. (2008) *Learning to Read the World through Other Eyes.* Derby: Global Education.

Antia, B. and Dyers, C. (2019) De-alienating the academy: Multilingual teaching as decolonial pedagogy. *Linguistics and Education* 51, 91–100.

Anzaldúa, G. (2012 [1987]) *Borderlands/La Frontera: The New Mestiza.* San Francisco, CA: Aunt Lute Books.

Benor, S. (2010) Ethnolinguistic repertoire: Shifting the analytic focus in language and ethnicity. *Journal of Sociolinguistics* 14 (2), 159–183.

Blommaert, J. (2005) *Discourse.* Cambridge: Cambridge University Press.

Busch, B. (2017) Expanding the notion of the linguistic repertoire: On the concept of *Spracherleben* – the lived experience of language. *Applied Linguistics* 38 (3), 340–358.

Canagarajah, A.S. (2007) Lingua franca English, multilingual communities, and language acquisition. *The Modern Language Journal* 91 (focus issue), 923–939.

Canagarajah, A.S. (2018) Translingual practice as spatial repertoires: Expanding the paradigm beyond structuralist orientations. *Applied Linguistics* 39 (1), 31–54.

Christie, P. and McKinney, C. (2017) Decoloniality and 'Model C' schools: Ethos, language and the protests of 2016. *Education as Change* 21 (3), 1–21.
Copland, F. and Creese, A. (2015) *Linguistic Ethnography: Collecting, Analysing and Presenting Data*. London: Sage.
Fanon, F. (2017 [1952]) *Black Skin White Masks*. London: Pluto Press.
Goodwin, M.H. and Goodwin, C. (2001) Emotion within situated activity. In A. Duranti (ed.) *Linguistic Anthropology: A Reader* (pp. 239–257). Chichester: Wiley-Blackwell.
Gutiérrez, K. (2008) Developing a sociocritical literacy in the third space. *Reading Research Quarterly* 43 (2), 148–164.
Hibbert, L. and van der Walt, C. (eds) (2014) *Multilingual Universities in South Africa: Reflecting Society in Higher Education*. Bristol: Multilingual Matters.
Lillis, T. (2008) Ethnography as method, methodology and 'deep theorising': Closing the gap between text and context in academic writing research. *Written Communication* 25 (3), 353–388.
Makalela, L. (2018) 'Our academics are intellectually colonised': Multi-languaging and fees must fall. *Southern African Linguistics and Applied Language Studies* 36 (1), 1–11.
Makalela, L. (2019) Community elders' narrative accounts of *Ubuntu* translanguaging: Learning and teaching in African education. *International Review of Education* 64, 823–843.
Makoe, P. (2007) Language discourses and identity construction in a multilingual South African primary school. *English Academy Review* 24 (2), 55–70.
Makoni, S. and Pennycook, A. (2007) Disinventing and reconstituting languages. In S. Makoni and A. Pennycook (eds) *Disinventing and Reconstituting Languages* (pp. 1–41). Clevedon: Multilingual Matters.
Maldonado Torres, N. (2007) On the coloniality of being: Contributions to the development of a concept. *Cultural Studies* 21 (2–3), 240–270.
McKinney, C. (2017) *Language and Power in Post-Colonial Schooling: Ideologies in Practice*. New York: Routledge.
Mignolo, W. (2007) Delinking: The rhetoric of modernity, the logic of coloniality and the grammar of de-coloniality. *Cultural Studies* 21 (2), 449–514.
Ngũgĩ wa Thiongo (1986) *Decolonising the Mind: The Language of African Literature*. London: James Currey.
Ortega, L. (2014) Ways forward for a bi/multilingual turn in SLA. In S. May (ed.) *The Multilingual Turn: Implications for SLA, TESOL and Bilingual Education* (pp. 32–53). New York and London: Routledge.
Rampton, B., Maybin, J. and Roberts, C. (2014) Methodological foundations in linguistic ethnography. Tilburg Papers in Cultural Studies No. 102.
Soudien, C. (2007) The asymmetries of contact: An assessment of 30 years of school integration in South Africa. *Race, Ethnicity and Education* 10 (4), 439–456.
Tlostanova, M. and Mignolo, W. (2012) *Learning to Unlearn: Decolonial Reflection from Eurasia and the Americas*. Columbus, OH: Ohio State University Press.
Wade, F. (2018) Ngũgĩ wa Thiongo and the tyranny of language. *New York Review of Books*, 6 August. See https://www.nybooks.com/daily/2018/08/06/ngugi-wa-thiongo-and-the-tyranny-of-language/.

10 Reinventing Literacy: Literacy Teacher Education in Contexts of Coloniality

Catherine Kell in conversation with Xolisa Guzula and Carolyn McKinney

> Catherine Kell has worked in the field of literacy studies for over 35 years, having begun her literacy work in adult education. Currently she is involved in teacher education, research and postgraduate supervision in the field. The breadth of her experience across adult education, early literacy, digital literacies and academic literacies has enabled her to develop innovative pedagogies to destabilise the prevailing deficit positioning of South African children, and their relationship to literacy, which are consequences of coloniality. Xolisa Guzula and Carolyn McKinney, as part of the younger generation of scholars in language and literacy studies, collaborated to interview Cathy about her understanding of the entanglements of literacy and coloniality in South Africa. In the interview, Cathy focuses on the 'invention' of literacy, the need for 'disinvention', and what this means for literacy teacher education.
>
> CK: Catherine Kell
> CM: Carolyn McKinney
> XG: Xolisa Guzula

Preface to the Interview

CK: By and large in South African higher education, student teachers and practising teachers come to their studies with powerful beliefs in universal ideas about literacy education and their roles in bringing such education to those who need it. They have heard the refrain from the public media about South Africa's performance in international testing regimes like the Progress in Reading Literacy Study (PIRLS). Many have had to subject their learners to such forms of testing, the results of which proclaim the dismal state of literacy education in South Africa and insist that the teachers themselves internalise the sense of deficit created by these regimes. The teachers want solutions. But, as Mamdani (2013) says, with reference to his teaching of university students in the United States, they are:

> ... like the modern counterpart of the missionaries. They are not particularly interested in the problem: they are there to give you the solution. By the time they leave the university they are imbued with a sense of what should be the solution. I always tell them that before you are unleashed upon the world let me have a chance to talk to you; get them to realise that the real question is not what's the solution, is what's the problem and the elements of any sustainable solution have to be found inside the problem. (Mamdani, 2013)

In my approach to teaching, which we focus on in the following interview, literacy itself is 'problematised'.[1] It is problematised through what Grosfoguel calls 'epistemological critique' of the invention of literacy and the possibilities for its disinvention and reinvention. It is problematised through detailed scrutiny of the students' personal experiences of, and orientations to literacy and those of others around them whose literacy practices may be quite different. As we engage in understanding these different practices (and often different literacies), we work on changing the prevailing idea that different practices are valued according to a hierarchy of values that is based on binaries such as educated/uneducated, literate/illiterate and so on.

Exploring the 'Invention of Literacy'

The invention of literacy: The development of orthographies

CM: Cathy, in preparing for this interview you talked about the decolonial context providing challenges for literacy work which are also challenges for literacy teachers. I wondered if you could talk to us a little bit about the invention of literacy and what you call the need for the 'reinvention of literacy'.

CK: I am drawing obviously on Makoni and Pennycook's (2007) concept of the 'the disinvention of languages', which I think is very relevant to the debates about delinking from coloniality, and which they elaborate on significantly in a recent book (Pennycook & Makoni, 2020). In *Disinventing and Reconstituting Languages*, Makoni and Pennycook's position is that languages are 'inventions' in that, before colonialism, people did not necessarily conceptualise their range of communicative practices as 'languages', but that after the arrival of missionaries and colonial settlers, languages started to be identified as named and distinct entities. This, in itself, contributed to the divisions of people, spaces and boundaries constructed under conditions of conquest and colonisation. Often, the processes of description and separation into named categories called languages were done by 19th century European linguists and by missionaries. And it was Europeans who constructed notions of African languages and traditions in ways that made sense to them and to their interests. The project of 'disinventing languages', then, is to understand the complex histories of language construction with a view to rethinking them and providing alternative constructions – what Makoni and Pennycook call 'reconstituting languages'.

> '... as part of any critical linguistic project, we need to disinvent and reconstitute languages [and literacy], a process that may involve becoming aware of the history of invention, and rethinking the way we look at languages [and literacies] and their relation to identity, geographical location and other social practices. Given that we acknowledge the very real contemporary effects of these inventions, our intention is not to return to some edenic pre-colonial era, but to find ways of rethinking language [and literacy] in the contemporary world.' (Makoni & Pennycook, 2005: 138, [CK's additions])

One of the problems with their argument is that it's not extended further to engage with what that means in terms of the invention and the disinvention of *literacy* (which I view as the practices involving written language). So, when I work with this idea in my teaching, I insert the words '... and literacy' or '... literacies' (as can be seen in the above quote), and I think about the 'critical linguistic project' as a way of engaging with decoloniality. They are referring to the work of Hobsbawm and Ranger (1983) on the 'invention of tradition' and Mudimbe's (1988) 'invention of Africa' when they talk about the invention of languages, but I think their use of the terms 'disinvent' and 'reconstitute' is highly generative for teaching.

In my view, there are three main threads in the idea of the 'invention of literacy' and they are all associated with ideas about universal 'truths': first, the colonial invention of literacy; second, the 'great divide' or myths about what literacy 'is' and 'does' in society; and third, the way in which literacy has become 'schooled'. The first is therefore the colonial invention of literacy which happened through the development of orthographies (writing systems) for African languages by the different missionary groups that came to southern Africa. We need to ask – what sort of understanding of language were the missionaries bringing to the development of orthography? In some cases, they did this together with local people, but often they did it themselves through the way they heard and viewed the local languages, bringing very particular understandings of orthography to the way African languages became written languages. Constructing orthographies is about how exactly the process of codification and standardisation took place as sounds were rendered in alphabetical symbols and in the combinations of symbols into syllables. So, in a sense, already, there's a kind of alienation that happens for local speakers of language because they weren't fully in charge of the ways in which their languages became written languages since it was already happening through the epistemological lenses, the morphologies and the sounds of the missionaries' languages, their forms of writing and their preconceptions about literacy. I think you've touched on that in some of your work, Xolisa, and others are starting to look at what happened in the development of those orthographies, how particular varieties were codified and became the standard.

XG: In isiXhosa, it was the Gcaleka and Rharhabe –
CK: – and the Bhaca and isiMpondo were marginalised –
XG: – the IsiHlubi, isiNtlangwini and others too.
CK: Yes, these dialects were not actually codified through writing as 'language', and one particular dialect of isiXhosa became the selected standard. So, in a sense then, if you don't see yourself in the standard written form – ... at that very material level, of the relationship between the sound and the symbol. I wonder about the effects of this –
CM: – yes, to what extent can you take hold of literacy where it's not capturing the sounds in your language?
CK: Yes, historically we don't (yet) know of any Indigenous writing systems or scripts in southern Africa. There are one or two recent attempts to construct scripts, like the isiBheqe sohlamvu in South Africa (2020) and the Mwangwego (1979; Omniglot, n.d.) in Malawi, neither of which have had much traction. But you don't have to go very far north to find a multiplicity of other writing systems through which people's languages became written, many of which were erased by colonialism as they were seen as lacking in the efficiency and precision of the Roman alphabet. A really interesting example is the writing system that was developed by the Vai people in Liberia which led Scribner and Cole (1981) to their crucial study called *The Psychology of Literacy*.[2] We also know that violent erasure of local scripts happened, for example, in other parts of the Global South when the colonisers and missionaries arrived. Writing about colonisation and languages in Latin America, Mignolo (1992: 303) says: 'Unfortunately the foundations on which European men of letters built their paradigm of the civilizing process prevented them from understanding networks of similar complexity within the Amerindian cultures'. He notes the story of one such person who when 'noticing that Nahuatl lacked seven letters was acting under the assumption that the Latin alphabet was a universal model to represent linguistic sounds and when it so happened that Nahuatl did not have all the that can be

represented by the Roman alphabet the language was at fault' (Mignolo, 1992: 345). We can therefore see that decisions about the standardisation and codification involved in developing orthographies have, and continue to give rise to passionate struggles, which are about the desire for writing to represent selves, the dream of a perfect transcription, the symbols to capture it and the ideal sound-symbol correspondences which will enable meaning to be made without reference to context. As Irvine (2019: 33) who quotes Grout (1853: 434–435) says with reference to the development of an orthography for Zulu: 'And when introducing writing to Africans, it was especially important to keep the orthography rational and orderly – unlike the disorder of English conventional spelling'.

> 'Such ambiguities, unsteadiness and inconsistency in orthography [as in English spelling conventions], are serious hindrances, among any people, to learning to read, but especially so to those whose dark, undisciplined minds are yet to receive almost the first ray of light, and the first rudiment of discipline.' (Grout, 1853: 434–435, in Irvine, 2019: 33)

XG: Maybe something else to think about is black people's agency in the writing of their own languages as well at the time. Some argue, when we bring up the arguments of languages having been invented by missionaries, they say 'But black people were not just sitting and folding hands. They were also writing'. So perhaps you are saying that we need to look into what they did in their writings, for example, people like Tiyo Soga. Often their writings were rejected if they didn't fit or conform to the standard and people like Soga were really upset that their writings were rejected.

CK: Yes, that's the kind of work I think of when I talk about disinventing and reinventing literacy: helping people understand how orthography itself involves a lot of choices and carries histories, many of which are ideologically driven and involved the erasure of certain ways of writing. In the very materiality of the way the sounds are rendered in symbols, those choices and histories are there. Doing some of that kind of excavating is crucially important to understanding literacy as a central feature in coloniality.

XG: There are people like Pumla Gqola, for example, who refuse for their names to have an H. Because 'Pumla' writes it P-U, rather than the more common P-H-U. And I have a friend, Pumza, also who refused to put an H in her name. It would be interesting also to find out why and to tell those stories as to why is it that they are refusing to add an H, for example.

CK: People might decide to write their name as M-A-T-U-T-U. However, they might decide to say it as, and understand it to mean MA-THU-THU (ashes) rather than MATUTU (which means thieves). As people make these new choices and uncover how choices have been made, we see actions that are starting to be taken that make that invisibilised history more visible.

The invention of literacy: What it is and what it does in society

CK: So, even at the level of the way that languages start to be rendered in written form, a whole baggage of ideologies is present and this brings me to the **second point**, which is that the development of literacy has been accompanied by a whole set of ideologies about what literacy *is* and what it *does* in society. These have been and are still associated with what are called 'great divide theories of literacy'. The great divide theories constructed the idea that literacy in and of itself had epochal consequences for societies and brought about the shift from primitive to civilised societies, from communitarian to individualised ways, and played a key role in instituting modernity. A foundational component of these theories is the idea that when people learn to break language down through learning writing, they develop a certain kind of higher order thinking, a sort of meta-knowledge about language as a system. The proposition is that people start to be able to see bits of language (and the things that language refer to) as parts of a system, to see language categorically, and thus they are able to develop more abstract thinking because they are implicitly finding this in the way language is written. This, of course, is an ideology of literacy and has been shown through numerous anthropological studies to be very, very questionable.

CM: Is that what's called 'the literacy myth'?

CK: Yes, this is one key tenet in the 'literacy myth', the idea that becoming literate has *cognitive consequences* in and of itself; that people can be divided into the 'advanced' who are literate with different ways of thinking due to their familiarity with alphabetical literacy and the 'primitive' who are not. And this carries very deep legacies of colonialism – its basic premises which were founded on binaries like the primitive-civilised; pre-modern-modern; divides between people, races –

XG: – as well as educated-uneducated, literate-illiterate.

CK: Yes, these are hugely powerful tropes which continue to circulate through much thinking about literacy, right through to the present.[3] Often, local people also started to take on that myth and internalise it themselves. So, in the early 1980s, when I was a literacy teacher among migrant workers in Cape Town, people would say that 'when I become literate, it's like seeing the light'.

XG: Yes, that does come out in some of your writings – how literacy is seen as enlightenment, as coming from darkness, which is colonial, of course.

CK: Absolutely, a very literal kind of enlightenment! It's tied up with religion as well – about leaving behind the kinds of belief systems that people had before the settlers and the missionaries brought Christianity, and the taking on of new sets of beliefs. In colonial contexts, the 'bringing of literacy' was very deeply intertwined with these massive social processes and was seen as central to the instantiation of the modern subject. That's one of the reasons why I always get students to read Patrick Harries' study about missionaries and Mozambican mineworkers which so clearly reveals the way in which the Swiss missionaries replicated the 'great divide' ideologies about literacy directly, but also how literacy was 'taken hold of' by the mineworkers in their own ways which were not what the missionaries expected at all![4]

> '[The missionary-anthropologist, Henri-Alexandre Junod] considered the skills of reading and writing universal ... as they were the historical product of the accumulated talents of a wide range of peoples. Junod believed that Africa's isolation from this world of reading was one of the major reasons for the continent's material backwardness. Only writing could transfer to Africa the ideas and experiences needed to engage the continent's potential. Junod felt that deciphering the characters printed on a page not only concentrated the mind and encouraged reflection; it also constituted a marker of intellectual evolution .... Junod was convinced that by immersing Africans in a written language structured by a disciplined grammar and a regular orthography, the missionaries would raise their charges to think in the manner that had led to the development of Europe.' (Harries, 2001: 410)

XG: The missionaries brought the belief that literacy is being reflective.

CK: Yes, this is a powerful theme in literacy studies, and it goes back to a particular interpretation of literacy, which is that reading the written word allows a person to reflect more deeply and personally, with a kind of interiority (this is also linked with the idea of silent reading). But that was simply an ideology that developed through particular literacy practices which were associated with forms of Christianity in Western Europe at the time, some of which were also associated with the development of Swiss Calvinism and the modernising and secularising state there (this is the strand of southern African missionary work that Harries focuses on). These entrenched the idea that a deep hermeneutic type of reading was necessary for one to be truly religious. I don't want to undermine the importance of that kind of reading for one moment, as it is very important –

CM: – but it's not the only way of reading. In fact, you have other philosophies which will say in order for deep reflection you need to rid yourself of all material objects. So, you shouldn't have any text, it should be completely internal, working within the mind.

CK: Yes, and how do we think about language and the text, then?

XG: It reminds me of coming from a Catholic Church and reading from the hymns. So, in church, people would say: 'Page 165'. And then we would sing the song. But then a critique came from the Zionist Church in our village, and the children from the Zionist Church were always teasing us, the Catholics, saying: 'Oh, you can't sing from the heart. You've got to go to a page, you've got to go to a page'. It's fascinating, now that I think about it. It's like they saw it as not something real because it came from a book.

CK: Well, it's one kind of real and this issue itself is deeply bound up with the theories of modernity and processes of representation. One is also reminded perhaps of other histories like the longstanding conflicts between what were called 'red' people and 'schooled people' in parts of the Eastern Cape, which represented the tensions between the custom-bound 'red' people and the 'schooled people' who embraced 'modernisation'.

> To understand these tensions and processes it's valuable to look at the work of writers like Mqhayi and A.C. Jordan who wrote about them at length. Mqhayi himself wrote in his preface to the famous book, *The Twins* (2020 [1914]), that the 'language and culture of the Xhosas is gradually disappearing because of the Word and the enlightenment that have come among us – which things have come with the nations of the West'.

CM: That helps us understand the invention of literacy then, and the ideologies that went with it and how those are linked to coloniality. And, of course, that's not only historical, that comes into the present day, which is, I suppose, why you are saying we need a reinvention of literacy. What might that mean? A reinvention?

CK: For me an important strategy in the work needed to delink from coloniality involves excavating that history, as I suggested earlier. Here, I am talking about the kind of research that can be done, as well as the work that can be done in teaching. First, as I've said, this problematising of literacy can involve excavating the history of the development of orthographies and the sort of alienation that people might have felt or not felt, or might still feel, in terms of how the orthography has captured their languages or not. Second, it can involve deconstructing the great divide theories and understanding how they were constructed as part of what Europe saw as its civilising mission.

XG: [In terms of this idea of reinvention] do you have something to say about literacy and the actual content of whatever is written? How are ideologies also at play in terms of the content that is being taught through literacy teaching materials that got written, for example?

The invention of literacy: The schooling of literacy

CK: Yes, and this is the **third thread** in the idea of invention, the ways in which written texts came to play a central role in what's been called the 'schooling of literacy'. Obviously, the earliest example is the Bible. It is useful to examine how particular understandings of ways of reading the Bible took hold. For the missionaries, these involved a deep and personal and individual reading between the subject and their own God, a kind of hermeneutics or exegesis, when you're supposed to do that very personal internal kind of reflection in relation to the text.[5] So, to think about how to relate this to some of the early texts in schools is important. There were very particular kinds of 'primers' or 'readers' which enshrined certain ways of taking on texts[6] and certain meanings contained in the texts –

XG: – yes, in one of Patricia Schonstein's books which is about teaching 'isiXhosa cultural grammar' (Schonstein, 1994), she gives as the very first statement, using the disjunctive spelling to fit the English orthography: 'Ii nko mo zon ke ze zi kaTixo'. In English it means 'All cows belong to God'. So, taking the cows from people could be justified through the use of the words 'Iinkomo zonke zezikaThixo' as the content of the reading!

CK: That's it! You can never separate off literacy from what content it is encoding. That's why the literacy myth cannot claim that there is a universal literacy, because alongside the obvious denotational functional are always (at minimum) the connotational and indexical functions – there always has to be something that is being written, with its associations, as well as something that is being said in the way it is written and what the text is 'pointing to'.

XG: So, if literacy was part of Christianising people, it was about erasing some of their beliefs. Of course, the content of what people themselves believed wouldn't be put in the texts, so people were having to learn new sets of knowledge at the same time.

CK: Exactly! So, there is erasure of the cultural knowledge that goes with the development of a written canon and particular ways of writing, and also in the way that writing is used to regulate practices. Because there were so few texts written in South Africa in that early period, the texts that did become written became quite influential, became about enshrining particular types of knowledge and dispositions.

XG: I know that in some of your earlier research you argued that along with the establishment of 'autonomous literacy', there is what you've called 'an evacuation of content' in teaching, and its replacement with the teaching of skills. How is this related to the erasure of cultural ways of knowing?

CK: In the form that the invention of literacy has taken, what Street (1982) called 'the autonomous model of literacy', it's possible to believe that you can teach literacy with some degree of separation from the content of what's encoded in the text. The current emphasis on phonics[7] is a great example of that and is part of the so-called 'back-to-basics' movements that have taken hold in schooling systems across the world, especially among conservative governments.[8] Along with this goes the dominant structuralist view of language that sees it as discrete units that are part of a bigger abstracted system, standing outside and above the flow of everyday communication. Such skills-based pedagogies suggest to learners that language and literacy are 'things' that need to be mastered, outside of the learners themselves. The claim is made then that these are universals about language and literacy.

At a basic level, it's quite an easy thing to believe, this idea that you can teach literacy as skills. You can see how it happens – the letter <a> is the sound <ah> and as an alphabetical symbol it's written like this <a> (although in handwriting the symbol is generally different). It seems like it's universal. But as soon as you start to look at how that <ah> or that <a> is mediated in the teaching of writing, it becomes part of a text, while it's being read or written. It's part of a word; let's take a verb starting with the sound <ah> – 'abolish'. You know, once something is entextualised, you don't get letters or parts of speech by themselves. Letters and parts of speech always come as a text. If, as a teacher, you are focusing on 'language as system' then you are immediately inserting a barrier between the meaning of the text and the engagement with it. But as soon as there's a text, there's a message, there's meaning, there's culture. So, you can't really think about those letters or parts of speech without it. As you say, the very first sentence 'Iinkomo –

XG: – zonke zezikaThixo' [laughs]. So that's also a particular way of saying that if this is how you're going to teach children at school, they will not question why the cows belong to certain people. I think now you are taking us to your work in literacy before 1994, before democracy and just afterwards, especially in adult literacy learning and critical literacy. In your study on letter-writing (Kell, 2000) you talk about the teaching of the writing of personal letters in adult literacy classes and how teaching adult literacy became so technical during the mid-1990s, so without content. Whereas literacy for unschooled people was rich in content. So, can you talk about the significance of that history and the shift that happened, for the current period?

CK: I would love to talk about that! I started as a literacy 'co-ordinator' with a literacy NGO that we set up in the early 1980s, called the Adult Learning Project, which was founded on the ideas of Paulo Freire. Freire understood literacy as reading the word and the world and so the concept of reading the world takes you immediately to a deeply cultural and political understanding of what literacy is. We saw reading and writing as enabling people to engage in political struggle, that learning to read and write was part of being able to take part in processes that are textually mediated. I was teaching adults who had never been to school. Many of them were older and had got by without really reading and writing. So, what we were enabling them to engage with were texts that helped them to understand more about their history and about the political struggle and so on, and especially to write and circulate their own stories and their own histories.[9] I now view what we were doing in enabling that kind of writing and publishing as a kind of insurgent citizenship, even though it was happening during the darkest period of apartheid.[10]

What started to happen towards the end of apartheid was that there was a massive attempt by organisations associated with what was called the mass democratic movement to develop adult education policies for those who were viewed as 'illiterate'. In this process, the currency of qualifications became important, the idea that all of those who did not go to school should now be able to get qualifications that would enable them to become more mobile. It was a very instrumental view and although the work was being done by the progressive trade unions and NGOs, it carried echoes of the earlier tropes we discussed about the development of the modern state and the instantiation of the modern subject. In this way, a very individualised and cognitive conception of literacy started to develop – if you can't read and write individually and cognitively, you're not going to be able to achieve mobility, which is part of the literacy myth again.

> 'It is estimated that about 15 million Black adults (over one third of the population) are illiterate .... The lack of access to basic education, including literacy and numeracy has consigned millions of our people to silence and marginalization from effective and meaningful participation in social and economic development.'
> (Centre for Education and Policy Development, 1994: 1)

One of the key exercises I do with my students is to present them with the story of a woman called Winnie Tsotso (see Kell, 1996) who, despite not being able to read and write, played a powerful role as a political and community leader in the informal settlement where she lived. After presenting the multiple further roles that Winnie played and the literacy practices that she engaged in through forms of mediation of the texts by those around her, I ask the students to consider whether we can say that Winnie is 'illiterate' and 'consigned to silence and marginalization'. Without exception, they say no – in fact, quite the opposite. This is one of the ways in which we problematise literacy.

CK: The myth of the cognitive consequences of literacy was all wrapped up with the huge move (which we know about from schooling as well) towards outcomes-based learning. In the mid-1990s, a whole army of people was mobilised to write outcomes for the new curriculum for the rapid formalisation of adult education. I was completely astonished at what I thought of as the hubris contained in the idea that we could boil everything down to sets of outcomes which, once attained, would have certain sets of results – how suddenly you were given the exact type of language that you should use in order to write outcomes. I am reminded of what Mignolo calls the 'hubris of the zero point' (Mignolo, 2009: 162), the assumption that one can speak from a universal, anonymous position. But in this way and suddenly, conceptions of adult literacy became schooled, became atomised and reified. In my letter-writing paper (Kell, 2000), I contrasted the teaching of letter writing in adult literacy classes with the actual letters between migrant workers and their families. I showed exactly how this took a particular form in literacy classes where literacy teachers (who would have known that what they were teaching wasn't necessarily the way that letter writing took place in communities) found themselves teaching the genre of letter writing according to a specific, Western, cultural standard.

XG: It's almost like a scripted way of teaching a letter.

CK: Completely. So, I studied a small sample of letters that migrant workers (who worked on the railways) showed me which had been sent to them by their wives in the rural areas. The children had actually written the letters for the wives and this is still a common practice in rural areas. Literacy mediation was therefore an absolutely central part of these practices. And the letters took completely different forms from what was being taught in the classroom. In the classroom, the learners were being told they had to write letters in very particular ways: they were to learn how to write their address at the top of the page and on an envelope; they were expected to use particular forms of greeting, of constructing the body of the letter and so on, to use what were called salutations –

XG: [Laughs] – and, as you showed, declarations of love!

CK: Yes, I went into the experience of 'hlonipha', which is a set of linguistic rituals followed among isiXhosa speaking married women which involve avoiding the use of terms of affect. So, deeply rooted cultural practices were being overwritten by standardised ideas of how writing should be done, even at the very intimate level of how people should write to their loved ones.

XG: So, were these teaching practices creating a binary then between schooled texts and unschooled texts?

CK: Yes, this contrasted with the kinds of writing the learners did in the Adult Learning Project before the end of apartheid. I term this kind of writing 'insurgent', where we were concerned with enabling the learners, in a sense, to write their worlds, without reference to standardised genres or writing conventions. In the letter-writing case (which was observed in around 1996 after the end of apartheid), when I interviewed the teacher, who was an isiXhosa speaker herself and who originated from a community much like the ones the railway workers were from, she was adamant that the learners had to learn the 'standard', the 'correct' way of writing letters. I am reminded of what Weth and Juffermans (2018: 15) describe as 'the tyranny of writing'.

> 'The examples of written language practices and ideologies around the written word demonstrate that writing can indeed be tyrannical. It seems that writing is rarely "tyrannical" by or in itself. Tyranny constructs, as much as it is constructed by a particular social and political order. To summarize, there are at least five ways in which writing can be tyrannical: Writing can be tyrannical in its capacity to influence speech. Standard orthography can be tyrannical when it is embedded in political power and enforced in formal education. Writing can be tyrannical – even in spoken language – as a source of prescriptive language norms. Writing can further be tyrannical when it is used as a vehicle for societal distinctions, particularization and nationalisms. Neglecting writing in education, finally, can also be tyrannical, as when learners are deprived of the resources they need to participate in their respective societies.' (Weth & Juffermans, 2018: 15)

CK: Now, I'm not wanting to suggest (and Makoni and Pennycook also caution against this in their quote at the start of this chapter) that we 'return to an edenic, pre-colonial era', nor do I think that we need to over-celebrate people's achievements without writing. But we do need to recognise that rather than looking at the ways in which literacy impacts on people we need to examine the multiplicity of ways of taking hold of literacy and recognise that these ways of 'taking hold' are highly contingent and are always embedded in deeply rooted cultural, political, historical and, above all, social, patterns. This idea of 'taking hold of literacy' has become a key theme in my work and the work of many of my students, and it leads to very different ways of understanding literacy.

I do think, though, that we have to be very careful when we talk about the schooled/unschooled binary and I have two stories that were hugely powerful learning experiences for me in this regard. There I was, this young activist, a radical Freirean, a 23-year-old white woman teaching much, much older black men and women. We followed the typical Freirean approach where we used what were called 'codes', which attempted to capture problems in people's lives which we worked on through discussion to understand the causes of the actions that could be taken, and we developed the texts for reading and writing out of those discussions. But one day one of my older learners, she must have been about 58 or so, came to me with a book in her hand. It was an ancient copy of Milton's *Paradise Lost*. She said to me: 'Cathy, this is what you must teach us. This is what we want'. There I was teaching them about the politics of bus boycotts … I mean, not teaching them [laughs], 'facilitating discussions' about the politics of bus boycotts and the history of the ANC (which was still banned at the time). And she brings me *Paradise Lost* and says: 'This is what we want'. And then one day, she also brought me a stick and she said: 'Cathy, you have to use this stick. When people don't do their homework, this is what you've got to use'. For adults! I'm supposed to use the stick on adults!

For me, these were hugely powerful and humbling moments. I could easily have dismissed them as the acts of a conservative woman, but they threw my own supposedly radical pedagogical practices and my own education into relief against the sense of loss, desire, yearning that someone like that felt for what she had never had, even though this was expressed through the surface 'signs' of it. We were trying to dismantle the extant views and pedagogies of literacy, but here I was being brought the very tools that stood for those views and pedagogies. In thinking about this, I found Audre Lorde's (1984) idea helpful when she said that 'we cannot use the master's tools to dismantle the master's house', and Mignolo and Walsh, drawing on Lewis and Jane Gordon, discuss this further in very productive ways.

> 'Slaves have historically done something more provocative with such tools than attempt to dismantle the Big House. There are those who used those tools, developed additional ones, and built houses of their own on more or less generous soil. It is our view that the proper response is to follow their lead, transcending rather than dismantling Western ideas through building our own houses of thought. When enough houses are built, the hegemony of the master's house – in fact, mastery itself – will cease to maintain its imperial status. Shelter needn't be the rooms offered by such domination.' (Lewis Gordon & Jane Gordon, in Mignolo & Walsh, 2018: 7)

I have another example from around 1995, 1996, when there was all of this policy development in education in South Africa. Everything was focused on what the new adult education system was going to *deliver* for people and in this we see the idea of the developmental state and of quite top-down forms of social engineering, which I believe have laid the basis for some of the problems we now have in South Africa. I remember talking at a well-attended policy workshop with activists about some of the work I'd been doing, and how my perspective on literacy had changed. And I remember an angry young man saying: 'So, now … you know … What is all this talk about *literacies* now? Those of us who were denied literacy under apartheid, those of you who have literacy, it must be given to us now. We need it. There is no talk about literacies. We want literacy now'. And that was also hugely powerful for me, although it was also evidence of how the reification of literacy had taken hold, often through the work of what were generally seen as progressive organisations.

XG: This argument is similar to the way to the way people still say: 'Well, we were denied English. So, we want English for our children'. Even when you try to bring other ideas about language, they say: 'No, don't deny us English –

CM: – because you've got it'.

XG: 'You've got it. So, I also want that'.

CK: Yes, so, this is part of what James Gee wrote about so powerfully and poignantly back in 1990, when he said that teachers need to accept the paradox of literacy. Janks (2004) calls it 'the access paradox'. In my work with teachers, we discuss this paradox over and over again. As teachers cognisant of the need for the reinvention of literacy but aware of the power that autonomous models hold (especially when they are entangled with the hegemony of English), and if we are to work with agency and with vision, *in the borders*, we have to do double or triple the work. Way back in 1999 (Kell, 2001), I published an article on how we needed to 'dwell', drawing on Bhabha's third space idea, in between the 'prescriptions of literacy' and the forms with which people practise reading and writing and its tangled, often sad and violent history.[11] Facing up to this complexity, on how things have come to be (rather than normative concerns about what they ought to be) involves a loss of innocence, a loss of the idea that literacy be seen as an unqualified good, and as a universal. Recognising and acknowledging the affective issues here is also part of the reinvention of literacy, in my view. Issues of affect (and embodiment), as the critique from decoloniality points out as well, are so neglected in teaching.

> 'English teachers, who take issues of language, power and identity seriously, confront the following irresolvable contradiction. If you provide more people with access to the dominant variety of the dominant language, you contribute to perpetuating and increasing its dominance. If, on the other hand, you deny students access, you perpetuate their marginalisation in a society that continues to

> recognise this language as a mark of distinction. You also deny them access to the extensive resources available in that language; resources which have developed as a consequence of the language's dominance.' (Janks, 2004: 33)

Epistemological Critique and the Challenges in Current Directions in Literacy Studies

CK: In literacy studies what can be called 'epistemological critique' (Grosfoguel, in Pennycook & Makoni, 2020: ix) to me is part of the reinvention of literacy. There have been strong traditions of such critique in South Africa in the past, but after the end of apartheid, as we discussed before, there was a need to unify the country and to build the modern state, and along with this went a need to almost recapitulate what were seen as the processes that led to modernity. So, with adult education that was seen as 'the people need to go back to school'. And I think this played some part in what's happened to the ability to critique over the past 25 years.

CM: Yes, it didn't matter what people had learnt in struggle, if they didn't have Grade 4, they were seen as not being able to participate as you said earlier, so not recognising what they had as a legitimate form of knowledge.

XG: Or knowing things that schooled people didn't know, like politics and revolution, which you are not going to learn at school.

CK: But there was also an element of fear – that in putting these so-called modern structures in place we couldn't disrupt them with too much critical engagement! The student protests from 2015 onwards and the global uprisings around Black Lives Matter have ruptured this. But I still have the sense that epistemological critique seems to have been largely evacuated from the field of literacy studies and even from education in general, in favour of superficial and self-evident folk theories of what literacy is and how it should be taught, which generally default to the psycholinguistic and cognitive approaches. I have a further story to illustrate this. At a very recent workshop on a particular approach that is being taken in early literacy work, I remember asking one very prominent university-based academic what theory of literacy he was basing his arguments on. His answer was that 'we don't need a theory of literacy'. While in a way, I completely understand how this perspective comes to be, I completely dispute it.

In the field of education in South Africa, we do have deep theorising around education in some theoretical traditions: we have what is called 'powerful knowledge' with its base in social realism; we have social constructivism and activity theory; more recently, we have the growing influence of posthumanism in education, especially in early childhood education. But these three traditions theorise literacy learning or literacy pedagogies rather than theorising literacy itself. The lack of attention to literacy in African languages that has been a key characteristic of coloniality in South Africa as well as our existing and dominant theoretical paradigms in education have thus naturalised a conception of literacy that is based largely on English literacy. This is slowly changing. We also have a very strong tradition of research and teaching in higher education in South Africa that draws on New Literacy Studies and the Academic Literacies paradigm which view literacy as social practice. These paradigms have been quicker to take on the implications of the medium of instruction debate and the politics around it.

CM: So, you had indicated that you wanted to talk about 'powerful knowledge' and about posthumanism –

CK: – yes, I think it is important to signal that in the field of early literacy (but not in the field of adult literacy) there are two different and really rather diametrically opposed paradigms that exert influence in the field of early literacy research and teaching in South Africa, at the moment. The powerful knowledge argument is based on the idea that knowledge itself has not played a central enough role in education and it theorises knowledge in a particular way, contrasting 'knowledge forms' with 'knower forms'. Knower forms are viewed as being bound up with identity and positionality, whereas, drawing on social realism, 'knowledge' forms stress the idea that there is a body of knowledge out there that people need to have access to, for example, disciplinary thinking, which involves systematic and generalisable tenets that lead to specialist knowledge, which is divergent from what is called 'everyday knowledge'. For knowledge to count as knowledge in this view, it needs to be seen to be decontextualised, and it is counterposed with 'everyday knowledge' which is seen as contextualised. And those forms of disciplinary knowledge are seen as being sequential, what Bernstein (1996) would call 'vertical knowledge structures'. The argument goes that if teaching does not enable learners and students to gain access to those kinds of knowledges, they are not going to be able to specialise and develop the ability to abstract (and of course this is associated with the idea of universals in not unproblematic ways).

There is a lot that I am sympathetic to in this argument. There is also a major critique of it from the perspective of decoloniality. But when we focus on the ways in which this approach has been taken up in the field of literacy studies, the argument starts to run into problems. There are two important problems. The first problem is the content issue. As we discussed before, written language never just refers to itself; writing always 'says something'. A clever cartoon by Sam Gross published in *The New Yorker* shows two men confronting a huge billboard with the words 'STOP AND THINK' written on it. The one man says to the other, 'It sure makes you stop and think, doesn't it?' But the irony is that you can never stop and think unless you are thinking about something. So, literacy always comes along with something else. In school literacy teaching, it always has to have some content, so literacy learning is best learnt in the context of other subjects; it is always therefore contextualised. And it always draws on everyday language as specialised forms of language, like scientific registers (which are of critical importance) are developed. In addition, there is always an interplay between what could be called 'everyday language' (although I don't like these differentiations) and the development of abstract concepts. We also know from the work of scholars like Latour that abstract concepts are always situated or contextualised, developed within particular practices. I sometimes think of this with regard to Street's (1982) 'autonomous and ideological models of literacy' – the autonomous model is always ideological in that it conceals its Eurocentrism and its situatedness. If it weren't for the extensive anthropological research done on this problem in the 1970s and 1980s and subsequently by scholars in the tradition of the New Literacy Studies, we would not have been able to deconstruct this view. So, there are many contradictions in what the powerful knowledge advocates view as important in literacy theory and teaching.

The second problem is: What disciplinary area does literacy fall under? If it is linguistics, then we know that the discipline of linguistics has bequeathed us very limited and contested conceptions of literacy which echo the *langue/parole* distinction going back to Saussure. In these, language is seen as an abstract system, consisting of elements which, when combined, make meaning. The way this has translated into current theories of literacy is through the very staged and sequenced pedagogies based on what are called the 'Big 5' (phonemic awareness, phonics, vocabulary, comprehension and fluency). Ironically, the 'powerful knowledge' approach is very critical of the notion of 'skills', but the approach to literacy most closely associated with it is the one that most rests on the Big 5 skills. The concept of literacy as staged and sequenced along a developmental trajectory is still –

CM: – very powerful – it's still there, even though there's no evidence for it [needing to be taught in that way].

XG: There is also the critique [made by those who subscribe to the powerful knowledge approach] of the role of teachers, that in the OBE [Outcomes-based Education] period, teachers were seen more as facilitators without actually or sufficiently mediating learning. The critique was that not enough actual learning was taking place.

CK: Yes, and again I have a lot of sympathy for that critique and it goes along with a critique of the 'whole language' approach, which argues that the 'knowledge' needed for literacy development (for example, the phonemic awareness and phonics which were seen as the building blocks) was not given sufficient attention by teachers. Now this can be a problem and the whole language approach can be criticised for this, but as we have argued in the bua-lit Collective (bua-lit, 2018), the binary between the Big 5 approach and the 'whole language' approach is not helpful. Literacy teaching does need overt instruction, along with systematic work on the development of specialised registers, for example. But the problem is more to do with the fact that in the building blocks approach the bigger picture of what literacy is for and what it is doing can so easily get lost. Engaging in literacy activities is not about practising meaning-making for some other time – the *real* time when meaning will need to be made. Meaning needs to be made in the here-and-now; otherwise it is hollowed out and stifled, becoming a rote practice of chanting and scribing.

CM: You also indicated that another, completely different influence in the literacy field comes from posthumanism. Can you explain that, and bring it back to the idea of reinventing literacy?

CK: The influence of posthumanism in research in early childhood studies is very evident in the US and the UK and is starting to become more evident here in South Africa. Posthumanism argues that all previous theoretical paradigms have put humans at the centre of everything in ways that have been very problematic for the planet and for the future survival of life. Posthumanists would argue that we need to de-centre humans in relation to the not-human world and the material world. The concept of the 'child' changes and the child's positioning in the world. This changes the way we understand classrooms, pedagogy and curriculum. And this then has influences on the way literacy is conceptualised, researched and perhaps taught. Again, there is much that I support in this theoretical shift, but I have also been critical of the way that issues of politics and inequality seem to have been evacuated from much of the research in early childhood education in this tradition, along with the urgent need to address our multilingual classes and often impoverished pedagogy and curriculum for literacy learning in South Africa. It may be too easy to gloss over the desperate situation in our schools, with celebrations of children's ways of being in the world and the assemblages that are created between children, texts, material objects and the natural world.

CM: So, Cathy, can we ask how we bring this back to working with teachers?

CK: So, as I've said, I think that helping teachers understand the invention of literacy and take part in its reinvention is crucial. In this, it's crucial to stress the historical, how things have come to be, and therefore how they can be changed. When I refer to the access paradox, the dilemma for literacy teachers is: How do they position themselves in this space of entanglement in order to do this complex work of translating between discourses and sets of practices? They have to engage with the children's (and adults') everyday practices and linguistic and cultural resources. But they do have to work with bringing in this new knowledge and the forms of overt instruction and having to work with reframing and transforming. So, it involves, on the one hand, working with children's existing repertoires and resources and, on the other, helping them gain access to the sort of specialised registers and texts that they need to engage with as they progress through schooling.

XG: Or perhaps how teachers become more able to defend what they're doing because many teachers aren't empowered enough to defend the practices they use. For example, they use code-switching or they translanguage in the classroom. But as soon as an official comes they feel like a small child who is going to get punished rather than stand their ground –

CK: – that is so much part of the politics of what we have been talking about! We need to understand that building the modern state and whatever required us to be certain kinds of subjects or very compliant subjects in the imperative of building the new nation-state. But the losses have been huge. And one of them is the narrowing of theoretical perspectives, leading to the limited set of perspectives that have framed our thinking about literacy and language. Literacy teachers are largely informed by the common-sense folk ideologies of literacy that I referred to earlier and are not exposed to alternative theories which can enable them to make choices in their teaching and argue for the choices they make.

But it's risky. There's always a sense of risk in the work. We have to help teachers understand that being a teacher involves risk. Because how did the teachers in the 1970s fight against apartheid and create the kinds of vibrant, critical and questioning spaces that involved the epistemological critique that I mentioned above? There were a lot of organisations that teachers belonged to in the 1970s and 1980s that helped them gain strength. And there were progressive teacher unions which were set up in opposition to the existing unions. So, teachers saw themselves as political agents in a way. I think we're starting to get a sense of that again and I do see a change in our own student group, far more questioning and challenging. And much of this has come out of processes of struggle, of the hard struggles that the student movement undertook in 2015, 2016 and 2017. I believe these struggles had a huge effect in changing consciousness, much as they did during the 1980s. So, I am hopeful that we are entering exciting times in education again.

Postscript to the interview

CK: I have aimed to pose dilemmas about how literacy and literacy teaching can be understood in relation to the range of binaries that have been characteristic of the literacy field and that are entangled in the practices and the pedagogies of reading and writing in contexts of coloniality. These include 'literacy versus orality', 'literacy versus illiteracy', 'top-down versus bottom-up approaches', 'whole language versus phonics' and so on. Since the emergence of writing in early history these binaries have preoccupied teachers, as well as philosophers, anthropologists and policy developers, and much of their work has involved the quest for a single, generalised and unified approach to understanding and researching written language and to literacy teaching. Engaging in such a search and the conception of literacy implied in it involves the epistemic injustice which erases the experiences and resources of subjects that have been racialised and are situated historically and politically. At the same time, it involves a challenge for those who disavow the single, universal and generalised approach. In teacher education, working with students around this challenge means that they, in a sense, have to engage with a loss of innocence – the idea that literacy is a reified 'thing' and that they will 'bring literacy to those who need it'. Working through the history of the ways in which literacy has been invented and working to reinvent it offers exciting challenges for futures in which all people can live in a world of literacy that values who they are, the ways in which they communicate and the multiplicity of resources they bring to all of their forms of expression, representation and communication.

Notes

(1) In the mid-1990s the concept of 'problem-solving' was circulating widely in education. This contrasted starkly with Paulo Freire's approach to literacy education which focused on the concept of 'problem-posing' and which influenced the way in which I think about problematising literacy in my teaching.

(2) Scribner and Cole's work was a crucial move in deconstructing earlier universal theories about literacy and in pointing to the importance of the concept of *practices* in literacy studies. A key issue for their study was that the same group of people made use of three different scripts – the Indigenous script of the Vai people, Arabic and the Roman alphabet.

(3) In a very recent popular article (Taylor, 2020), a well-known commentator on education in South Africa, Dr Nick Taylor, finished his article by saying: 'A government too illiterate to learn from the literature and too proud to admit its own mistakes, is doomed to repeat them, to the great detriment of taxpayers and the poor'. It is important to examine the associations that are carried by the use of the term in this way and the effects of those associations. In my teaching I get students to constantly examine and question the use of the term 'illiterate'.

(4) These ways of taking included: collective acts involving evangelical bands, lively sermons, brandishing of the Bible, recitals, learning by heart and singing aloud from it; transactional exchanges around reading and writing; the use of Biblical passages to reinforce beliefs in witchcraft or polygamy, the belief that dreams were a vehicle of divine communication and so on. In this way, they were 'reworking the missionaries' stories into their own cosmos' (Harries, 2001: 418).

(5) This does not mean that this is the way it was taken up by local people; in fact, as Harries' work shows, it was quite the opposite.

(6) Again, I wish to stress that these were not always what the 'bringers' of the texts intended. The idea that people 'take hold of' literacy in ways consistent with their own cultural, social, political and economic situations is a key tenet in the New Literacy Studies and leads us to the idea that literacy is always 'placed'.

(7) Menezes de Souza (in Makoni & Pennycook, 2007: 152) writes eloquently about this as involving the 'fetishization of the phoneme': '[the methodology which yielded the concept of the phoneme] was considered to be rational, precise and scientific, and the role of the linguist involved in the transposition of speech into writing was considered to be neutral'.

(8) Duboc and de Mello Ferraz (2020: 445) outline this within the context of changes made to literacy policy under Bolsonaro in Brazil. They quote Bolsonaro's National Literacy Secretary (who they argue is a phonics-based method aficionado), who issued a set of decrees as part of Brazil's new National Literacy Programme and claimed: 'Cognitive reading theory presents a set of robust evidence-based arguments on how people learn to read and write as it points out to the most effective reading and writing teaching methods. The NLP tends to place Brazil among the countries which have chosen science as the basis for their literacy national policies, carrying the findings of cognitive science to classrooms towards effective literacy teaching practices all over the nation'.

(9) For a description of the way we viewed literacy in the Adult Learning Project, see Karl von Holdt's (1986) article, 'Literacy and liberation: Towards a workers' school' in *South African Labour Bulletin*.

(10) The magazine we brought out was called *Ukhwelo*. It contained writing by the adult learners and only a handful of issues were produced between 1983 and 1984. Ukhwelo means 'a call' and by this we meant a call to learn. But at the same time, it is also the word used in rural areas to whistle for the cows, to call the cows home. It was very important to us that it carried that meaning as well, one that pointed to the richness of local practices.

(11) A key element in my own teaching is a deeply affective focus on students' own powerful literacy experiences and histories, in which they can write in very personal ways and use multiple modes of communication (for example, using handwriting changes the way they feel about their communication). In this work, their backgrounds and the different orientations that each of them holds, towards literacy, are revealed. We also explore the ways in which this impacts on their own ways of 'taking hold of' academic literacies and the difficulties they experience with reading and writing at university. In this way we focus on difference rather than deficit and highlight the intransigence of the academy in enabling students to find forms of expression and communication that work for them.

References

Bernstein, B. (1996) *Pedagogy, Symbolic Control and Identity: Theory, Research, Critique*. London: Taylor and Francis.

bua-lit Collective (2018) Why are we failing our children? Reconceptualising language and literacy education, accessed on 5 August 2020. https://bua-lit.org.za/our-position/ bua-lit Collective (2018) *Why Are We Failing our Children? Reconceptualising Language and Literacy Education*. See https://bua-lit.org.za/our-position/ (accessed 5 August 2020).

Centre for Education Policy Development (1994) Report of the Task Team on ABET: Adult Basic Education and Training as a Force for Social Participation and Economic Development. May, 1994.

Duboc, A.P. and de Mello Ferraz, D. (2020) What's behind a literacy war? A discursive and political analysis of the neoconservative Brazilian literacy policy. *Journal of Multicultural Discourses* 15 (4), 436–457.

Gee, J. (1990) *Social Linguistics and Literacies: Ideology in Discourses*. Abingdon: Routledge.

Harries, P. (2001) Missionaries, Marxists and magic: Power and the politics of literacy in south-east Africa. *Journal of Southern African Studies* 27 (3), 405–427.

Hobsbawm, E. and Ranger, T. (1983) *The Invention of Tradition*. Cambridge: Cambridge University Press.

Irvine, J. (2019) Minerva's orthography: Early colonial projects for print literacy in African languages. *Social Dynamics* 45 (1), 26–52.

isiBheqe Sohlamvu (2020) *Ditema Tsa Dinoko*. See https://isibheqe.org.za/ (accessed 20 August 2020).

Janks, H. (2004) The access paradox. *English in Australia* 139, 33–42.

Kell, C. (1996) Literacy practices in an informal settlement in the Cape Peninsula. In M. Prinsloo and M. Breier (eds) *The Social Uses of Literacy* (pp. 235–256). Cape Town and Amsterdam: Sached and John Benjamins.

Kell, C. (2000) Teaching letters: The recontextualisation of letter-writing practices in adult literacy classes in South Africa. In D. Barton and N. Hall (eds) *Letter Writing as Social Practice* (pp. 209–233). Amsterdam: John Benjamins.

Kell, C. (2001) Literacy, literacies and ABET: On a knife-edge, thin end of the wedge or new cutting edge? In L. Tett and J. Crowther (eds) *Powerful Literacies* (pp. 98–112). London: National Institute for Adult and Continuing Education (NIACE).

Lorde, A. (1984) *Sister Outsider*. Berkeley, CA: Crossing Press.

Makoni, S. and Pennycook, A. (2005) Disinventing and (re)constituting languages. *Critical Inquiry in Language Studies: An International Journal* 2 (3), 137–156.

Mamdani, M. (2013) *Interview with Bhakti Shringapure*. See http://www.warscapes.com/conversations/conversation-mahmood-mamdani (accessed 20 September 2020).

Menezes de Souza, T.L.M. (2007) Entering a culture quietly: Writing and cultural survival in indigenous education in Brazil. In S. Makoni and A. Pennycook (eds) *Disinventing and Reconstituting Languages* (pp. 135–169). Clevedon: Multilingual Matters.

Mignolo, W. (1992) On the colonisation of Amerindian languages and memories: Renaissance theories of writing and the discovery of the classical tradition. *Comparative Studies in Society and History* 34 (2), 301–330.

Mignolo, W. (1998) *The Darker Side of the Renaissance: Literacy, Territoriality and Colonization*. Ann Arbor, MI: University of Michigan Press.

Mignolo, W. (2009) Epistemic disobedience, independent thought and decolonial freedom. *Theory, Culture and Society* 26 (7–8), 159–181.

Mignolo, W. and Walsh, C. (2018) *On Decoloniality: Concepts, Analytics, Praxis*. Durham, NC: Duke University Press.

Mqhayi, S. (2020 [1914]) *The Lawsuit of the Twins* (T. Mabeqe, trans.). Cape Town: Oxford University Press. (Original work published in 1914 by Lovedale Press.)

Mudimbe, V. (1988) *The Invention of Africa: Gnosis, Philosophy and the Order of Knowledge*. Bloomington, IN: Indiana University Press.

Omniglot (n.d.) *Mwangwego*. See https://omniglot.com/writing/mwangwego.htm (accessed 16 August 2020).

Pennycook, A. and Makoni, S. (2020) *Innovations in Applied Linguistics from the Global South*. Abingdon: Routledge.

Schonstein, P. (1994) *Xhosa: A Cultural Grammar for Beginners*. Cape Town: African Sun Press.

Scribner, S. and Cole, M. (1981) *The Psychology of Literacy*. Cambridge, MA: Harvard University Press.

Street, B. (1982) *Literacy in Theory and Practice*. Cambridge: Cambridge University Press.

Taylor, N. (2020) School closures: A triumph of special interests over social justice. *Daily Maverick*, 27 July. See https://www.dailymaverick.co.za/opinionista/2020-07-27-school-closures-a-triumph-of-special-interests-over-social-justice/ (accessed 17 October 2020).

von Holdt, K. (1986) Literacy and liberation: Towards a workers' school. *South African Labour Bulletin*.

Weth, C. and Juffermans, K. (2018) *The Tyranny of Writing*. London and Oxford: Bloomsbury.

Part 3

Conversations with Teacher Educators in Brazil, Canada and Chile

Part 2

11 Teacher Education amid Centralising/Colonial and Decentralising/Decolonial Forces

Cloris Porto Torquato

I write here from the position of a professor whose work is included in graduate and postgraduate courses in Language Studies (focusing on teacher education) in a public Brazilian university in South Brazil.[1] Like South Africa, Brazil is a country founded on and characterised by profound inequality and social injustice. From my position, the main aspect I would like to highlight was presented by Carolyn McKinney and Pam Christie (Chapter 1, this volume) as questions:

> How might initial teacher education programmes best prepare students to work for social justice in one of the most unequal societies in the world, with a divided and variably performing schooling system of which they themselves are products? How, in times of crisis and polarisation, might the professional requirements of qualifications be met, and students from different backgrounds and with different beliefs be supported to build their knowledge for teaching and to be prepared to teach in the complex and unequal schooling system?

Despite the answers being situated and provisional, the questions enunciated by the authors in relation to South Africa are also appropriate to the Brazilian context. The colonial process – based on the racialisation, exploitation and (as a result) dehumanisation of Indigenous and Black people – made racism structural in Brazil; consequently, racism constitutes our educational system as part of Brazilian society. Racialisation was developed as the main way to categorise and dehumanise colonised people; it continues to operate in the colonial matrix of power, in coloniality. In this sense, the first question proposed by McKinney and Christie echoes as 'How might initial teacher education programmes best prepare students to work' against coloniality (of language, being, knowing and power) in this context? As the authors of the chapters showed, there are many possible answers in situated decolonial praxis. I would like to add some personal experiences lived in Brazil to the research presented by the scholars in this book and to suggest some other situated questions.

Teacher Education in the Context of the Brazilian COVID-19 Pandemic

I am writing this text one year after COVID-19 spread in Brazil. Since the first cases were identified, in March 2020, schools and universities were temporarily closed and activities suspended. Activities resumed in remote teaching-learning mode three months later, and classes returned online in August. Many teachers in schools and professors at universities felt that it was necessary to redesign our courses. It was not possible to maintain the same aims, topics, reading lists and learning activities and the same methodologies as in face-to-face courses.

Usually, I discuss the course description with my students, and we design the syllabus of the course together. While the official university course description cannot be changed, I negotiate the course syllabus with my students, departing from what is set. I ask them to read the description and to take notes of the insights and questions that they have, connecting to their experiences and knowledges developed inside and outside the academic context. They share these reflections with their classmates, and we group common questions and insights; we decide together the topics that will be added to or excluded from the outline, and the questions or themes that we are going to focus on. In 2020, however, I did not have this opportunity to work collectively and I was anxious about the online classes. Many students were excluded from classes, not having internet access. Others evaded participation because they did not feel comfortable with this online system. To avoid more students giving up, our university decided not to compel the students to follow the classes synchronously, and helped many students to get devices and internet access. Classes would be recorded and made available to students in Classroom Platform. Students could access the recorded classes at any time until the end of the academic year.

Considering this new scenario, I presented to my students a syllabus previously prepared along general lines and discussed with them any changes that they considered necessary or important. We did not have enough time or opportunity to complete the process of designing the programme. The course was called Thematic Seminars (about Brazilian schooling realities), and it was related to identities and differences in language education. I proposed to my students that we begin with attentive listening to the voices that have been silenced in our society. I suggested that they listen to, view and read Black, Indigenous, feminist and LGBTQ activists and scholars on YouTube, Instagram, Twitter, blogs and podcast platforms, reflecting on identities, social struggles in Brazilian society and education. Academic written texts would come after this first movement of attentive listening.

While most had not discussed the syllabus, one student I had taught before asked: 'If the idea is to listen attentively to some silenced voices, why don't we start by listening to our voices?'. The students present in the synchronous online class agreed with him. Therefore, I asked him to share his idea with the colleagues that were not with us, writing his proposal in the Classroom stream. He wrote the following text:

> Hello people, as discussed in the classroom, my proposal to start the work of the discipline of Thematic Seminars is to start listening to our voices. How is the experience of each one in this context of pandemic, confinement, distance learning (in the roles of teacher and student)? This is because I understand that it is a need for the students to verbalize all that they are feeling, even because everyone will be teachers – or at least they will have education for this – and these are extremely relevant issues, because how are we going to understand our students if at this moment of our training we do not understand ourselves? In the best way to think about how it will be from now on, will the classes be all online and will we have to become youtuber teachers? is it good or is it bad? are we prepared for this? or if we don't agree what will we do about it? please give your opinion.
>
> Thanks (Samuel)

Samuel's response exercises agency, as Makoe (Chapter 3, this volume) argues of some of the young storytellers. His agency was followed by another student in the Classroom chat, Murilo, who suggested that we focus on the human right to education and the exclusion of so many students. He answered Samuel's call and wrote:

> Based on Samuel's reflection on our current educational scenario, I believe it is necessary to discuss how this new form of teaching has reached students, especially those who cannot access the material disseminated through television and the internet. Considering Article 6 of the Constitution, is the right to education for ALL being respected? (Murilo)

Murilo's question dialogues with the second question posed by McKinney and Christie (Chapter 1, this volume) about supporting students from different backgrounds and with different beliefs to build their knowledge, since the student argued for the right to education and highlighted exclusion due to socioeconomic conditions. Students in elementary schools and students in undergraduate initial teacher education were being excluded from education in remarkably similar ways. Murilo highlighted that we need to listen to the point of view of students in basic (primary and secondary levels) and higher education systems about distance and remote education. His question showed that we need to prepare teachers to be sensitive to students' views and voices, to socioeconomic constraints to educational access and success, able to comprehend students' social positions and to understand education in broader social, cultural and historical contexts. Preparing sensitive teachers in this way leads us to reinforce the idea that 'actions and events are located in, and influenced by, multiple historical and socio-political contexts', as stated by Rochelle Kapp (Chapter 7, this volume), citing Donohoe (2015: 802).

The voices of these students in initial teacher education led us to understand the centrality of an education that would consider the wellbeing of students and, thus, the inseparability of mind, body, emotions and spirit (hooks, 1994). Samuel expressed 'the need to verbalise' their feelings and to understand themselves in order to understand their students in future; Murilo called our attention to students whose voices were not being heard because they could not participate in education. His question provides a glimpse of the division between those students included and those excluded and unheard. It was a challenge for us. Unfortunately, we failed in this project; we were not able to create spaces of dialogue with excluded students.

Coloniality and the Production of Hierarchies

The separation of mind, body, emotions and spirit is part of the project of modernity/coloniality, and has generated the focus of educational practices on the mind, separating knowledge from body, feelings, emotions and spirit.

> The cornerstone of Eurocentrism and scientism is the formulation of 'I think, therefore I am', by Descartes, elaborated in 1637 [...] At the time of the elaboration of the Discourse on method, Descartes inaugurates a tradition of thought that imagines itself producing universal knowledge, without bodily determinations nor geopolitical determinations. In other words, it is believed that the knowledge produced within this tradition has universal validity. (Bernardino-Costa *et al.*, 2019: 11–12)

Bodies entered the scene in the colonial context within the production of racialisation and gendering, processes of hierarchising based, above all, on race and gender/sexuality. This produced 'the dichotomous hierarchy between the human and the non-human as the central dichotomy of colonial modernity' (Lugones, 2010: 743). The production of the non-human is operated mainly as a racialisation process. According to Veronelli (2015), racialisation refers to 'the processes of dehumanization that reduce people by putting them in situations and relations that strip them of their humanity'; these processes operate through 'modern institutions, laws, treatments, practices, and desires that place those who are disfranchised in situations and relations adequate only to beings/societies who are inferior, in contrast with the superior civilized, human, colonizers' (Veronelli, 2015: 113, quoted as in original). This dichotomy of human and non-human 'was accompanied by other dichotomous hierarchical distinctions, among them that between men and women' (Lugones, 2010: 743).

Language is part of this dichotomous and hierarchical world created by coloniality, since coloniality implies hierarchising people and their knowledges, world views and practices. Languages were hierarchised as well. Languages, in the decolonial option, are seen as inseparable from knowledges, because '"Science" (knowledge and wisdom) cannot be detached from language; languages are not just "cultural" phenomena in which people find their "identity"; they are also the location where knowledge is inscribed' (Maldonado-Torres, 2007: 130).

The decolonial option emphasises the entanglement of language and knowledge. Within this perspective, Garcés (2007) proposed that the geopolitics of knowledge generated the coloniality of language, which refers, first, to the centrality of European languages and knowledge and, second, to practices of evaluating other languages and knowledges using the European[2] as the parameter of reference of the highest value, devaluing Indigenous and Black languages and knowledges. In this way, coloniality of language is constitutive of coloniality of being and knowing: '[...] the privilege of the knowledge of some has as a corollary the denial of the knowledge of others, in the same way that the affirmation of the existence of some has as a hidden side the denial of the right to life of the other' (Bernardino-Costa, 2018: 123).

Ngũgĩ wa Thiong'o (1997 [1987]) and Fanon (1967), similarly to Bakhtin (1981), see language as world view; consequently, imposing a language means imposing a world view, and denying or depriving a people of a language means depriving people of a world view or denying their world view (Torquato, 2020). Ngũgĩ wa Thiong'o (1997 [1987]: 16) emphasised this aspect: 'The domination of a people's language by the languages of the colonising nations was crucial to the domination of the mental universe of the colonised'. In this perspective, (dominant, colonial) languages carry out an essential role in dehumanising processes. Considering the role of language in racialisation and dehumanising processes, Veronelli (2015) also proposed that coloniality of language could be seen as the fourth vertex of coloniality, configuring the colonial matrix of power: coloniality of being, power, knowing and language.

Coloniality of language is characterised by: (1) hierarchising people, knowledges and languages; (2) the imposition of colonisers' languages on colonised peoples; (3) silencing and delegitimising the knowledges and languages of colonised people; and (4) hierarchising 'social languages'/heteroglossia (Bakhtin, 1981), including what have been called linguistic varieties by sociolinguistics. In this sense, monolingual ideology and standardisation ideology and practice can be seen as procedures of coloniality of language. The concept of Anglonormativity (McKinney, 2017), whose constitutive practices and effects are investigated in this book, is a process of coloniality of language.

Centralising and Decentralising Forces of Coloniality

As decoloniality emerged within and concomitant with modernity/coloniality (Walsh, 2018), decoloniality of language can be seen as the counterpart of and response to coloniality of language, as decentralising forces that resist, challenge and oppose centralising forces (Bakhtin, 1981). The unequal and constant action of these forces in the articulation of coloniality and decoloniality can be understood when we focus on the power and the violence of colonialism and the consequent maintenance of coloniality. The chapters of this book show procedures of centralising forces (coloniality) as well as processes of decentralising forces (decoloniality). Indeed, this book works as a decentralising force while exposing, analysing and contesting coloniality of language, power, being and knowing; it also operates as a decentralising force while revealing, analysing and reinforcing decolonial practices in decolonising minds and languages, not only in the language education context but in broader educational contexts.

Centralising and decentralising forces operate differently in different contexts. Since in Brazil and South Africa we suffered distinct colonial processes and we have various social, historical and cultural human organisations, our decolonial responses can and will be different. That is the reason why Ramon Grosfoguel (2015)[3] insists on highlighting that we have heterogeneous decolonial critiques and projects (in the plural), not a single decolonial project.

The decentralising forces and decolonial responses focused on by the authors and social actors in this book are situated in the South African context. In the Brazilian context, we are living in severe economic, pandemic, social and political crises and polarisations. I am writing this text when well over 400,000 people have succumbed to COVID-19 at the time of writing. Some important political leaders denied the danger of the virus, discouraged the population from mask wearing and social distancing, and encouraged them to use ineffective medicines as preventive methods or treatments for COVID-19, neglecting all recommendations and studies in health science. The COVID-19 pandemic has been politicised,[4] an object of dispute between those who support the federal government and those who oppose it.

The politicisation and polarisation of the pandemic are the most lethal polarisation that we are living, but they are not unique. We are experiencing political polarisation in many different aspects of our lives: any position against domination and exploitation based on gender, sexuality, race, ethnicity or class has been delegitimised by the government (and its supporters) as 'communism' or 'leftist'. The current federal government can be positioned as ultra-right. From this perspective, calling people 'communists'[5] is an insult that positions them as subversive, dangerous to society, perverted, sick. Many of those so-called 'communists' are, in racial and ethnic aspects, Black and Indigenous people; in relation to gender and sexuality, many are women and LGTBQ; in professional and educational aspects, many are professors and teachers (mainly in the Social Sciences and Humanities), artists, and graduates of the Social Sciences and Humanities.

To better understand this scenario, it is important to know that the election of many politicians to positions of power (at federal and state levels) was a battlefield where fake news was constantly used: messages spread via WhatsApp affirmed that schools were teaching children to be LGBTQ, feminist, anti-Christian and, consequently, 'communists'. These messages were spread especially in Brazilian businessmen's and medium and large-scale farmers' groups and in some Christian groups, which are the major electoral base of the current president and of many politicians. Accusing schools of indoctrinating students was a strategy to mobilise part of the population against education (elementary and higher levels) and against all forms of resistance to homophobia, sexism, racism and other types of oppression and discrimination. Professors,[6] teachers[7] and activists have been persecuted for denouncing these oppressions.

Education is in the eye of the hurricane; thus teacher education is in the same challenging place. Because of this, funds for public education and science in Brazil have been drastically cut. These can be seen as reactions of centralising forces in opposition to decentralising forces, since in the final years of the 1990s and first decade of the 2000s the federal government created educational policies to address inequalities of race, gender/sexuality and ethnicity. Official documents and laws were produced: (1) to guarantee that African, Afro-Brazilian and Indigenous histories and cultures would be considered in education; and (2) to seek gender and sexual equality, suppressing oppression and violence through education. Within the context of this struggle, mainly in the second decade of the 2000s, we are seeing policies that limit and prohibit schools from addressing gender[8] and sexuality issues. We are experiencing the upsurge of centralising forces, and we are seeing how strongly coloniality keeps acting in our context.

Completing this critical scenario, there is a violent and lethal manipulation of the environment, especially the invasion of Indigenous lands and preserved areas (the remaining forests) in the name of 'development and progress'; in fact, we see the continuing colonial logic of exploitation of the invaded and colonised lands. In present times, these lands are being invaded by large-scale farmers and for the illegal extraction and commerce of wood and minerals. The predatory use of the environment holds hands with the violence against Indigenous people. The empowerment of Indigenous voices is proportional to the effort to silence them. Decentralising and centralising forces are in battle, but it is an unequal battle because Indigenous people are fighting against international agrobusiness capital and against historical bias and a historical process of dehumanising and extermination.

Teacher education and language education in the Brazilian context are positioned among these centralising and decentralising forces in dispute. How do we prepare teachers to face coloniality and to produce decolonial praxis, aware that their/our acts are not definitive, but contingent on and related to how they/we defy or handle these forces? How would we strengthen decentralising forces and produce decolonial praxis in teacher education in this complex scenario?

In the pandemic scenario and in distance/remote education, my students Samuel and Murilo showed me that the first step might be to listen to the students' own voices about their feelings related to what they are experiencing in order to support them in understanding themselves. Another step might be reaching spaces where we can listen to the voices of those students who are excluded. Listening to these voices implies dialoguing with multiple voices, world views and social languages (Bakhtin, 1981; Fanon, 1967; Ngũgĩ wa Thiong'o, 1997 [1987]), overcoming the division of body, mind, emotions and spirit, and overcoming hierarchies of knowledges and people. But there are more questions than answers.

Would the understanding that these crises and polarisations are our objects in teaching-learning language and teacher education be a step towards answers to these questions? Would multiple voices/discourses about these crises and polarisations help us to access pluriversality (Mignolo, 2007, and as highlighted in this book), overcoming and challenging hegemonic voices and knowledges? The observation of these multiple voices would help us to know how social languages/heteroglossia/world views are built upon, valued and shared under the tensions of centralising and decentralising forces, reinforcing or challenging the vertexes of coloniality, and enabling pluriversality in teacher education and language education.

Notes

(1) Brazilian Applied Linguistics has focused on linguistic/discursive practices as the object of study. These practices are produced by subjects socially, culturally, historically and politically situated, subjects situated in contexts of social struggle, since we are in a context of inequality and social injustice, in power relations that are characteristically intercultural. In this field, our focuses are the subjects and their actions related to each other acting through, in, with, for and to language(s)/discourses. That is the perspective that guides my work on teacher education. But this perspective is in dispute with other perspectives of language for power positions in the context of teacher education in Brazil, and it is not the dominant perspective. Teacher education is a space of tensions of centralising and decentralising forces.
(2) Mignolo asserts that six modern colonial European languages are seen as the languages that produce knowledge: Italian, Spanish and Portuguese, which were the languages of the Renaissance; and French, German and English, which were the dominant languages from the Enlightenment to the present day; 'they remain the hegemonic languages of scholarship and world literature' (Mignolo, 2000: 290). These Imperial languages lead the hierarchy of languages.

(3) See https://www.youtube.com/watch?v=IpIfyoLE_ek&t=3985s.
(4) See https://www.opendemocracy.net/en/democraciaabierta/project-authoritarian-bolsonaro-pandemic-erosion-democracy-brazil-en/.
(5) Calling someone communist or leftist is also related to the long period of the Labour Party (Partido dos Trabalhadores; PT) being in power at the federal level in Brazil (2002–2016). Members of this party and its supporters have been called 'the reds' as well.
(6) See https://brasil.elpais.com/brasil/2021-03-06/no-futuro-vao-se-lembrar-que-professores-foram-processados-por-criticar-o-governo-bolsonaro-e-uma-mancha-na-historia-do-pais-diz-alvo-de-censura.html.
(7) See https://extra.globo.com/noticias/educacao/professora-denunciada-por-pai-de-aluno-por-passar-filme-sobre-cultura-negra-22797872.html; https://istoe.com.br/canal-para-denunciar-professor-e-anunciado/; https://www.jb.com.br/pais/2018/10/951863-deputada-do-psl-pede-que-alunos-gravem-videos-para-denunciar-professores.html.
(8) See https://theloop.ecpr.eu/academic-feminists-beware-bolsonaro-is-out-to-crush-brazils-gender-ideology/

References

Bakhtin, M.M. (1981) *The Dialogic Imagination: Four Essays*. Austin, TX: University of Texas Press.

Bernardino-Costa, J. (2018) Decolonialidade, Atlântico Negro e intelectuais negros brasileiros: Em busca de um diálogo horizontal (Decoloniality, Black Atlantic and Brazilian Black intellectuals: In search of a horizontal dialogue). *Sociedade e Estado (Society and State)* 33 (1), 117–135.

Bernardino-Costa, J., Maldonado-Torres, N. and Grosfoguel, R. (eds) (2019) *Decolonialidade e pensamento afrodiaspórico (Decoloniality and Afrodiasporic Thinking)*. Belo Horizonte: Autêntica.

Donohoe, A. (2015) Reflective writing: Articulating an alternative pedagogy. *Procedia – Social and Behavioral Sciences* 186, 800–804.

Fanon, F. (1967) *Black Skin, White Masks*. New York: Grove Press.

Garcés, F. (2007) Las Políticas del Conocimiento y la Colonialidad lingüística y Epistémica (The policies of knowledge and linguistic and epistemic coloniality). In S. Castro-Gómez and R. Grosfoguel (eds) *El Giro Decolonial: Reflexiones para una diversidad epistémica más allá del capitalismo global (The Decolonial Turn: Reflections for Epistemic Diversity beyond Global Capitalism)*. Bogotá: Siglo del Hombre Editores; Universidad Central, Instituto de Estudios Sociales Contemporáneos y Pontifícia Universidad Javeriana, Instituto Pensar.

Grosfoguel, R. (2015) *De la crítica poscolonial a la crítica descolonial (From Postcolonial Critique to Decolonial Critique)*. See https://www.youtube.com/watch?v=IpIfyoLE_ek&t=3985s.

hooks, b. (1994) *Teaching to Transgress: Education as Practice of Freedom*. New York and London: Routledge.

Lugones, M. (2010) Toward a decolonial feminism. *Hypatia* 25 (4), 742–759.

Maldonado-Torres, N. (2007) On coloniality of being: Contributions to the development of a concept. *Cultural Studies* 21 (2–3), 240–270.

McKinney, C. (2017) *Language and Power in Post-Colonial Schooling: Ideologies in Practice*. London: Routledge.

Mignolo, W. (2012) *Local Histories/Global Designs Coloniality, Subaltern Knowledges, and Border Thinking*. Princeton, NJ: Princeton University Press

Mignolo, W. (2007) Delinking: The rhetoric of modernity, the logic of coloniality and the grammar of de-coloniality. *Cultural Studies* 21 (2–3), 449–514.

Ngũgĩ wa Thiong'o (1997 [1987]) *Decolonizing the Mind: The Politics of Language in African Literature*. Harare: Zimbabwe Publishing House.

Torquato, C.P. (2020) Challenging the coloniality of languages. *Alternation*, Special Edition 33, 457–500.

Veronelli, G.A. (2015) The coloniality of language: Race, expressivity, power, and the darker side of modernity. *Wagadu: A Journal of Transnational Women's and Gender Studies* 13, 108–134.

Walsh, C. (2018) Decoloniality in/as praxis. In C. Walsh and W. Mignolo (eds) *On Decoloniality: Concepts, Analytics, Praxis*. Durham, NC and London: Duke University Press.

12 Education for Depth: An Invitation to Engage with the Complexities and Challenges of Decolonizing Work

Vanessa Andreotti and Sharon Stein

The editors of this book start the text with the question of how we might prepare teacher candidates to both meet professional qualifications as well as meet their ethical and educational responsibilities in complex and unequal schooling systems. They also ask how we might do this in a way that recognizes both the unprecedented elements of crises, uncertainty, insecurity and polarization, *and* the fact that this moment is part of a longer history of colonial violence in which Indigenous and racialized communities have long been subject to these experiences as the price of others' stability, certainty, security and consensus. As the editors note, there can be no easy or simple solutions to these questions, only partial, imperfect, contextually specific efforts to intervene and interrupt colonial patterns in the short term, and a commitment to wrestle with the impossibilities, paradoxes, tensions and uncertainties of decolonizing work in the long term. The chapters in this book primarily offer rich examples of the former, and in this afterword we offer our brief reflections on the latter.

In any discussion of decolonization, it is important to attend to the ways in which the term has come to mean different things to different people (Andreotti *et al.*, 2015; Stein & Andreotti, 2016). These differences of course include the tokenistic institutional efforts to co-opt and commodify the term in order to ensure the continuity of business-as-usual while offering a public image of transformation (Jimmy *et al.*, 2019). But they also encompass internal disagreements among those who feel themselves deeply committed to a decolonial project, but who have different understandings of what that project entails and how to achieve it. Thus, in our work as scholars and as members of the Gesturing Towards Decolonial Futures research/arts/ecology collective, we have emphasized the need to consider where different approaches to decolonization are coming from, what they assume, what they enable and what they foreclose. This includes self-reflexively examining our own decolonizing efforts, rather than assuming our own benevolence, and considering the ways in which these efforts might paradoxically be driven by colonial desires and contribute to the reproduction of colonial harms.

Like many others, we have come to understand the interdependent relationship between modernity and coloniality. In this dynamic, the shiny promises of modernity are subsidized by the violent underside of coloniality, and this colonial violence persists even in contexts where formal political colonization has ceased (Andreotti, 2011; Byrd, 2011; Coulthard, 2014; Mignolo, 2011; Silva, 2014; Spivak, 1988). However, we have also found that, while having this intellectual analysis is indispensable to our decolonizing work, the awareness of this analysis does not necessarily lead us somewhere different. If our intellectual frames of reference have been developed within a colonial system, then even our critiques of colonization are not immune to reproducing colonial tropes. Indeed, we have generally found that any critique of modernity/coloniality that is intelligible within modernity's epistemic frames and institutions inescapably reproduces many of modernity's harmful traits.

In a dialectical fashion, most critiques of modernity seek to delegitimize modernity and propose a replacement to the modern/colonial system. This is partly because most traditions of critique within modernity are dialectically set to offer an antithesis to an opposing view and a synthesis, rather than to wrestle with paradoxes, complexities and uncertainties. The idea here is to replace one universal and exceptional system with another; the inevitable continuity of universalism and exceptionalism are rarely questioned. This creates a situation where, for example, critiques that aim to challenge the arrogance of modernity's universalism (to 'dethrone' modernity and to try to get rid of thrones) are invariably interpreted as seeking to trash modernity altogether and to replace it with a different universal project (one that seeks modernity's throne for itself). Critiques that point to insights and horizons that are unintelligible within modernity are rendered incoherent, implausible and pointless. In this sense it is impossible to use modernity's logic and mode of knowing and being as a way out of modernity: no matter what we do to reject or resist modernity, we are still conditioned by its grip, which is partly because the dialectics of rejection and resistance are also constitutive of modernity itself.

In the work we do with our collective, we have critiqued the onto-metaphysics of modernity/coloniality where the certainty of knowing grounds the security of being. This onto-metaphysics grounds the grammar of understanding of modernity/coloniality in which Cartesian, logocentric, dialectic, teleological, universal, utility-maximizing, anthropocentric and allochronic forms of reasoning determine what is intelligible and legitimate within modernity. When this grammar is also universalized, onto-epistemologies that may not privilege knowing over being (like many Indigenous ontologies) are outright ignored, dismissed or mis-translated (see Ahenakew, 2016; Mika, 2017). One common mis-translation is when people understand 'the land as a living entity' as a 'concept' or a descriptive representation of reality, rather than something that precedes and exceeds human conceptualizations. One of the ways our collective has found to address this issue is to attempt to shift how we conceptualize pedagogy, teaching and learning, based on insights from Indigenous communities and scholars we collaborate with. For example, while modern/colonial schools understand learning to happen in the head/mind in order to regulate and control the emotions, behaviors and relations of the individual body, we have been taught that Indigenous education happens both individually, collectively and metabolically (with and through the land) in the 'guts', then travels to the heart, and it is the head/mind that follows suit. We have also learned that the education of the hearts and guts is suggestive rather than descriptive/prescriptive; that is, it is not about accumulating knowledge or indexing ourselves and the world in an encyclopedia, but rather about supporting people to move as part of the metabolism of the world in more responsible and accountable ways (Ahenakew, 2017).

We have tried to translate these teachings into pedagogical approaches that attempt to interrupt colonial patterns within modernity/coloniality. We mostly fail, but the pedagogical failures are also 'successes' (Kapoor, 2004) in that they are extremely useful for showing us time and time again that the problem is much deeper than we think it is. In these pedagogies, we understand learning as happening through a nested system where an intellectual layer is embedded in an affective layer that is embedded in a relational layer that is embedded in a 'metabolic' layer. For those of us whose lives are subsidized by the violences and unsustainability of modernity/coloniality, this affective layer is saturated with the fears, insecurities, fragilities, projections and unprocessed individual and collective traumas that modernity has ill-equipped us to process or to release. The affective and relational layers are largely socially conditioned and work primarily through our unconscious (they precede our rationalizations). Unless we find a way of clearing or decluttering the affective layer ('the heart' in the Indigenous analogy), losing the satisfaction that we have with the (often pleasurable) compensation mechanisms we have created to deny or avoid dealing with that saturation, our intellectual layers ('the head') will be caught in a circular loop where critique is consumed and epistemic additions are made, but very little changes in the affective or relational layers and we are back to the same allegedly universal ontology. In this case, the relational layer ('the guts'), where change needs to happen for genuinely new ontic possibilities to emerge, becomes inaccessible since it requires the affective space to be in motion for anything to 'land' so that we can show up differently to each other and in the world at large.

Through this learning framework, we have created and translated many educational experiments (see, for example, *Education 2048* [GTDF, 2020a]) that seek to denaturalize and de-universalize modernity. We note that these materials both interrupt *and* reproduce modern grammar to varying extents. The same can be said of many other scholarly efforts in this area, including this afterword and the other chapters in this book. None of this diminishes the value of this work; indeed, these paradoxes and circularities are likely an inevitable part of any decolonization effort. But for these failures to be generative, we need to consider and be accountable for the ways in which our efforts to both resist coloniality and make space for other possibilities might also be contributing to the reproduction of the very violences we seek to challenge. This does not mean that resistance is not worthwhile, but that we should not assume that we are transparent to ourselves, nor presume that we are outside of the problems we identify. Therefore, part of the work is to interrupt desires to celebrate decolonization as a point of arrival and develop stamina for the long haul of decolonial futures that are multigenerational processes characterized by uncertainty, paradoxes, complexities and abundant contradictions.

Another complexity of decolonizing work we often find is that our critiques of modernity/coloniality usually focus on one of its many aspects, ignoring how interrelated its different dimensions are. For example, someone who critiques the ways in which cognitive imperialism is imposed upon a community in the Global South may propose that the solution to this problem is a strong form of nationalism grounded on local knowledge systems that may counter the epistemic violence of modernity/coloniality. However, the formation of the nation-state and of nationalism are also part and parcel of the same modern/colonial project and the relationship with knowledge that focuses on the preservation of knowledge and meaning precisely reflects modernity's ways of knowing and being. Again, the resistance to modernity, to be intelligible within modernity, must necessarily manifest through modernity's grammar and reproduce its traits. Therefore, critiques of modernity tend to promote the replacement of a specific configuration of modernity with a different configuration of modernity. Another example of this trend is the discussion about teacher- versus learner-centered education. Each approach is a different configuration of modernity that upholds modernity's promises in different ways. Many educators would claim that the learner-centered approach can 'decolonize' traditional aspects of schooling, particularly the unequal power relations between teachers and students. While traditional power relations can be challenged in this case (when students are placed at the center), modernity is also firmly reproduced in the centering of students as autonomous consumers who choose according to their preferences and convenience, and this is seldom problematized.

This leads us to our final observation about different approaches to decolonization and the ways in which decolonization efforts can reproduce dimensions of coloniality, which has to do with human exceptionalism. Our learning around this matter has been significantly informed by our collaborations with Indigenous communities in Canada and Latin America, through the network Teia das 5 Curas. In their approach to decolonization, these communities emphasize the fact that many of us have forgotten or numbed our sense of entanglement with the earth as a living entity, which they also call a metabolic system. In doing so, these communities remind us of both the limits of human agency in the enactment of decolonial futures, and the importance of allowing the intelligence and intention of the earth itself to shape these futures. In other words, rather than framing education as either teacher or learner centered, the Indigenous communities that we collaborate with emphasize earth-centered education. Earth-centered education acknowledges that we are also a part of this earth and thus we are accountable to it and to all living beings (both human and other-than-human). This comes from an analysis that colonization entails not just the subjugation of certain human groups by other human groups, but also the subjugation of the earth itself and the fantasy of separability that promises people that they can be independent individuals who are only accountable if they choose to be. In other words, modern ontologies of separability promise unrestricted autonomy, thus leading to the denial of responsibility and the privileging of humanity and its dreams and desires at the expense of other living beings.

As we mentioned before, the communities also remind us that honoring the earth as a living entity of which we are all a part is not something that can be done through conceptual shifts or intellectual analyses – that is, shifting our 'heads'. It also has to be (primarily) done through shifting our hearts and our 'guts'. This requires that those of us socialized within modernity interrupt and lose our satisfaction with our perceived colonial entitlements and exceptionalism. This step is necessary before we can even begin to sense that we are missing something, let alone actually hear the silenced possibilities for knowing, sensing, being and relating otherwise. That is, we cannot simply 'add' the knowledges and practices that have been made absent within the modern/colonial system onto colonial ways of being, and hope for the best (Ahenakew, 2016). We have to denaturalize, interrupt and ultimately 'compost' modern/colonial ways of being in order for something truly different to be possible (see also Stein *et al.*, 2020). Thinking educationally, this requires a different kind of education from the kind of education that is naturalized within modernity/coloniality – a shift from what we call education for mastery to education for depth. Below, we elaborate on this distinction and review how it relates to our discussion above as a means of closing our contribution in this afterword.

Often within our modern/colonial system, we assume that 'education' is synonymous with formal schooling, whether in primary, secondary or post-secondary institutions. We also assume that education is something to be transferred by educators, and accumulated and mastered by learners – skills, facts, competencies, information. Generally, it is felt that this process of education as mastery facilitates the development of fully functional members of modern societies, making their labor and social contributions more valuable and meaningful. Particularly in the contemporary moment and the current swing towards learner-centered education (Biesta, 2015, 2016), we find that education for mastery (which can also be understood as education for conquest) is also rooted in consumption. Students have been encouraged to treat education as a menu of options from which they can chose in order to feel *comfortable, hopeful, inspired and empowered.*

Education for depth offers an entirely different invitation. Education for depth invites learners, as well as teachers, to dive into the complexities, contradictions and complicities that characterize the modern/colonial system as we know it so that we might begin to sense the limits of this system alongside its gifts and confront the difficulties of imagining and enacting something otherwise. This mode of education also offers us a reminder of our responsibilities to denaturalize, interrupt and ultimately disinvest from this system if we wish to honor our metabolic entanglement with everyone and everything. Education for depth seeks to prepare learners with the stamina and the dispositions to be able to hold complexities, contradictions and complicities of ourselves and the world, rather than try to either repress or immediately resolve them. This entails not just the intellectual work of critique, but also affective and relational work that is often sidelined or even dismissed and delegitimized within institutions that are focused on providing education for mastery. By *decentering* the learner, the teacher and also humanity in general, education for depth can be understood as 'ego-disarming', inviting people into a space of *humility, maturity, sobriety and responsibility.*

Our scholarly engagement with postcolonial and decolonial scholars like Gayatri Spivak and Jacqui Alexander, as well as our learning alongside Indigenous communities, has taught us that education for depth is not something that we practically can nor ethically should force upon anyone. It is a difficult, often painful process, and while this process can mobilize many different possibilities and relations in the world, it can offer no guarantees, assurances or preconceived alternatives to the modern/colonial system. Unlike education for mastery, education for depth is not focused on outcomes, arrivals or fixed forms, but rather is focused on the integrity of the process, the quality of relationships and the capacity for movement that is enabled. Thus, education for depth can only be offered as an invitation; generally, this invitation is taken up with most interest by those who are not only dissatisfied with the modern/colonial system, but also with many existing critical and decolonial responses to that system. While education for mastery tells us that 'not knowing' is a problem to be resisted and remedied with more knowledge and information, education for depth suggests that not knowing can be an extremely generative starting place for diving deeper, without projections about what we will find and without the promise that the complex predicament we find ourselves in can ever be 'resolved'. The first step of education for depth is to expand our capacity to hold space for difficult and painful things without being immobilized and overwhelmed or wanting to be rescued. This first step, in itself, is a major challenge for all of us (writing or reading this text) who have been conditioned by education for mastery.

While we understand that education for mastery can still be the most effective form of resistance for Indigenous, Black and racialized people in many contexts where it is still possible to negotiate access to the benefits of modernity/coloniality, it is important to note that it only works (as a form of resistance) while the architectures of modernity/coloniality are firmly in place. As this architecture begins to fracture, education for mastery may leave us unprepared and ill-equipped to address multiple crises, uncertainty, insecurity and polarization (see GTDF, 2020b).

There is a popular saying in Brazil that states that, in a flood situation, it is only when the water reaches people's hips that it becomes possible for them to swim. Before that, with the water up to our ankles or knees, it is only possible to walk, or to wade. In other words, we might only be able to learn to swim – that is, to exist differently – once we have no other choice. But in the meantime, we can prepare by learning to open ourselves up to the teachings of the water, as well as the teachings of those who have been swimming for their lives against multiple currents of colonial violence. As the water levels continue to rise in our own and other contexts, there will be a point where we will need different approaches – even beyond depth education, to face this flood together in more generative ways.

References

Ahenakew, C. (2016) Grafting Indigenous ways of knowing onto non-Indigenous ways of being: The (underestimated) challenges of a decolonial imagination. *International Review of Qualitative Research* 9 (3), 323–340.

Ahenakew, C.R. (2017) Mapping and complicating conversations about Indigenous education. *Diaspora, Indigenous, and Minority Education* 11 (2), 80–91.

Andreotti, V. (2011) *Actionable Postcolonial Theory in Education*. Dordrecht: Springer.

Andreotti, V.D.O., Stein, S., Ahenakew, C. and Hunt, D. (2015) Mapping interpretations of decolonization in the context of higher education. *Decolonization: Indigeneity, Education & Society* 4 (1), 21–40.

Biesta, G. (2015) What is education for? On good education, teacher judgement, and educational professionalism. *European Journal of Education* 50 (1), 75–87.

Biesta, G. (2016) The rediscovery of teaching: On robot vacuum cleaners, non-egological education and the limits of the hermeneutical world view. *Educational Philosophy and Theory* 48 (4), 374–392.

Byrd, J.A. (2011) *The Transit of Empire: Indigenous Critiques of Colonialism*. Minnesota, MN: University of Minnesota Press.

Coulthard, G.S. (2014) *Red Skin, White Masks: Rejecting the Colonial Politics of Recognition*. Minnesota, MN: University of Minnesota Press.

GTDF (Gesturing Towards Decolonial Futures Collective) (2020a) *Education 2048*. See https://decolonialfutures.net/portfolio/education-2048-v2/.

GTDF (Gesturing Towards Decolonial Futures Collective) (2020b) Preparing for the end of the world as we know it. *Open Democracy*, 24 August. See www.opendemocracy.net/en/oureconomy/preparing-end-world-we-know-it/.

Jimmy, E., Andreotti, V. and Stein, S. (2019) *Towards Braiding*. Guelph, ON: Musagetes Foundation.

Kapoor, I. (2004) Hyper-self-reflexive development? Spivak on representing the Third World 'Other'. *Third World Quarterly* 25 (4), 627–647.

Mignolo, W. (2011) *The Darker Side of Western Modernity: Global Futures, Decolonial Options*. Durham, NC: Duke University Press.

Mika, C. (2017) *Indigenous Education and the Metaphysics of Presence: A Worlded Philosophy*. London: Taylor & Francis.

Silva, D.F.D. (2014) Toward a Black feminist poethics: The quest(ion) of Blackness toward the End of the World. *The Black Scholar* 44 (2), 81–97.

Spivak, G.C. (1988) Can the subaltern speak? In C. Nelson and L. Grossberg (eds) *Marxism and the Interpretation of Culture* (pp. 271–313). Champaign, IL: University of Illinois Press.

Stein, S. and Andreotti, V.D.O. (2016) Decolonization and higher education. In M.A. Peters (ed.) *Encyclopedia of Educational Philosophy and Theory*. Singapore: Springer Science + Business Media.

Stein, S., Andreotti, V., Suša, R., *et al.* (2020) Gesturing towards decolonial futures. *Nordic Journal of Comparative and International Education (NJCIE)* 4 (1), 43–65.

13 Transnational Connections in the Global South: A Reflection on this Book's Reception

Natalia Ávila Reyes

I had the pleasure of being an early reader of this book in the meridional summer of 2021. As a literacy researcher, I was deeply moved by the perspective this book offers on the conditions of teaching and learning language in post-apartheid South Africa, by the ethical and epistemological constraints posed by the enduring colonial structures and, above all, by the impressive number of connections that as a researcher, teacher and teacher educator, I could establish with my own country, Chile.

Andreotti and Stein (this volume) explain the interdependence of modernity and coloniality, even in contexts where colonization has ceased. This idea expands our usual understanding of power structures and social dynamics when researching literacy in Latin America, particularly in Chile. For example, the main decolonial claim of the professional association I participate in, ALES (Latin American Association of Writing Studies in Higher Education and Professional Contexts), has centered on the demand to occupy visible places in the scientific production from the South, to foster South-South exchanges, and to reposition the value of our languages in the construction of knowledge (Ávila Reyes, in press). The reading of this book pushed me further, to read the structures of domination that implicitly pervade the teaching and learning of writing in my country in a decolonial key. My research gravitates around higher education writing in a system that has long kept certain social groups excluded, and the discourses that label these new students as lacking 'competencies' that are supposed to be prerequisites for higher education, such as academic reading and writing 'skills'. Indeed, the normative imaginaries (Lillis, 2017) that construct these students as subjects of deficit start earlier in the school trajectories, and this book offers a comprehensive framework to understand these imaginaries as coloniality structures.

Thus, I am pointing to an implicit deficit thinking that operates in a predominantly monolingual society or, at least, in a monolingual university system.[1] It is mainly a structure of class domination, although in Chile aspects of race, linguistic varieties and other forms of minoritization are conflated (and hidden) in the socioeconomic divide. Both the reflections on the construction of bilinguals as deficient monolinguals whose expressive resources are invisibilized (Guzula, this volume), and on the restrictions on students to draw from their own experiences when writing (Makoe, this volume), advocate for structurally rethinking how we teach language and writing at school. Both studies underline the importance of creating third spaces (Gutiérrez *et al.*, 1999) to include subjects and to challenge the directionality of the language knowledge imparted at school. In widening higher education systems, the construction of third spaces that value and actively use students' knowledge as a teaching repertoire is also relevant to start pushing for a structural change in academic literacy teaching and, overall, to embrace social diversity (Ávila Reyes *et al.*, 2021).

Students Can Write (Revolutions)

Another striking nexus of this book with current educational challenges in Chile is the civic unrest and historical role of students in reshaping education. In the brief overview below, which does not do justice to the magnitude of student movements in Chile, I attempt to show how protests have attested the variety of communicative and expressive resources, agency and rhetorical savviness of students – along with underlining the coincidences with the South African social movement that originated this book. This section offers a brief synopsis of 21st century student movements in Chile and the strength of their discursive devices and resources.

The Chilean educational system constitutes an extreme case of market-oriented educational policies. The architecture of the country's education system lies in national vouchers, mixed public-private provision, competition for students, and parental choice (Carrasco & Gunter, 2019), which has resulted in increasingly segregated schools in which academic performance strongly correlates with students' socioeconomic status (Valenzuela *et al.*, 2014). This architecture was consecrated by the country's Constitution of 1980, approved during Augusto Pinochet's dictatorial regime, and enshrined by an Education Constitutional Law, LOCE, enacted on the last day of Pinochet's rule. In 1980, a higher education reform introduced private universities and set up a self-funding policy for existing universities. Non-profit, tuition-free and state-funded institutions started to charge tuition and fees (Espinoza, 2017).

This order remained unchanged long after the return to democracy in 1990. It was only in 2006 that the school reform movement known as la revolución pingüina (the penguin revolution)[2] defied the school system.

The movement, furthered by high school students, advanced an unprecedented public conversation about quality, equity and profit in the school system and influenced policymaking to the point of the abolition of the Constitutional Law of Education, LOCE (Bellei *et al.*, 2010). The movement gained people's support and influenced new educational legislation, although the structure of the higher education system remained unaltered (Fernández Darraz, 2015).

Despite its limited effect on the structural market orientation of the educational system, 'the penguin revolution' of 2006 established a precedent in Chilean politics after the return to democracy. It was not until the pingüinos took to the streets that a structural demand put into question the ideological orientation of the educational system as a whole and, indeed, achieved the symbolic victory of repealing a law. Moreover, 'they also developed innovative forms of political organization, sophisticated mass-media communication strategies … [and] the intensive use of new communication technologies and instant messaging' (Bellei *et al.*, 2014: 430).

The 2011 student movement was a series of student protests that achieved even more impact and social support than in 2006. The first national demonstration took place on 12 May 2011; more than 20,000 students congregated in the capital city. The number of demonstrators increased after each march, because the dissatisfaction had accumulated over the years. The movement claimed that democratic governments had so far focused on increasing coverage by subsidizing demand, while leaving the system's architecture unchanged. As a result, the higher education system remained segregated, most private institutions offered quantity over quality, and an alarming level of student indebtedness affected graduates.

As Salinas and Fraser (2012) highlight, an explanation of the social impact of the movement was the capacity to frame and communicate educational grievances. During the year of protests, demonstrators coined a motto for demanding 'a quality, public, and free education', our version of 'free, decolonized education'. As a whole, the movement promoted a view on education as a social right, which translated into concrete demands such as equity in access to higher education, strengthening and expansion of public institutions, stronger financial and educational regulations for institutions, end of profit –which was forbidden by law but still occurred through loopholes– and more student participation in institutional governance.

By the end of the year, around 2,194,609 people had participated in the students' protests (Salinas & Fraser, 2012). This movement represents an extraordinary example of students' agency, which shaped a narrative of an epic victory using unprecedented rhetorical strategies, new technologies as a platform for disseminating the message, and creative means of protesting, including parties, marathons, installations, flashmobs and art actions that appeared across the cities. Secondary and tertiary students articulated a common set of demands and worked collaboratively in assemblies across the country. As Salinas and Fraser argue, 'the movement's frames – that is, the interpretations and discursive choices made to present claims and demands – highlighted clear educational problems, were displayed through innovative repertoires, and were communicated by highly articulate and critical leaders' (Salinas & Fraser, 2012: 29).

Lastly, the movement had a strong influence on higher education public policies (Bellei *et al.*, 2014; Fernández Darraz, 2015), shaping a new context for higher education that continues to change rapidly, such as focalized free tuition (known as gratuidad) and many affirmative action programs that are currently widening participation in selective institutions.

In 2018, a new social movement, 'the feminist wave', arose among high school and university students. More than 30 universities and many high schools went on strike and started occupations. The primary demand of this wave of protests was to create response protocols for cases of sexual harassment and accusations of sexual abuse. Navarro (2018) chronicled the rhetorical nature of the movement in one elite university, recording how manifestos and petition statements were crafted. Through sophisticated techniques of collective composing and intertextuality, students were able to create petitions, respond to official requests from authorities, formulate demands and, eventually, change the fate of a dean's election. 'Feminist writing is collective, grounded, dialogic and action-oriented. It is a complex and effective rhetorical action that changes reality' (Navarro, 2018, my translation). The author also claims that such a complex rhetorical action must contest the narratives of students' deficits. I would add that such a display of resources is a visible example of the grassroots literacy practices that comprise the repertoires of Chilean students, understated in traditional writing pedagogies. Students have continuously proven that they can be agents, learn to write for new settings, and participate in a vast array of literate practices – academic or not.

The last event that I would like to recall happened very recently. In October 2019, high school students protested for weeks over the rising costs of urban transport and the precarization of life. On 18 October, the general public expressed their support and took to the streets to participate in demonstrations and roadblocks that led to violent protests as night fell. This movement led to a sudden interruption of everyday civic life, something unseen since the return of democratic rule. A State of Emergency was declared, and the military took control of various regions. In Santiago, public transport was destroyed and suspended for weeks, which interrupted work and school activity. This civic life interruption led to the closure of many universities, including the one where I work. The visual essay by Angier, McKinney and Kell triggered in my memory some episodes of the moving and uncertain period of 2019. The movement, known as estallido social (social outburst), played a crucial role in furthering the current constituent process in Chile as, for many people, the 1980s Constitution has been the legal frame to perpetuate structural inequities. Although this movement grew as a generalized discomfort and did not respond to organizational structures, it allowed university federations to reposition the longstanding demand to put an end to outsourced contracts for university maintenance personnel – yet another of the many similarities I have found throughout this book. To date, several prominent universities in the country have begun contracting out their service personnel.

In the wake of the protests, I conducted the fifth of six series of interviews on academic literacy in a longitudinal project about student writing with a diverse group of university students. Unavoidably, this topic impacted participants' in and out of school literacy practices. We learned about students' use of diaries to cope with feelings, their increased participation in social network debates, and their spontaneous choice of topics related to the social upheaval for class papers (Ávila Reyes *et al.*, 2021). In particular, this experience allowed us to verify, this time with concrete students who participated in our research, the richness of their interests, ethical commitments, expressive repertoires and agency, all valuable inputs to build bridges between students' literate lives and academic literacy.

This brief overview of the recent history of the student movement aims to counteract the commonplaces with which the new students who try to access the university are constructed. Family, religious or political literacy practices in which many of the new students engage might become invisible, irrelevant or even stigmatized to university instructors, even when they represent legitimate forms of participation, citizenship and identity expression, such as the ones displayed in social movements by Chilean students across generations. It is imperative to solve this paradox through strategies that allow us to conceptualize youth in their highest diversity as subjects with valid knowledge, and desist from the deficit view as the driving force behind language and literacy teaching at the university.

Closing Thoughts

In this reflection, I have tried to capture the strength with which the student movement strains and exposes inherited structures of domination. Ultimately, the students are the ones who have confronted us, educational researchers and teacher educators, with ethical and educational imperatives. The fact that this book has emerged from a similar juncture invites us to rethink the ways of researching education and teaching language that may be common to the social needs of the Global South, understood not as a clearly charted geographical region, but rather as a set of commonalities in terms of economic and power inequalities, and which happen to be mostly located in the South (Rigg, 2007).

Chile has still a long way to go to democratize full access to quality education. Moreover, the changing landscape of the student body, fostered by recent migratory waves, has brought multilingualism to a school system that is scarcely prepared. Thus, *Decoloniality, Language and Literacy* offers a broad framework for understanding and redefining these emerging challenges alongside the existing ones. Its ideas make a contribution far beyond the borders of South Africa and offer a conceptual underpinning for emerging issues in the Global South in an era unprecedentedly signed by crisis and uncertainty.

A decolonial perspective in teacher education can contribute to understanding inequity and educational segregation under a common framework in the Global South countries. The reach of these bridges goes far beyond the borders of my country. However, I have been careful to not tokenize the Chilean experience, so as to avoid overlooking the complexity and specificity of the experiences of my Latin American colleagues – with whom, I am sure, this text will also resonate significantly. I am deeply grateful to the editors for inviting me to think about these transnational connections and build new directionalities to create knowledge.

Notes

(1) As researchers and educators, we must begin to deconstruct the dominant ideology of Chile as a monolingual Spanish speaking country, a pervasive idea that has been addressed in the literature as the 'monolingual mindset' (Weber & Horner, 2013) or as 'implicit monolingualism' (Shuck, 2006). In Chile, Indigenous languages had long been invisibilized by the monolingual educational policies (Quintrileo Llancao & Quintrileo Llancao, 2018), and the new multilingualism resulting from recent waves of immigration is scarcely addressed by schools (Gelber *et al.*, 2021). Additionally, primary and high schools have experienced an increase in the migrant population of more than 600% since 2014 (Toledo Vega *et al.*, 2020), but maybe because of social economic segregation, not many bilingual immigrants have made their way to universities. These emerging challenges are a matter of great breadth that would deserve a deeper analysis than I can offer in these pages. This is another of the contributions that this book can offer to researchers in Chile.
(2) The name 'penguin' makes reference to the secondary school students' uniform.

References

Ávila Reyes, N. (in press) Multilingual insights into a complex field of study: An introduction to the aims of this book. In N. Ávila Reyes (ed.) *Multilingual Contributions to Writing Research: Towards an Equal Academic Exchange*. Fort Collins, CO: WAC Clearinghouse.

Ávila Reyes, N., Calle-Arango, L. and Léniz, E. (2021) Researching in times of pandemic and social unrest: A flexible mindset for an enriched view on literacy. *International Studies on Sociology of Education*. doi:10.1080/09620214.2021.1927142

Bellei, C., Contreras, D. and Valenzuela, J.P. (2010) Viejos dilemas y nuevas propuestas en la política educacional chilena. In C. Bellei, D. Contreras and J.P. Valenzuela (eds) *Ecos de la revolución pingüina: Avances, debates y silencios en la reforma educacional*. New York: UNICEF.

Bellei, C., Cabalin, C. and Orellana, V. (2014) The 2011 Chilean student movement against neoliberal educational policies. *Studies in Higher Education* 39 (3), 426–440. doi:10.1080/03075079.2014.896179

Carrasco, A. and Gunter, H.M. (2019) The 'private' in the privatisation of schools: The case of Chile. *Educational Review* 71 (1), 67–80. doi:10.1080/00131911.2019.1522035

Espinoza, Ó. (2017) Privatización de la educación superior en Chile: Consecuencias y lecciones aprendidas. *EccoS Revista Científica* 44 (September–December), 175–202. doi:10.5585/EccoS.n44.8070

Fernández Darraz, E. (2015) Políticas públicas de Educación Superior desde 1990 hasta el presente. In A. Bernasconi (ed.) *La educación superior de Chile. Transformación, desarrollo y crisis* (pp. 173–217). Santiago: Ediciones UC.

Gelber, D., Ávila Reyes, N., Espinosa Aguirre, M.J., Escribano, R., Figueroa Miralles, J. and Castillo González, C. (2021) Mitos y realidades sobre la inclusión de migrantes en aulas chilenas: El caso de la escritura. *Archivos Analíticos de Políticas Educativas* 29 (74), 1–27.

Gutiérrez, K.D., Baquedano-López, P. and Tejeda, C. (1999) Rethinking diversity: Hybridity and hybrid language practices in the third space. *Mind, Culture, and Activity* 6 (4), 286–303. doi:10.1080/10749039909524733

Lillis, T.M. (2017) Resistir regímenes de evaluación en el estudio del escribir: Hacia un imaginario enriquecido. *Signo y Pensamiento* 71, 66–81.

Navarro, F. (2018) Escribiendo la revolución feminista en educación superior..Centro de Investigación Periodística (CIPER) Opinión Publicado: 13.06.2018.

Quintrileo Llancao, C. and Quintrileo Llancao, E. (2018) Desafíos en la enseñanza de lenguas indígenas: El caso del mapudungun en el Programa de Educación Intercultural Bilingüe (PEIB) de Chile TT. *Trabalhos Em Linguística Aplicada* 57 (3), 1467–1485.

Rigg, J. (2007) *An Everyday Geography of the Global South*. New York: Routledge. doi:10.4324/9780203967577

Salinas, D. and Fraser, P. (2012) Educational opportunity and contentious politics: The 2011 Chilean Student Movement. *Berkeley Review of Education* 3 (1), 17–47. http://escholarship.org/uc/ucbgse_bre.

Shuck, G. (2006) Combating monolingualism: A novice administrator's challenge. *WPA: Writing Program Administration* 30 (1–2), 59–82.

Toledo Vega, G., Quilodrán, F., Olivares, M. and Silva, J. (2020) Perspectivas actuales para el fomento del aula transcultural en Chile. *Nueva Revista Del Pacífico* 53, 164–185.

Valenzuela, J.P., Bellei, C. and de los Ríos, D. (2014) Socioeconomic school segregation in a market-oriented educational system. The case of Chile. *Journal of Education Policy* 29 (2), 217–241. doi:10.1080/02680939.2013.806995

Weber, J.-J. and Horner, K. (2013) Multilingual universities and the monological mindset. In I. de Saint-Georges and J.-J. Weber (eds) *Multilingualism and Multimodality: Current Challenges for Educational Studies* (pp. 101–116). Leiden: Brill.

Index

Academic literacies: 1, 16, 19, 31, 37, 49, 59, 119, 120, 131, 138–139, 141, 165, 131, 187
African languages: 5, 10, 15, 23, 25–34, 45, 47–48, 51, 64–66, 106, 128, 136, 155–159, 163, 169, 171, 175–177, 187–188, 193, 216, 218–219
Agency (and student agency): 14–16, 46, 48, 58–59, 118, 120, 125–126, 131, 133
Anglonormativity: 9, 29, 66, 70, 157, 159, 170, 201
Assemblage: 82, 161, 190
Autonomous model of literacy: 50, 181, 186, 189

Bilingual (and bilingualism): 13, 24, 26–27, 29–32, 34–35, 37, 39–43, 47, 63–64, 67–69, 72, 106, 113, 161, 163, 165, 170–171, 216, 220
Borderlands: xiii–xiv, 11, 14, 18, 66, 69, 70, 74–75, 157
Borders: 2, 12, 14, 24, 63, 69, 82, 107, 111, 118, 131, 156, 186, 220
Boundaries: 12, 13, 32, 36, 64, 69, 74, 99, 100, 112, 118, 130
Brazil: 15, 192, 197–198, 202, 203–205

Canada: 15, 211
Chile: 15, 16, 215–220
Coloniality: xiii, 1–3, 5, 7, 9, 11, 12–16, 21, 23, 30, 48–50, 59, 66, 83, 86, 96, 136, 156–158, 161, 170, 173–175, 177, 180, 186–188, 191, 197, 200, 201–204, 208–212, 215, 220
Coloniality of language: xiii, 9, 30, 201–202
Colonialism: xiii, xiv, 3, 9, 16, 47, 49, 58–59, 81, 82, 155–156, 174, 176, 178, 202
Contact zones: xiii, 11, 58, 81–82

Decoloniality: 3, 13, 48–49, 59, 66, 136, 175, 186, 188, 202, 220
Decolonisation: 5, 83, 99
Decolonization: 207–208, 210, 211
Deficit and deficit thinking/framing: 12, 16, 125, 129, 133, 216
Democracy/Democratic/Democratization: 3, 26, 52, 106, 182, 216–218
Denaturalize: 210, 212
Discourse appropriation: 47, 65, 67, 72–75
Distance/remote/blended learning: 2, 16, 96, 198–199, 204

Earth–centred education: 16, 211
Education for depth vs education for mastery: 16, 207, 211–213
Education funding: 4, 10, 216
Emergent bilinguals: 24, 28, 31
Epistemic/epistemological violence: 1, 6, 9, 208–210
Epistemological critique: 174, 187, 191
Eurocentric pedagogies and epistemologies: 13, 28, 49, 59, 157
Europe/Eurocentrism/European languages: 15, 18, 25, 28, 46, 49, 57, 72, 156–158, 175, 176, 179–180, 189, 200, 201, 204
Expressive – language, resources, repertoires: 16, 124, 216, 219

Fallist: 6, 83
Fees Must Fall (#FMF): 5, 18, 82, 83, 152

Gender based violence: 14, 81, 90, 132
Global South: 1–2, 8, 15, 59, 176, 210, 215, 219, 220

Hierarchy/Hierarchical/Hierarchization: 5, 11, 15, 36, 72, 82, 91, 102, 124, 156, 164, 165, 174, 200, 201, 204

222

Identity: 13, 27, 35, 41, 46, 50, 59, 63–69, 72, 73, 74, 75, 101, 114, 117, 119, 138, 175, 186, 188, 201, 219
Identity meshing: 13, 65, 69, 71–72, 74–75
Imperial/Imperialism: xiii, 5, 25, 50, 81, 158, 185, 204, 210
Indigenous: 5, 15, 47, 50, 51, 53, 67, 101, 102, 104, 109, 110, 111–112, 113, 157, 159, 176, 192, 197, 198, 201–203, 207, 209, 211, 212, 213, 220
Inequalities: 3–5, 8, 14, 30, 18, 24, 25, 27, 28, 39, 48, 51, 57, 93, 98, 101, 118, 125, 129, 131, 144, 190, 197, 203, 204, 219
Invention of literacy (and reinvention of literacy): 174–175, 178, 180, 181, 190

Knowledge/Knowledge making: 2, 12, 13, 36–41, 48, 50–51, 57–59, 63–64, 66, 67, 109, 119, 122, 132, 165, 170, 189

language policy: 13, 23–25, 69–70, 72, 106, 170
Language ideologies: 13, 48, 65, 157
Language of instruction: 10, 19, 23, 24, 26, 27, 39, 47, 51, 100, 114, 136
Lesson plan: 136, 141–143, 145–146, 148–150, 152
Linguistic ethnography: 32–34, 65, 157, 160
Linguistic repertoire: 8, 13, 28, 30, 31, 37, 39–41, 44, 46, 47, 48, 49, 51–52, 55, 60, 65, 66, 68–69, 101, 104, 106, 113, 132, 155, 158–159, 162, 164, 170, 176, 184, 190
Literacy practice: 117, 119–122, 125, 131, 133, 159

Medium of instruction (see *language of instruction*)
Modernity/coloniality: 4, 5, 16, 18, 178, 179, 187, 200, 202, 208–211, 213, 215
Monoglossic/monolingual ideology: 10, 23, 26, 28–29, 44, 46, 47, 64, 65, 156, 157, 162, 165, 201, 216, 220
Multiliteracies: 30–34, 37, 40, 47
Multimodality: 1, 11, 30, 32–35, 40–41, 47, 60, 68, 136–143, 145, 152, 159, 161, 165–166

Orthography: 175–181, 184

Pandemic: 15–18, 81, 198, 199, 202, 204
Pluriversality: 2, 10, 12, 66, 204
position/positioning: 18, 24, 30, 34, 48, 58, 64, 72, 74, 111, 117–122, 125–126, 147, 155, 156, 160, 171
privilege: 817, 46, 50, 72, 87, 89–90, 96, 99–100, 128, 132, 155–157, 201, 209

'race': xiii, xiv, 3, 5, 8, 18, 46, 64, 82–83, 87, 96
Racialization: 15, 25, 51, 144, 158, 159, 162, 163, 169, 171, 191, 197, 200–201
Reflection/reflective writing: 2, 12, 14–16, 53–55, 96, 99–100, 103, 110, 117, 118–126, 129–133, 152, 179, 180, 198, 199, 207, 216, 219
Repertoire: 10, 13, 14, 16, 30, 34, 37, 39–41, 44, 46–48, 56, 58, 67, 68, 70, 75, 77, 111, 113, 136, 137, 147–150, 152, 157–159, 161, 163, 169–170, 208, 216, 218, 219
Rhodes Must Fall (#RMF): 5, 16, 18, 19, 82, 83, 155
Rural/semi–rural schools: 4, 10, 14, 27, 44, 48, 98–100, 102, 106, 110, 113–114, 155, 167, 183, 192

Semiotic repertoire: 13, 34, 39–41, 47, 67, 68, 70, 75, 111, 150, 161
Silent conversation: 86–87, 90
Social justice: 2, 8, 52, 96, 98–100, 103–104, 106, 109, 110, 118, 197
Storytelling: 13, 46, 48, 52–55, 57
Student protests: 2, 3, 5, 6, 9, 14, 90, 152, 187, 211, 216–219

Teach–in: 186
Teaching practice/school experience: 10, 14, 92, 98–100, 102–103, 109–110, 117–132, 137, 140, 147
Third space/s: 136–137, 139, 144–145, 147, 152
Translanguaging (and trans–languaging): 30, 34, 41, 48, 68, 70, 74–75
Trans–semiotising: 68, 72, 74, 111

Uyinene Mrwetyana: 90, 94

Violence: 1, 3, 48, 93, 119, 130, 202, 203, 207–208, 209–210, 213